NON CIRCULATING

THROUGH THESE
PORTALS

THROUGH THESE
PORTALS
A Pacific War Saga

Wayne C. MacGregor, Jr.

WSU
PRESS

Washington State University Press
Pullman, Washington

Washington State University Press
PO Box 645910
Pullman, Washington 99164-5910
Phone: 800-354-7360
Fax: 509-335-8568
E-mail: wsupress@wsu.edu
Web site: www.wsu.edu/wsupress

Library of Congress Cataloging-in-Publication Data

MacGregor, Wayne C., 1925-
   Through these portals : a Pacific war saga / Wayne C. MacGregor, Jr..
     p. cm.
   Includes bibliographical references and index.
   ISBN 0-87422-255-9 (pbk. : alk. paper) — ISBN 0-87422-256-7 (hardbound : alk. paper)
     1. MacGregor, Wayne C., 1925- 2. Soldiers—United States—Biography. 3. World War,
   1939-1945—Campaigns—Pacific Area. 4. World War, 1939-1945—Personal narratives,
   American. 5. Spokane (Wash.)—Social conditions. 6. United States—Social conditions—
   1933-1945. I. Title.

   D767 .M16 2002   2002013187

Front Cover: 77th Division infantrymen fording the Tagbong River on Leyte in the Philippines. *U.S. Army*

Division patches: (l. to r.) 1st Marine Division, 27th Infantry Division, 2nd Marine Division, 77th Infantry Division, 6th Marine Division, 96th Infantry Division, 7th Infantry Division.

TABLE OF CONTENTS

DEDICATION

This book is for all those men and women who
went into World War II and never returned;
for those who did return but are no longer with us;
and for the remainder who in a few short years will also
be gone, leaving only a memory of their service.

A Foreword by the Editor

I well remember the World War II generation when they still were young, mainly in their 30s and 40s, and yet had eyes set on future goals in a prospering America. They were heroes to those of us born not long after the war ended. In the 1950s and 1960s, it seemed that practically every youngster's father had been a soldier, sailor, or airman.

When families met, veterans sometimes moved off to the side and quietly discussed their military experiences. My brother and I eagerly listened in on these stories—the Native American severely burned in a submarine accident; the airman shot down by Axis gunners and held in a German *stalag;* the Coast Guardsman wounded during fighting in the Aleutians; a female relative who served in the Navy's Women Reserves; our own father clearing obstacles for attacking tanks on Okinawa; an uncle in the Navy whose machine gun helped blast a kamikaze plane into oblivion just 100 yards from his ship. Other uncles, too, served in the Merchant Marine, one of whom I'm named after, Glen Wyley, who perished in 1942 during the Battle of the Atlantic.

Often close to the surface in these tales, too, were hints of incredible horrors, seldom openly discussed. Our parents, mothers and fathers alike, also recalled growing up during the Great Depression—a period of national tribulation as intense as the war itself. Because of the World War II generation's dedication to duty, it seemed to me, when a youth, that Americans of every generation were destined for trial and adventure—in my time this was exemplified by President Kennedy's call to national service, the Peace Corps, and our struggle in the Cold War. Could we measure up, as our heroes had?

The long Vietnam conflict, particularly in the years 1965–72, regretfully changed much of this. Whereas World War II had ended in a costly but great triumph, Vietnam seemed to be an endless quagmire. Despite this, many young Americans followed the example of their patriotic parents and willingly served in the military. Many other sons and daughters, however, heeded their fathers' stories of war's horror, which no doubt contributed in some measure to the Vietnam War protest movement. The Vietnam conflict's deep perplexities tended to divide the generations—neither parents nor their offspring really understood the vastly different geopolitical and social realities that divided the 1940s from the 1960s.

Fortunately, these divisive issues have greatly softened in recent years, and again the younger generations are giving their World War II era parents and grandparents the respect and gratitude they deserve. I'm sure I speak for many when I say it's an especially gratifying reconciliation. We feel honored to hear their stories—and Wayne MacGregor's is one of the best.

It might be worth noting that I, the book's editor and historian, and Tom Thompson, one of the manuscript's outside reviewers, both have fathers who served with the 96th Infantry Division, which stood shoulder to shoulder with Wayne MacGregor's 77th Division on Okinawa. Sylvan R. Thompson was a tank man, and Melvin C. Lindeman, a combat engineer. I'm grateful to Wayne MacGregor for providing profound insight into the challenges faced by our fathers and the other men who served on Okinawa. Tom Thompson and I, too, have both served in army infantry units (peacetime duty) and have enjoyed discussions with Wayne about equipment, small-unit tactics, etc. Also, a dozen photos from our fathers' collections supplement Wayne's extraordinary pictures in *Through These Portals*.

In the 1950s, it still was common to hear the respectful expression, "He's a man's man." Cultural and gender sensitivities have changed in recent decades, of course, and such usage now is seldom heard, but this was a linguistic holdover from the time when our parents grew up. The qualities embodied in the term, "being a man," included self-respect, courage, honesty, cordiality, hard work, backbone, responsibility, and self-sufficiency. No matter what his occupation or station in life, a "man" was someone you respected. I've heard it said that my Uncle Glen was "a man's man." In the long process of preparing this book for publication and developing a friendship with the author, I can truly say the same about Wayne MacGregor.

Setting the Stage for *Through These Portals*

Like peoples everywhere, the Japanese have had their enigmas. In their period of modernization in the late 19th and early 20th centuries, they retained their admirable sensitivity to nature, profound philosophical disciplines, strong familial affiliations, and exceptional artistic traditions while at the same time practicing the harshest kind of xenophobia, militarism, and exploitation of outside populations.

Being one of the world's most dynamic peoples, they were a dreadful enemy to reckon with in World War II. Of course, the Allies' main foe in Europe, the Germans, also were extremely formidable, and the Italians, too, could be tough opponents when well led, such as by Nazi General Erwin Rommel in North Africa. But, as Wayne MacGregor so aptly points out, Japanese soldiers in the Pacific simply were in a class of their own—they were "tremendous adversaries."

Some understanding of their haughtiness, fatalism in combat, cruelty, and primal adoration of the Emperor can be gained by briefly looking at their history. In the early 1600s, after a period of initial contact with Dutch, Portuguese, and

English mariners, traders, and missionaries, Japan's leaders abruptly closed their country to all outsiders. Shut off from the world for the next two centuries, the Japanese retained a stolid, rather feudal-like social, political, and economic order; uninvited foreigners landing on their shores were summarily executed.

By the 1850s, however, it became obvious to many in the hermit kingdom that the growing influence of the Western colonial powers in Asia would make it impossible for Japan to maintain its exclusion policy. Consequently in the 1860s–70s, Japan grudgingly opened its doors to the outside world in a volatile period of internal revolts between reactionaries and progressives, and occasional coastal bombardments by Western navies.

Emperor Meiji's court took a lead in forming the new policies. The objective now was to achieve complete equality with the Western powers. From this period came impressive economic, commercial, social, and political modernization, but ingrained feelings of racial and cultural superiority and specialness, disapproval of outsiders, and a brutal, feudal-like obedience to authority still remained in the national character, particularly among members of the armed forces.

Needing natural resources for industrial development and feeling destined to lead Asian populations out of Western bondage, the Japanese had begun expanding territorially both by diplomatic and military means, particularly against their Chinese neighbor. Meanwhile, initial stirrings by populations all across Asia to throw off the West's unfair trading policies and foreign yoke also had begun. A strong and technologically modern Asian power, like Japan, might have been an especially influential element in this movement. Ironically, as arrogant Japanese political and military leaders extended their new empire in the decades ahead, they established harsher colonial regimes and imposed even more onerous demands on their Asian neighbors than the Western powers did.

Japan's long record of aggression began in the late 1870s when occupying the Ryukyu Islands (Okinawa) despite China's protest. Elsewhere, the Kurils in the north and other western Pacific islands fell into Japanese hands. This was followed in 1894–95 by a successful war against China and the acquisition of Formosa and the Pescadores. Japan then sided with the Western nations in China's Boxer Rebellion of 1900. Next came conflict with Imperial Russia in 1904–5, started by a Japanese "surprise attack" against the Russian fleet at Port Arthur. Japan's naval and ground forces were victorious and the Russians conceded southern Sakhalin Island and a Japanese presence in south Manchuria. Korea, too, was annexed in 1905–10.

During World War I, Japan opportunistically grabbed German possessions in China and Micronesia, including the Marshall, Caroline, and most of the Mariana islands. Next, all of Manchuria was seized militarily in 1931, followed in 1937 by a massive continuing assault against China proper, and two border battles with the Soviet Union in the late 1930s. In 1940–41, Japan diplomatically wrested French Indo-China from a German-defeated French nation. Everywhere, except for the non-consequential clashes with the Soviets, Japan's imperial ambitions and armed forces had long triumphed, giving them feelings of invincibility.

Also in the late 1920s, as much of the world slid toward economic chaos, fascism, and nationalistic aggression, jingoistic Japanese militarists were in ascendancy over the more liberal and progressive elements of society and government. By 1936, they had taken full control of Japan's leadership.

Cognizant that their mostly mountainous homeland lacked sufficient natural resources to support an expansive imperialistic policy, the Japanese eyed the vast oil, rice, rubber, and mineral deposits of British Malaya and Burma, the Philippines (acquired by the U.S. in the 1898 Spanish American War), and especially the Dutch East Indies (essentially today's Malaysia and Indonesia). Here were the rich resources needed to sustain a vast empire and to economically and militarily displace Western influence in Asia. A critical time of decision had arrived for the island nation.

Japan's continued armed aggression in China had increasingly aggravated the United States. By 1940–41, the American government had imposed the severest kinds of trade sanctions and warnings against Japan. A showdown clearly was imminent; either Japan had to restrict its further imperial ambitions and withdraw in China, or serious confrontation with the United States was inevitable. At this juncture in mid 1941, Japan's leaders made the fatal decision to invade the rich southern resource area and fight a war of attrition against the United States in the vast Pacific Ocean. They realized, too, that their Pacific neighbor, the Soviet Union, no longer was a threat, as the Russians were locked in a death grip with German armies outside of Moscow. Final planning began for the early December 1941 surprise attacks on Hawaii, the Philippines, and British-held Malaya.

Japanese arrogance toward the Chinese, their anti-Westernism, and their sense of destiny in establishing a "new order" in Asia are clearly evident in Emperor Hirohito's declaration of war on America and Britain. This extraordinary document—providing a clear insight into the thinking of Japan's wartime leadership—is presented on page 212 of *Through These Portals*.

It is, then, in this context of the Great Depression and an expanding worldwide conflagration that Wayne MacGregor's remarkable personal story, and that of millions of other young Americans, unfolded in the 1930s and early 1940s.

Glen W. Lindeman
Editor in Chief
Washington State University Press

PREFACE

Trying to recall events of over a half-century ago with clarity and accuracy is a difficult feat. The memories in this chronicle are mine. They may or may not be bent by the passage of time, and they might differ in some ways from the remembrances of friends, family, and comrades in arms. I realize that sometimes we recall events not as they actually happened, but rather as we wished they had. However, to the "best" of my recollection and awareness, everything occurred in the way and manner that I've recorded it.

I've also attempted to chronologically correlate my personal experiences with the broader historical developments that occurred at the same time. However, since this primarily is not meant to be a history, but rather a memoir, reference notes are limited. For those wanting more detailed historical information, there is a suggested reading list at the back of *Through These Portals* that includes works that I've found especially valuable or well-written.

Time is a common denominator and age eventually equalizes all of us. Ultimately, we come to the point where, as our mortality triumphs, our wins and losses no longer count so much for or against us. More than 75 years have swept past me, like the high-beam lights of an on-coming car in the night. For a long time, its approach is lucent, taking an interminable time in coming, and illuminating everything before it with great clarity. Then suddenly it's past, leaving only an aching darkness in what had been a bright, shining radiance. So, too, my life has been brightened for these past many years, anticipated and anxiously awaited. Suddenly, however, comes the realization that it's almost past—that one's life does not, and will not, continue indefinitely. We fade away, leaving for posterity only what remains of us in the "memories" of those we leave behind.

This conclusion reminds me of my father-in-law, Thomas Rex Walenta, who was born in Iowa in 1901. When five years old, he traveled with his family in a covered wagon to northwest South Dakota. There, his father homesteaded and eventually raised cattle and sheep on several thousand acres of prairie near the Standing Rock Sioux Indian Reservation. When Rex was 14, being the youngest of two sons, he was sent off to high school and then college, while his older brother stayed on the land and ranched with their father.

Rex was born with a bright and active mind that he finely honed in college, ultimately earning education and law degrees from the University of Idaho, and master's and doctor of law degrees from the University of Illinois. After engaging in private practice for several years in Minnesota and Colorado, Rex brought his family to the University of Idaho where he served as a professor of law for 18 years.

Rex's lifetime spanned an era: from when people still traveled west in covered wagons to a time when men walked on the moon. Being of Irish lineage (his mother was a Nolan from County Cork, Ireland), he had innate ability as a fine teacher and communicator. A raconteur, he loved to talk to people and his narratives always were enthralling, often interspersed with the brilliant sense of humor that's so characteristic of the Irish.

We often urged him to write down his stories, and later, as he aged, to record them on tape, but he did neither. Rex passed away in 1995, his lifetime having nearly spanned the 20th century. Now, almost all of his engrossing stories—so many connecting his life with prominent personages and significant events—are unfortunately dimmed or lost by the inevitable passing of people and time.

Perhaps that's why my children have urged me to leave something in writing—a memoir—for them to pass on to their descendants. Accordingly, I've recorded as best I can the recollections of my youth. My life started in the mid 1920s when our nation experienced much promise, joy, and prosperity. Then suddenly in the 1930s, America was cast into economic and social darkness and despair. Then came the first half of the 1940s—an age of wickedness, death, and destruction of a scope never before experienced in world history. But destitution and evil finally were overcome by a generation of young Americans who wouldn't quit, couldn't be defeated, and who left a bright and shining future for their descendants. It will require patience, hard work, and dedication to maintain that legacy—the challenge is there for succeeding generations if they are up to it.

1 HARD TIMES

*A*S A BOY OF ABOUT FIVE OR SIX, I remember when Dad worked in a sawmill not far from our house. I'd wait for him every afternoon to come home and I always could hear him whistling before he walked into the yard. I'd run to meet him, he'd take my hand, and we'd walk into the house together.

Mother stayed home and cared for us kids—Norma, Joyce, and myself. When she and Dad separated, no one told me why it happened, it just occurred. Dad never sat me down and gave an explanation of any kind. All that Mother said was that he didn't want to live with us anymore, that he was leaving and wouldn't be coming back.

When Dad came home to get his clothes, he gave me a tube of airplane glue. He knew I was working on an airplane model and needed cement for the balsa wood pieces. When he left, I put it on an apple crate next to my bed. I never touched it again. After two or three years, it became hard and brittle, and I couldn't have used it anyway. But, it was one of the last things he ever gave me. It was a reminder of those times when I had a father—someone who lived with me, that I could turn to for comfort, who was there when I needed him.

I never really had a relationship with him after that. Not that he didn't try to see me occasionally. He did, but I never forgave him for leaving Mother, my sisters, and myself. Now that he was gone, I somehow felt I had to take his place in the family and to do that I needed to shut him completely out of my life. I believed that he had deserted us and I wanted nothing to do with him.

Dad's trouble was his attraction to women. He was a big, tall, handsome man—about six feet three and two hundred and twenty pounds. "Moose," as he was known, looked and acted like a movie star. He had a warm, outgoing personality and a deep, resonant voice. He liked to talk and did so capably. For years, he worked as a part-time sports broadcaster and was known as the voice of the Spokane Indians, the local professional baseball team.

Then, as now, young women were drawn to men's athletic events. Baseball players were physically imposing and attractive, and when women came to see them play, Dad was no less impressive. Sitting in the press box, the spotlight often was on him while announcing the game, or when singing the national anthem along with the crowd in a sweet, Irish tenor voice. "Moose" became a recognized part of the Spokane baseball scene.

Unfortunately as time went on, some of the women—observing that handsome, stirring man with the microphone in his hand, calling every play and commenting on the players—began to be attracted to him. Inevitably, women got in his way as an announcer, the same as it did with being Mother's husband and our father.

★★★

I was born on May 27, 1925, at the Astor Apartments on North Astor in Spokane, Washington, right across the street from the Western Pine Mill where Dad worked. He was a sawyer and had been employed there since he was fourteen years old. Like many young men in those days, he hadn't attended high school and had started working after completing grade school. Being big and strong for his age, he had no trouble finding a job. He was a good worker, never was fired or laid off from any job, and never took any type of government assistance. The social programs we now call "welfare" were then referred to as "being on relief." He refused to have anything to do with government work relief programs or any other kind of aid or assistance. He was a proud man—proud of his size and strength. Asking for, or receiving, help was a sign of weakness in his eyes. He always said he could find work no matter how hard the times were, and he did.

Being a mill worker, he was proud of the fact that he still had all of his fingers. When his friends came to visit, I noticed how many of them had lost thumbs and fingers—almost everyone! There was no OSHA in those days and safety regulations were unheard of. In the late 1920s and early 1930s, production was the most important goal of any manufacturing plant or factory. Production, production, production—to hell with safety and working conditions! This was the time of the Great Depression and if a man wasn't prepared to work long hours, six days a week, under any conditions, there were plenty of other men standing in line outside the mills, factories, and employment offices ready to take his place. They'd jump at the chance, fighting for any available job. They didn't ask about the safety conditions, working hours, or wages. They were only interested in getting a job—any work, any time, anywhere.

When I was seven or eight, Dad switched to a job driving for the Spokane Crematorium, which is just another way of saying he drove a garbage truck. Not that there was anything wrong or demeaning about this. During the Depression, holding any long-term job was considered a wonderful achievement. With so much unemployment rampant, men who had a permanent job were looked up to and envied. I was proud that my Dad was working. Besides, this had other hidden benefits. Bakeries threw away old rolls and bread, and other businesses and shops discarded stale candy, soiled clothes and fabrics, and used towels. Dad went through these items and brought home what he thought was useable. We kids especially enjoyed the candy even though it was old, hard, and broken up.

One unfortunate thing, however, resulted from our use of scavenged fabrics—Dad brought home bedbugs. One morning while Norma helped Mother make the beds, she noticed little red spots along the mattress seams. When Mother examined them, she exclaimed in anger and disgust, "Bedbugs!" She always had carefully washed the soiled fabrics that Dad brought home, but even so, she thought that was the source of the bedbugs. She spent days washing all of our clothing, scrubbing the floors, and sprinkling bedbug powder in every corner, along the edges of the walls, and under the beds. Finally, she was satisfied that they were exterminated.

As we went to bed at night, we children now understood what Mother meant when, wryly smiling, she'd say, "Goodnight, sleep tight, don't let the bedbugs bite."

I was ten when Mother noticed my grades falling off at Logan Elementary School. She took me along to talk to Miss Major, my fifth grade teacher, who said, "I believe he needs glasses."

Although any extra expense was a real hardship for a family like ours, Mother took me to an optical shop and had me fitted for glasses. I still remember the day! At that time, we lived in an old clapboard house on 2226 N. Cincinnati Street. After Mother and I stepped on a streetcar to go home, I looked out the windows, seeing things I never knew existed. I read signs that I didn't even know were there. I could recognize drivers in cars for the first time. It was a miracle and I was the happiest kid in town. I'd worried about being called "four eyes" and that my friends might think me a "sissy," but none of that mattered now. I could see!

From our house on Cincinnati Street, it was only a few blocks west to North Astor Street where the Western Pine Mill was located. Further west, just beyond the mill, stood the old Union Iron Works, which the Depression had shut down. Behind it was a storage area containing all types of discarded steel culverts and an unimaginable jungle of old, rusting, and abandoned machinery of all kinds. It was an iron cemetery, where young boys could spend hours in a fantasyland crawling through pipes and culverts, and climbing up to the seats and controls of corroded tractors, cranes, backhoes, and other heavy construction equipment. We fought make believe wars and explored a strange, weird, but dangerous world—a place where our mothers feared we'd get hurt or injured and had told us to avoid.

The Hillyard streetcar, which went near our house on 2226 N. Cincinnati Sreet, Spokane. *Northwest Museum of Arts & Culture/EWSHS, Spokane, WA (L87-113.63)*

Also located here was a large empty field where a circus erected its tents during annual visits to Spokane. The circus arrived on its own train at the railroad siding north of Trent, near Division. They'd unload there and form a huge caravan that paraded north on Division to the empty lot next to the Union Iron Works, in effect offering a preview of the coming show.

People who wouldn't be able to afford tickets to see the performances stood among hundreds of spectators lining Division Street and watched the procession. Circus musicians marched in the caravan to the crescendos of drums. Tigers, lions, leopards, and even a hippopotamus were pulled along in cages mounted on large, wagon-like flatcars. Alongside walked clowns and acrobats, together with elephants, camels, horses, or even ostriches. When this multitude of circus animals, people, and equipment reached the empty lot, men immediately began erecting the "big top," a huge tent that covered bleachers and the "three rings" for the shows. "Hawkers" instantly called out in high, shrill voices, offering free tickets to any boys who'd carry water for the elephants, which seemed to have an unquenchable thirst. For several years, I always volunteered and earned tickets for admission in this way.

After the huge circus tents were raised up, they were outfitted inside with high wires, trapezes, and brightly painted collapsible bleachers, along with booths, food stands, and sideshows. Suddenly, in addition to the sharp, pungent odor of sawdust and animal manure, the irresistible smell of popcorn, cotton candy, hamburgers, and hotdogs filled the air, which added to the excitement, stimulation, and fascination that seemed to permeate the circus environment.

Even today, a thrill goes through me when I see a circus, and I wish I were nine or ten years old again, hauling water to the elephants.

★★★

In 1933 Dad purchased a used 1927 Dodge. We'd never owned a car before. How wonderful! That summer we took a trip to visit Dad's cousins in Montana. The Dave Sweet ranch was up along the Canadian border, east of Sweetgrass, in the rolling, high-line, cattle country of northern Montana.

Dad told me his cousins were "real cowboys" and I could ride horses at the ranch. I was so excited; it was all I thought about. After all, the adults in the neighborhood where we lived had given me the nickname "Two Gun Harvard Hooligan." "Two Gun" because everywhere I went I pretended to be a cowboy and always wore two holsters with my cap guns in them; "Harvard" because they said I was bright and always had an answer for everything; and "Hooligan" since I continually was getting into some kind of trouble. Norma, my older sister, was as excited as I was, but sister Joyce was too little yet to understand.

Joyce and "Two Gun Harvard Hooligan."

Mother prepared all the food we'd need for the trip—everything was either baked or canned. There were no fast food "drive-ins" in those days, nor were there motels with full services. Travelers stayed at "auto camps," which usually consisted of a cluster of small shacks on a lot next to a highway. Few auto camps had running water, other than a centrally located, communal spigot, and most had outdoor toilets. But staying at auto camps cost money and we didn't have any to spare. In fact, practically nobody had any extra money in those days, and most travelers, when nighttime came, simply pulled off to the side of the road and slept in their cars or on the ground.

Rising early, the Dodge was packed and we left Spokane for Montana. We tented the first night alongside the road in a little meadow by a creek, perhaps 25 or 30 miles north of Missoula, Montana. Dad cut a lodge pole, tied it between two trees, threw a tarp over it, hammered down the tent poles, and dug a drainage ditch. We were ready for the night.

The next morning when I got up, Dad already had prepared a fire and Mother was cooking hotcakes and bacon. I could smell the aroma floating into the tent and couldn't get dressed fast enough to get down to the creek, wash my hands and face, and come back to eat. After eating and packing our gear, we headed out. Dad regaled us with Wild West tales and descriptions of the magnificent scenery we'd be seeing when passing through Glacier National Park and the Blackfeet Indian Reservation. Dad explained that the Blackfeet always had lived on the Great Plains east of the Rocky Mountains. From time immemorial, they'd driven buffalo herds over cliffs, butchering them where they fell and were killed. The Blackfeet country, he said, had been a land of plenty.

Among the first contacts that the Blackfeet had with white people was when Captain Meriwether Lewis entered their country in 1806, during the Lewis and Clark Expedition's return from the Pacific Ocean. Lewis with three men had undertaken a side trip north to the headwaters of the Marias River and entered what is now the heart of the Blackfeet Indian Reservation. Lewis's small party soon met a small band of young Piegans, one of three tribes comprising the Blackfeet nation, the other two being the Blood and Blackfeet proper. The Piegans, Dad explained, were probably the most proud, independent, and warlike of all Plains tribes. He said the Indians determined wealth by the number of horses they owned. The more horses a man owned, the more household necessities could be carried and the more wives he could have.

In any event, Dad explained that when Lewis met the young warriors he desired to be friends with them and wanted to establish future trading relationships between the tribe and the United States. Consequently, they camped together that evening. Early the next morning, however, the Indians suddenly attempted to make off with the Lewis party's horses and firearms. They grabbed a rifle and started to run, pursued by a couple of Lewis's men. In the ensuing struggle, one Indian was stabbed to death. Lewis attempted to halt other warriors by shouting to them, but one turned and fired his rifle at Lewis, who shot back and killed the man. The remainder of the party ran off.

Greatly alarmed and frightened by the encounter, and deep in what was now hostile country, Lewis's group quickly broke camp. With all possible speed, they rode for the far-off Missouri River where they eventually rejoined another detachment of the expedition and continued by canoe downstream toward St. Louis. Dad told us that we'd be passing close by the spot where this incident occurred. (Mother always told me that she thought Dad's mother, Grandma Crow, had Blackfeet blood. I asked Grandma a few times, but she never acknowledged it.)

We continued along the west side of Flathead Lake, where much of the road was under maintenance. It was rough and dusty. In Glacier Park, Dad said, we'd be traveling on the new Going-to-the-Sun Highway, which opened for the first time that summer (July 1933). He said it'd be something we'd remember all of our lives.

After entering the park and passing by magnificent Lake McDonald, we proceeded into the McDonald Creek valley, with its beautiful waterfalls and tumbling cascades. When making an eastward bend in the new roadway, we saw before us the continental divide and the Rocky Mountains, a sheer, great wall standing against the horizon. Dad said it was "the backbone of the United States." The Going-to-the-Sun Highway was unpaved—in fact, it largely consisted of large rocks, about four to six inches in diameter. Most of it hadn't been gravelled. Few, if any, hard surfaced roads existed anywhere in the West in those days, except in cities and towns like Seattle and Spokane.[1]

Also, automobile tires in the 1930s weren't the wonderful manufactured creations of today that last 60,000 or 70,000 miles before wearing out. They were thin and vulnerable to sharp rocks. We had flats twice on our way over Logan Pass in Glacier Park. Each time, everyone had to get out, Dad jacked up the car and removed the tire, and we'd repair the tube with a patching kit. After the inner tube was patched up and put back inside the tire, it was pumped up with a hand pump.

In mid summer, even in the high mountains, it was a hot job. I remember Dad with beads of sweat running down his forehead and nose. Although the old Dodge had an electric starter and battery, it often worked reluctantly or not at all, so Dad had to hand crank the engine. Sometimes the engine kicked back, which was dangerous if one weren't careful—the hand crank might break a thumb or wrist. Dad, being hot, dirty, and tired, on occasion used some pretty strong language. This enabled me to add a few choice words to my vocabulary that I later passed on to schoolmates.

Numerous tumbling, splashing creeks lined the road, and often there were concrete holding basins with pipes running from them for drinking water. We filled the car radiator at every opportunity. The water was ice cold and tasted wonderful. In those days, no one heard of Giardiasis, the diarrhea-causing intestinal disease usually attributed to drinking from streams polluted by wild or domestic animals.

Travel over the pass was slow and there were patches of snow alongside the road. Few cut-stone barriers lined the road's edge in those days. As Dad drove the old Dodge through some of the tight turns, you could look out the side of the car and see the treetops below, moving in the wind. One almost got dizzy watching them. We felt that it was a dangerous road. Mother was almost to the point of crying several times, but the scenery was absolutely awe-inspiring.

Wonderful grand hotels constructed by American and Canadian railroad companies stood in these mountains at the time—Many Glacier, East Glacier, and McDonald lodges in Glacier National Park, and the Prince of Wales Lodge in Canada's adjoining Waterton Lakes National Park—but we never stopped at any of them.[2] They were too expensive and, besides, the weather was warm and it was more fun to camp out. I believe my love of wilderness was initiated and nurtured during that trip over the Going-to-the-Sun Highway in 1933.

We continued past St. Mary Lake and out the park's east gate to the reservation town of Browning. From there, we went east through Cut Bank to Shelby, and then turned sharply north to Sunburst and on to the little village of Sweetgrass. Soon, we were warmly welcomed at Uncle Dave's ranch.

Like lonely sentinels on the immense prairie, the Sweet Grass Hills are towering bulwarks on the border between Montana and Canada. Just to the north, the Milk River flows in an irregular, wandering channel eastward to its far-off meeting with the great Missouri. Most people in Montana will tell you that the Sweet Grass Hills were named after the short buffalo grass that grows from the mid Dakotas to the Rockies, once the heart of the North American buffalo country and the hunting ground of the Blackfeet. By the mid 1880s, when the buffalo were hunted to extinction almost everywhere else on the Great Plains, a few small bands remained in the Sweet Grass Hills. These last remnants eventually were exterminated, too.

Dad at Dave Sweet's ranch in Montana, July 1933.

Uncle Dave's father had come into that country bringing cattle with him and staked a claim near the Sweet Grass Hills. While it was popularly acknowledged that the hills were named for the sweet grass, Uncle Dave told us, with a twinkle in his eyes, that this wasn't the case. He said, when his father's neighbors were asked by others whose land this was, they'd point at it, saying, "That's Sweet's grass." This is how the hills got their name—according to Uncle Dave!

One day, Uncle Dave said he'd take us to where there'd been a battle between two Indian tribes and we could look for arrowheads and other artifacts. We all loaded into Dad's old Dodge and Uncle Dave's ancient Model T Ford and took off to the northeast. There wasn't a road, just tracks and ruts going in the general direction that Uncle Dave and others had driven to the battlefield. Digging down where Uncle Dave previously found artifacts, we uncovered arrow points and the head of a war-club.[3] We also found larger projectile points and a number of small trade beads.

While searching through the short buffalo grass, which at this time of year was beginning to turn brown, we felt the weather changing as the wind picked up and the temperature dropped. A huge gray mass of clouds was coming from the north, reaching from horizon to horizon, and stirring up clouds of dust in front of it. Uncle Dave said we'd better pile into our rigs and get out of there because once it started to rain, we'd sink in mud up to the hubs and be lucky if we didn't have to walk back to the ranch. Fortunately, it was mostly downhill, but the rain began coming down hard. Soon, the tracks worn in the sod turned to thick mud and it was difficult to get through. We pulled out of the ruts onto the buffalo grass sod and kept driving until we finally reached the ranch.

Then the rain poured down in sheets and we ran for the cabin. Mother and I stood silently under the back porch roof watching the downpour. Water drained off the roof in rivulets, and inside the house it sounded as if someone were pounding on the ceiling. The next day, water stood in pools all around the yard, with the mud ankle deep. Only Uncle Dave and his sons ventured out— to milk cows.

I've often thought about that week spent at Uncle Dave's place and how he made us feel so welcome. I've wondered, too, about what this land was like when it belonged to the Blackfeet, and what an effort it must have been for the early ranchers, struggling just to survive in that often harsh, bitter country. How did they stand up to the winters when the wind blew across the frozen prairie and the cattle bunched up in fence corners, turning their hind quarters to the weather to protect themselves—with their nostrils filling up with ice and the temperature tumbling as low as −40°. Cattle sometimes died where they stood. This was a hard country and Uncle Dave and those families that lived there were tough people. I've lost all track of the Sweets and I don't know if any of them remain in that country. But that week of hospitality is ingrained in my memory as reminiscent of the traditional generosity once offered by isolated ranch people all across the American West.

Dad said we'd be leaving in a day or two, but we'd wait to watch the branding. Next morning, Uncle Dave and his sons brought cattle down from the hills

My mother, Estella, and Dave Sweet's son, with a "bummer" lamb at the Montana ranch.

to corrals next to the house. Dad had built a fire and kept the flames hot, maintaining the branding irons at the right temperature. We'd take the red-hot irons and hand them to the cowboys through the corral posts, and carried the cooled-off ones back to the fire. Dad's cousins stretched the calves out while Uncle Dave leaned into them with a branding iron. It sizzled and smoked as it touched hair and hide, and the little critters bawled. Castrating young bulls—turning them into steers—also was done at this time. It was dusty and hot, and the men worked hard. I sat on the corral fence watching it all. I know the rituals of branding still continue today as they did back then, but I've grown older and it wouldn't hold the same excitement for me as when I was a child watching, with fascination, "real cowboys."

Having finished seeing the branding, we said our goodbyes and left the Sweet Grass Hills, heading south to the oil towns of Sunburst, Oilmont, and Shelby. The Kevin-Sunburst oil field, stretching across the northern Montana plains from Shelby north to Canada, had been discovered in 1921, boomed for several years, and then slowed down. Shelby was a typical western cow town. Established in 1891 along the newly constructed Great Northern Railway, it was named after Pete Shelby, a railroad manager. When told about this distinction, Shelby reportedly said, "That miserable forsaken mudhole will never amount to a goddamn."

This assertion wasn't entirely correct because in 1923 a daring promotional event was undertaken at Shelby—a heavyweight boxing championship between reigning world champion Jack Dempsey and Tommy Gibbons, the number one contender. Several prominent cattlemen and bankers recently made wealthy by the oil strikes had personally guaranteed the financing needed to entice Dempsey and his entourage to come to Montana. A huge arena was built of locally sawn lumber with a seating capacity for 40,000 people. Shelby's population at the time was less than 2,000 and there were no paved roads in the town or vicinity.

Several causes contributed to a financial fiasco, but primarily the huge gamble didn't succeed because, right up to fight day, there were rumors that the bout wasn't actually going to be held. Consequently, many specially chartered trains cancelled their trips to Montana. Thousands of other fight fans, who'd intended on coming by automobile, stayed home. The championship bout, indeed, came off as scheduled. However, instead of a "million dollar gate" as some predicted, ticket sales apparently were only slightly in excess of $200,000. Reportedly after the fight, several Montana banks failed and a number of Shelby ranchers and businessmen filed for bankruptcy.

By the early 1930s, however, fresh oil strikes were rebuilding the fortunes of many local residents, and once again money flowed freely in Shelby. I remember when we stopped at a service station, I couldn't believe that water was being sold in pop bottles for 15 cents. Evidently, water was terribly scarce and trucked in from out of town. Shelby was crowded with oilmen from all over the country, particularly from Oklahoma and Texas. Speculators, planning on making thousands of dollars, were securing leases from local ranchers and farmers.

The dusty streets of the towns were crowded with horses, wagons, automobiles, and trucks of every kind. The whole population was "oil mad," thinking up ways to make money in the expanding petroleum fields. Ranchers ran back and forth selling leases, and oil company representatives were either buying up leases or trying to dispose of ones that hadn't proved out. Everything was expensive and there seemed to be a lot of money in circulation. Nobody seemed to talk or think about anything but oil. It worked a hardship on some ranchers seeking hired hands because all available local laborers were working for the oil companies. The activity was so hectic that I was glad when we left for Glacier Park. We arrived home two days later.

★★★

By late 1933, the Depression had ripened into a bitter harvest of despair in Spokane. More and more people were filled with doubts and skepticism over what the future held. For families, with it came the cruel, harsh challenge of putting food on the table and finding clothing for children during the uncompromising winter months. The destitute face of the country had a frightening aspect—particularly after the enthusiasm of the previous decade, when thousands of victorious young soldiers had returned from Europe in 1918–19, followed by the exhilarating prosperity of the 1920s.

Unlike today, the percentage of Americans in the late 1920s and early 1930s who had stock market investments was rather minimal. When the 1929 Wall Street Crash occurred, it didn't immediately decimate any substantial portion of the public with financial losses. Rather, along with the financial downturn came a general impression that there were going to be adverse impacts on the nation's economic activity. This thinking increased pessimism, and even contributed in part to the economic disaster that followed in a couple of years.

Wealth wasn't as equally distributed as today—consumer spending was low because most people had little money. Unemployment started rising, and shops and stores began to feel the effects when people didn't have cash to purchase the necessities of life, let alone luxuries. Businesses and factories began closing because they couldn't sell enough goods, money became ever scarcer, and banks failed. As fear and failure spread throughout the nation, nearly everyone began suffering. Hundreds of thousands of out-of-work young people began travelling across the country looking for employment. Most didn't have automobiles. They jumped on freight trains or put out their thumbs along the roadways, hitching rides wherever they could to go looking for jobs. Older adults, too, with no employment and little or no income, began to gather up their families and belongings in cars and drove out on the highways to seek a fresh start someplace else.

Throughout the winter of 1933 and into 1934, thousands of lonely, desperate people—moving from city to city, county to county, and state to state—stopped at hobo jungles, went from door to door asking for food, sought out soup kitchens, or stood on sidewalks asking for hand outs. Some resorted to stealing food, and crime began to increase in the countryside. In Spokane, unemployed people sat on the sidewalks, leaning against buildings, with their hands held out begging for money or food. They slept in alleys and on the streets, or huddled together in little groups under Spokane River bridges, sharing a fire and a can of stew. They'd pay a dime for a bed or a mattress in a flophouse, or sought out vacated houses, or crawled into abandoned cars or culverts to get out of the weather.

Fear pervaded most everywhere—fear that you'd lose your job if you had one, fear that you couldn't buy groceries for your family, fear that you wouldn't be able to heat your home. Children feared for their parents, who would hardly eat anything for three or four days so that there'd be sufficient nutrition for the kids. Despair passed over America like an Arctic wind, chilling hope and confidence, and leaving behind despondency and hopelessness. Unless someone has lived through it, this kind of fear can't be understood.

For a time, we still were fairly comfortable. Dad worked full-time and was managing to meet our family's financial obligations and keep our stomachs full, but then it began to fall apart. Dad's weaknesses brought devastation upon us. When his city crematorium route was changed from a residential area to the southeast side of downtown Spokane where dance halls, bars, taverns, and whorehouses lined the streets, he simply didn't have the will to withstand temptation. My sisters and I noticed that he wasn't coming home every night, and then we began to hear Mother and him arguing and shouting. It wasn't long afterward that he picked up his belongings and left, moving into a downtown hotel.

With Dad gone, Mother not only was taking care of us by herself, but she had to find employment. She managed to get a job candling eggs at the Washington Co-op, located just south of Sprague Avenue almost twenty-six blocks from where we lived on Cincinnati Street. Mother woke, dressed, and fed us each morning before leaving the house by 7 o'clock to walk the long distance to the Co-op. She'd sit all day at a table in front of a bright light, holding up eggs to determine whether good or bad yolks were inside.

To keep the eggs fresh, the building wasn't heated. Candled eggs were individually placed in cardboard egg cartons, which in turn were put in a box. When the boxes were filled and quite heavy, Mother lifted them as high as she could stack them. This process was repeated, with thirty minutes off for lunch, all day long—nine hours a day, and six days a week, for twenty-five cents an hour. Of course there wasn't any overtime pay, medical benefits, or vacation time. It was just a job—one of hard toiling labor.

After work, Mother walked the long distance home, rain or shine. I remember how weary she looked when coming into the house. If it hadn't been for my sister, Norma, Mother couldn't have handled it. Fortunately, Norma was someone Mother could lean on and who helped in many ways keeping the family going.

Groceries, of course, were expensive for people with little income. To cut costs many people constructed chicken and rabbit hutches in their backyards. We had a chicken pen, and I remember once when it was used for something else than hens or rabbits. My cousin Roy had been up to Uncle Pete's place in the Coeur d'Alenes and found a small black bear cub. Where the mother was, Roy didn't know, didn't care, and he didn't look for her. Knowing we had a chicken pen, Roy came by and asked Mother if he could keep the cub there. The cub was small and cute, and we fed it with a nipple and bottle.

Mother told Roy it was all right if he'd partition off part of the pen with chicken wire and take care of the cub. Roy promised to do so, and for the first couple of months he did take good care of it. But, bear cubs grow and this one put on weight like it was training to be a heavyweight wrestler. In what seemed like no time at all, he probably weighed thirty or forty pounds and wasn't as cute as when fed from a bottle. The cub wanted meat and this kept Roy busy going to the market for bones and scraps. Soon, antipathy arose between the bear and Roy. They didn't get along. In fact, the bear cub really disliked Roy. It would charge at Roy when he went into the chicken pen and do its best to try and tear down the wire barrier to get at him. Roy didn't help matters. He had kind of an ornery streak and got a kick out of teasing and tormenting the bear.

One day, Grandpa Smith, when seeing Roy poking a stick at the bear through the chicken wire, told him, "That's enough. You get my car, secure that bear, and take him back to where you found him."

Roy obediently said he would, and asked me to help him. After we put the bear in a wooden crate and in the trunk, instead of driving way out to Uncle Pete's place, he said, "Damn it, Mac, that's too far to go."

With that, we drove only to Minnehaha Park, a natural wooded area on the east side of Spokane. I tried to tell him that we were too close to town, but Roy said, "One place is as good as another," and turned the bear loose.

My apprehensions proved true. Just a few days later, Mother read in the *Spokane Chronicle* that a man bicycling in Minnehaha Park was attacked by a small bear. Mother never said a thing to Roy, but I'm sure she had a good idea where that bear came from.

As the local economy continued to decline, more and more people became unemployed, and Mother, too, was laid off at the co-op. She looked for other work, finding a job as a cleaning lady at the Cambern Creamery, located northwest of North Central High School. We moved to Washington Street so Mother could be closer to her work. I don't know whether Dad paid child support or helped in any other way, but I'm not aware that he did.

During this time, he continued his womanising ways, going out with one woman and then another. It's hard for me to remember their faces let alone their names, but over the next three or four years he was married four times. I'm not sure I even met all of them, except seeing them on the street with him. I believe his next wife was Viola, then Henrietta, Grace, and finally Rhetta. None of the marriages lasted long, and I recall little about these women except that they were leggy, flashy, swung their hips when walking, and were rather hard looking. The first two were peroxide blondes; Grace, a brunette; while Rhetta was a henna dyed redhead. Mother called them Chippys. That's just a more delicate name for a whore, but then she still felt pretty bitter about the whole situation.

I've heard it said, "The right woman can make you, the wrong one can break you." Dad ended up with too many of the wrong ones.

★★★

It's difficult for people today to understand just how hard times were in the mid-1930s. There were few gas or electrical stoves in those days; most homes were heated with wood or coal. Sometimes I'd go out with my cousins to cut cordwood in the backcountry.

The Madison Lumber Company was located a few blocks north of where we lived on Cincinnati Street. I remember as a small boy taking my wagon almost every day to the railroad tracks at the lumber company. I'd pick up pieces of coal dropped by trains when loading and unloading cargo. Other children carrying gunnysacks or pulling wagons also were there looking for coal. Sometimes we fought over the biggest pieces. My hard gained lumps of coal helped heat our house.

My uncle, Pete Kruse, owned land up in the Coeur d'Alene Mountains just southeast of Mica Peak near the Washington-Idaho border, where I spent the summer of 1937 with him and Aunt Grace. He ran a pack string carrying supplies to a sheep outfit that rented his land and other contiguous property for summer range. We lived in an old abandoned log cabin that Uncle Pete had cleaned up. It had a dirt floor and no electricity or plumbing of any kind. Water had to be hauled to the cabin in a pail from a creek about forty or fifty yards away. The toilet was a nearby one-seat outhouse.

It was at this time that I learned to hunt and trap. Pete had lots of traps for different kinds of animals—ground squirrels, badgers, coyotes, and bears. He told me he'd pay a nickel for each ground squirrel that I shot, but I killed so many he reduced the price to a penny. Most people called them "gophers," but they actually were ground squirrels. They dug holes in hayfields and could multiply like rabbits, eating the hay. Literally hundreds seemed to occupy every hayfield. Originally, I shot them with my .22 rifle; however, they eventually became quite wary, whistling a warning and ducking down into their holes as soon as I approached. Consequently, I set out a trap line for them, just as I did for coyotes and badgers.

Badger and coyote pelts were merchantable, and Pete sold them when he got them. Pete hated coyotes. Over the years, he'd lost a number of calves to them. A mother cow could fight off one coyote, keeping it away from her calf, but if there were two or more coyotes, a calf was a goner. Coyotes would work on a mother cow, nipping at her heels and snapping at her nose, while working

Uncle Pete on "Old Shorty," 1938.

her in circles away from her calf. Once this was accomplished, another coyote nailed the calf. A mother cow would stand exhausted, tongue hanging out, and too tired to struggle, and watch the coyotes tear open the calf's belly and start eating, often before the calf was dead.

Coyotes are smart and difficult to trap. A special coyote scent must be used to get them to put a foot into a trap. Uncle Pete prepared scent, which I believe

consisted mostly of coyote urine and blood from a female coyote's sex organs collected when she was in season, plus some contents from coyote intestines. There may have been other ingredients, but Pete never told me about it. He liked to keep the formula a secret. The county paid a $1.50 bounty for coyotes. Pete showed me how to kill trapped coyotes and badgers so that the hide wasn't damaged. Instead of shooting them, we'd carry a shovel, hit them on the head with it to stun them, and then we'd jump up and come down hard on their chests with our knees, crushing the life out of them. After skinning a coyote, we used the shovel to bury the carcass. It may sound cruel, but life was tough in those days, and everyone did whatever was necessary to just get by.

Coyote trapped near Uncle Pete's cabin.

No matter how bad the times were, Pete was sure they'd get better. Pete taught me to be an optimist. He'd say, "When things reach bottom there's only one way to go and that's up."

One rainy day, we pulled the pack string over one ridge after another while carrying supplies to one of the sheep camps. When evening came, we were wet, tired, and hungry. Being exhausted, I didn't think I could even help unpack the horses, let alone lead them off and tie them up, stack the saddle pads and blankets, cover the gear, grain the horses, and help pitch the tent. I just stood there unable to move with the rain running off my hat and down my neck.

Pete came over, put his arm around me, and said, "Mac, don't ever give up. When you've come to the end of your rope, tie a knot in it and hang on."

As the years went by, whenever I found myself in situations that I thought I'd done all I could and had reached "the end of my rope," I'd remember Pete saying, "tie a knot in it and hang on."

I worshiped Pete. He was everything I thought a man should be—honest, true, brave. If you've ever seen old movies starring Wallace Beery, then you've seen Pete. He looked and acted just like Wallace Beery. He had a rough, gruff, perhaps even cantankerous exterior, but underneath he had a heart of gold.

Uncle Pete was good to me. He showed me how to use an axe—how to make a deep cut downward, then one upward, alternating each stroke, and keeping the strokes even so that the cut was almost as smooth as if it'd been polished. He taught me how to use my wrists and put my shoulders into each stroke, delivering the most power at the point of impact. I learned how to ride and pack a horse—to "manty" a load and hump it up on a packsaddle, and throw a diamond hitch around it.

Packing is an art, and once it was the only way to get around in most of the backcountry. In the 1930s, there still were huge areas in Washington, Idaho, Montana, Oregon, and Wyoming where roads didn't exist and the only way of getting across them was on foot or horseback. The Coeur d'Alenes were covered with vast stands of pine, fir, tamarack, and ponderosa. Standing on a summit, one could see an infinity of timbered blue ridges, one after another, and with no logging clear cuts.

Uncle Pete was a good packer. When he "mantyed" a load, it stayed together. He was an artist at tying knots, something I never learned. When packing a horse, it's important to carefully balance a load on each side and the top. Three 50-pound packs are just about right, and never more than a total of 200 pounds.

Uncle Pete knew Mother was raising me by herself and there wasn't a man in the house. He did his best that summer to try and teach me things I should've learned from Dad. He taught me how to shoot a rifle—how to aim, to carefully squeeze the trigger and not pull it. Uncle Pete said I should squeeze the trigger so gradually that I wouldn't even know when the rifle would go off. He said it was more important to concentrate on the trigger squeeze than aiming. Also, not to use the tip of my trigger finger, but the muscle between the first and second joint of the index finger.

He taught me all of the shooting positions—prone, sitting, offhand, and kneeling. He said being prone was the steadiest and to use it mostly when varmint hunting, such as for ground squirrels or woodchucks. When big game hunting, Pete said I shouldn't ever shoot offhand provided there was time to find a spot to lie or sit down, because firing from these positions was much steadier. Most people shoot from an offhand position, but it's the least accurate.

I learned a lot from Uncle Pete, some of which I probably have forgotten, but one thing in particular stuck with me through the years—never climb a fence with a gun in hand. Pete said that if I did, someday I'd be climbing a fence with a loaded gun, and I'd slip, fall, or the trigger would catch on something, and either I or someone else would get shot. It would be too late to be sorry. He said that whenever I came to a fence, to lay my gun down (with the safety on) under the fence, and climb over about five or six feet away. After crossing the fence, go back, pick up the rifle, check the safety, and then continue. Uncle Pete made me safety conscious. When I got older and could afford a shotgun, I made sure it was a double barrel over-under. I always carried it broken, closing it to shoot only when I flushed a bird, raising it up and, in one motion, closing the breech and firing.

Pete gave me an old, single-shot Remington .22 and I used it all that summer, shooting almost anything that moved—ground squirrels, rock chucks, hawks, badgers, even a deer. I know it sounds irresponsible now, but most of what I killed, I equivocated, was because I was protecting Pete's land and stock or to get food. I was only twelve years old and that's the way it was in those days. All my friends thought the same—whatever wildlife there was in the woods, it would continue to be there forever. There were a lot of ruffed grouse and blue grouse in the area. Hardly a day went by that I didn't go out hunting and come back with at least one or two grouse for the dinner table. I got so that I could shoot their heads off with every shot and never damage the meat.

I didn't have a fishing pole, so Uncle Pete cut a long tree branch to which he tied a fishing line with leader. When not hunting, I fished in the nearby creek, or "crick," as Uncle Pete called it. The little stream, hemmed in by willows and alders, flowed around big fir roots. I learned to fish in a stooped position, silently moving among the thick brush and trees, trying to keep out of sight of the Brook trout, and finding open spots to cast my hook. I used angleworms and grasshoppers for bait. I'd catch several grasshoppers and put them in my pocket. Pete taught me how to read the water, and how to make a fly lure by cutting a piece of red flannel off my shirttails and tying it to a hook.

I looked for logjams or where undercutting of the bank had dropped a tree across the stream, holding back the water in dark, quiet pools. I'd drop my baited line, hoping to see a small swirl on the surface as a trout struck. I usually had good luck at an old, partly silted-in beaver pond where the water was dark among partly rotted logs. I also learned to fish close to shore, along the slightly undercut banks where the trout fed or where they rested in the dark shade of the willows.

The fish were small, never more than eight or nine inches long, but with beautifully colored speckles. At the cabin, Aunt Grace dipped the fish in flour and dropped them in a frying pan with bacon grease. They tasted wonderful. I was always bringing game for Aunt Grace to cook. Being a good shot later served me well in the Army when I was classified as an "expert," the highest ranking for marksmanship. That summer is one that I'll always remember, striding along the trails on the ridges and in the aspen clumps east of Mica Peak.

★★★

In the fall of 1938, Mother quit her job at the creamery and was out of work again. Her boss kept getting fresh with her, patting her on the rump, rubbing up against her when he walked by, and continuously asking her to go home with him. He began to get so aggressive that Mother couldn't stand it any longer. She only stuck it out as long as she did because jobs were hard to find. There were dark corners at the creamery and out-of-the-way places where she was afraid he'd

Grandpa Smith and Joyce—at Grandpa's house, 2017 N. Center St., Spokane, 1940.

push her or find her, and force himself on her. No matter how desperate the times were, she had to quit.

With no job, she couldn't pay the rent, so we moved into her father's house—Grandpa Smith's—on 2017 N. Center Street. We were lucky just to have a place to live. Not only were Mother, Joyce, Norma, and I living with Grandpa and Grandma Smith, but also Aunt Grace and her son Roy. We pooled resources to try to get enough to eat.

Grandpa Smith's house stood only about 200 feet from the railroad tracks where westbound trains slackened their speed to start up a grade. My cousin Roy taught me how to board a train as it slowed to climb the slight hill. Many times I'd jump on a freight car and ride down to Division Street, where the Great Northern and Union Pacific rail yards were located. I'd get off just west of the Division Street Bridge and walk through the nearby hobo jungle to downtown. I never let Mother know what I was doing, but I felt it was quite an adventure.

I'd talk to the men in the hobo camps, listening to their accounts about where they'd been and what they'd done. Many persons called them tramps and bums, but mostly they were unemployed, homeless, and out-of-luck transients, and they weren't bad people. Most were middle aged—their faces waned and wrinkled before their time, hair dishevelled, eyes sunken, and with teeth missing and tobacco stains running down the sides of their mouths. There were a lot of young men there, too, who'd also been riding freight cars all over the country, mostly from the East coming to the West. They'd drifted through the Central and Rocky Mountain states, but didn't stay because there was nothing for them there. They were continuing on to the larger cities out West, such as Spokane, Seattle, and Portland—hungry and downcast, old before their time, and moving from city to city looking for jobs that weren't there. Their clothes were dirty and ragged, their eyes listless, and their actions and hand movements were nervous and restless. As tough as they looked and as bad as their situation was, they never once abused or harmed me.

I enjoyed listening to their stories. Spokane was "hobo friendly" according to some that I talked to, but that wasn't true of many places where they'd been.

Soup line at the old Golden Age Brewery building during the Great Depression, 1934. This structure still stands on East Trent in Spokane. *Northwest Museum of Arts & Culture/ EWSHS, Spokane, WA (L93-18.62)*

They described beatings by railroad guards and some had been shot at. The railroad companies didn't want them riding on freight trains, and the police in most cities didn't want them in town, but to keep right on moving and never come back. Some were educated men, which you could tell by the way that they spoke. There always were a few women, usually young, but not many. I hardly ever saw a black.

The hobo jungle conveniently stood adjacent to the railroad yards and close to the city's missions and soup kitchens, about two or three blocks away. Several charitable organizations and churches also ran a free kitchen and had set up sleeping cots in the old Golden Age Brewery on Trent Avenue, several blocks east of the Division Street Bridge. The brewery had shut down when Prohibition ended the beer and liquor business. Here, as a last resort, an unemployed or homeless person could get something to eat and spend a night indoors.

Even in Spokane, however, railroad-hired "yard bulls" didn't let tramps stay too long. They'd make rounds through the jungle and kept people on the move. Anyone recognized as having been there three or four days was ordered to leave. If they didn't, usually they later were found beaten senseless. In some towns, men even were thrown under the wheels of a passing freight train—this wasn't all that unusual in those days.

★★★

One night in 1938, some acquaintances of Dad came to visit Mother. With them was Joe Towers, a man of medium height, broad and barrel chested, and muscular. His face was pitted from smallpox and he had a large wen behind one ear. In the next two or three months, he visited us several times and Mother dated him occasionally. Neither Norma nor I cared for Joe. I can't explain exactly what Norma disliked about him, but to me he seemed gross, ill tempered, and unattractive.

When Mother told us that she was going to marry him, we couldn't believe it. We talked to her several times, begging her to change her mind. She answered that Joe had a steady job (working as a "gandy dancer" for the Union Pacific laying ties and rails). He'd never been married before and was willing to assume the obligation of providing for us children. Mother said it was hard on Grandpa with so many people living together in the house and he wasn't well.

That gentle, loving woman! In the depths of the Great Depression, out of work, having no money or income, three children to care for, and a future that appeared to consist only of despair and hopelessness, she never once gave up or broke down crying. She promised us kids that things would get better.

"Besides," she'd say, "as long as we have a roof over our heads to keep out the rain, a bed with covers to keep us warm, and enough to eat, we should never complain."

Looking back, I remember how unbelievably tough the times were and I can understand why Mother did what she did. But, my God, what a sacrifice—what incredible love she showed us to enter into such a marriage so that her children had a place to live and enough to eat.

Although Joe was employed, living still was hard. That winter we ran low on firewood. Joe had been replacing ties on a railroad bridge over Hangman Creek on the southwest edge of Spokane, where the gandy dancers threw the old ties off the bridge into the water. Joe, my cousins Roy and Harold Hodges, and I went in Harold's truck to the creek to retrieve the ties for firewood. They lay in two or three feet of water, and it was 10° above zero in January with a foot of snow on the ground. We waded in the creek, breaking the ice, set choker chains around the ties, and the truck pulled them out, one by one. It was cold, exhausting, miserable work, but we had enough wood to last Grandpa Smith and us for the rest of the winter. Of course, the ties still had to be cut with cross cut saws and split by axe for stove wood at home.

Joe was a Finnlander, and a rough, hard man who kept to himself, had an ugly temper, and God help anyone that crossed him. He liked alcohol and we kids learned to stay out of his way when he was drinking, which was most of the time. Often when coming home, it was obvious he'd been fighting; his clothes were dirty and torn, and his face and knuckles bruised and lacerated.

Joe insisted that I learn how to fight, but Mother always said my hands were too small to be a boxer. Joe said you fought with your heart, not your hands. He felt everyone had to be able to protect themselves. He had some boxing gloves and made me spar with him. Every once in awhile, he'd let go and knock me on my butt. Then, he'd pick me up, wipe the blood off my lips, laugh, and say, "You're learning, Mac, you're learning."

One thing he told me I never forgot—if a fight starts and someone pulls a knife, back off and get out of there. He'd seen too many men so badly sliced up that they never were the same again. Unfortunately, Joe didn't follow his own advice. He and mother eventually separated, and after the war, along about 1950, while I was attending the University of Idaho law school, Mother said she'd read in the *Seattle Times* that "Joe Towers, a former Spokane resident, died in Valdez, Alaska." The article reported he'd been stabbed to death in a fight in a waterfront saloon. But, I'm getting ahead of my story. In 1939, Joe was sent to Pasco, Washington, to work laying rails. Mother and Joyce went with him, but Norma and I moved back into Grandpa Smith's house. Norma had a job clerking at Newberry's dime store and I'd be starting high school that fall.

★★★

Poverty afflicted most people, but they had pride and attempted to hide it, trying to act and appear as though things were normal. Before Mother left for Pasco, she still packed our school lunches in a paper bag, but instead of meat or cheese sandwiches, we had catsup or bean sandwiches. We ate bread without butter. In the summer we had cucumber, onion, or just plain lettuce sandwiches.

When I wore holes in the bottoms of my shoes, Mother cut up cardboard boxes, making shaped inserts for the inner soles. These didn't last long in rain or snow. The cardboard rapidly deteriorated and sometimes I'd replace the inserts two or three times a week. It was worse, though, when the heels of my shoes wore down, because nails pushed up through the soles, cut my stockings, stuck into my heels causing bleeding, and made me walk with a noticeable limp. No matter how hard the nails were hammered back down, they always seemed to work their way back up.

Our family clothes, particularly Joyce's and mine, were patched, often with patches over other patches. When clothing completely wore out and couldn't be repaired, Mother or Norma would tear the material into strips and knit thick rugs. In the winter, Mother gathered up throw rugs off the floor and used them as blankets, tucking us in when we went to sleep. We also wore stockings in bed to keep our feet warm.

In the 1930s, housework done by women such as my Mother, Aunt Grace, and Norma was back breaking. The many conveniences we have today barely had been invented. Dishes were washed and dried by hand. Clothes mostly were individually hand-scrubbed on a corrugated board, wrung out, and put on a line

Wraight's dime store. *Northwest Museum of Arts & Culture/EWSHS, Spokane, WA (L87-1.43789-30)*

to dry. There were hardly any automatic washers and dryers in those days, nor electric or gas furnaces for heating—wood had to be cut and split, and coal shoveled and carried in buckets, and hand fed into stoves. Electric refrigeration was rare. Electrical lines didn't exist outside of the cities, and farmhouses were lighted by kerosene lamps. Outhouses often served as toilets, even in town. In cool weather, food frequently was kept in an apple crate or wooden box attached outside of a window. When it was hot outside, perishables were kept in an icebox filled once a week from an itinerant iceman's truck. Hot water was heated in buckets on the kitchen stove and poured into galvanized wash tubs in the middle of the floor for Saturday night baths. The electric cooking range and bread toasters were relatively new innovations.

Hardly anyone knew what a vacuum cleaner was. At home there weren't any garbage disposals, power lawnmowers, sprinkler systems, garage door openers, self operating furnaces, thermostats, thermal-pane windows, power saws, electric typewriters, air conditioners, electric blankets, panty hose, Kleenex, disposable diapers, or electric hair dryers. The first ski lifts had just been built at the exclusive new Sun Valley resort, opening in 1936. Radios were common, but, of course, television, stereos, and cassette tapes hadn't yet been invented.

Babies mostly were born at home, not in hospitals, with a birthing often attended by relatives assisted by a mid-wife, not a doctor. Few people could afford dental work—a third of the population had black, decaying, or missing teeth. If you did visit a dentist, the pain was excruciating. Drills were slow, and the anesthetic so primitive and the side effects so bad that it often wasn't administered. Penicillin hadn't been invented, nor sulfa drugs. Infections were common, and appendicitis and pneumonia often proved fatal. Doctors made house calls, but no matter how attentive, babies still died of whooping cough, measles, and diphtheria.

★★★

We kids walked up and down the alley behind the houses in our neighborhood looking for empty pop bottles in the garbage. We'd return them to a grocery store for two pennies apiece. I worked some on Saturdays polishing shoes at a shoeshine stand next to the Orpheum Theatre. With the little money I earned, I bought marbles and became quite a marble shark for a little guy. Boys played for "keeps." That is, whatever marbles you won, you kept. Some that I won were agates and "cat eyes," which were coveted by marble players.

I gave my winnings to my cousin Roy, and he'd take the marbles to a small pawnshop next to the Rainbo Theatre on Washington Street between Riverside and Main. With the pawn money in our pocket, we'd go further downtown to Main and Post to the Westlake Market. It was an interesting place full of the aromas of baked bread, fish, fruit, vegetables, and damp sawdust thrown thickly over the floor between heavy, wooden, butcher blocks. None of the goods were pre-packaged in those days; it hadn't been invented yet. Rather, the meat, cheese, fish, vegetables and flowers were all sold fresh. I loved the market. It was an exciting place and there was a chance that a butcher would give you a wiener, a cut of cheese, or a dill pickle.

But it wasn't the market that we were mainly interested in; it was the pool hall located downstairs. Dark, damp, and full of cigar smoke and the stale smell of beer, here was where the action was. Roy still was in high school and hardly more than a kid, but, by God, he was a pool player and born hustler. He didn't look or act like a pool player and this let him sneak up on people. He had a way of getting into a game and initially stumbled when shooting eight ball. He was capable of running the table in almost every game, so he had to be careful not to show how good he was right off or he couldn't get anyone to play him. It wasn't unusual for Roy to win five or six dollars in an afternoon, sometimes playing for as much as a quarter a ball. He wasn't called "Slick" for nothing.

Looking back on it, I'm reminded of the saying, "Don't play cards with someone called 'Lucky,' pick a fight with anyone named 'Rocky,' or play pool with a 'Slick.'"

One thing though, even if Roy sometimes was a little on the shady side, he treated me fair. Whatever he won with my money, he gave me half. Roy always had money, but it wasn't a good thing because in his mind it was "Easy come, easy go." He was so skilled at shooting pool, rolling dice, and playing poker that making money seemed easy. Apparently cash burnt a hole in Roy's pocket because he couldn't keep any of it. He was a wild kid, looking for excitement wherever he could find it.

He always was spending money and unfortunately on all of the wrong things. He loved to gamble, particularly pool, dice, and card games, and liked to frequent the whorehouses on the southeast side of downtown Spokane at the Herald, St. Regis, Roxie, and other hotels. These actually weren't organized houses of prostitution, but rather were rundown hotels located in the seedy part of town where girls were working the streets on their own, and where they had a room to ply their trade. I got to know some of them because occasionally, when I was with Roy, he and his friends would go to the hotels and take me along, but I'd sit out in the car while they went inside and entertained themselves. Roy knew enough not to take me in.

Several times some of his friends said, "Come on, Roy, let's give Mac a chance. It's time he learned to grow up. Let's take him in and let him f__k one of the whores."

Roy wouldn't hear of it, and, of course, I really wasn't old enough yet to have much of an inclination anyway. In fact, it scared me when they talked about it.

Roy told them, "Listen, Mac is my cousin, he's not old enough to be going in there with us and quit talking about it. He's going to sit out in the car and that's where he's going to stay." And that's what I did.

Everyone liked Roy. He had a way about him. He was fun just to be around. He always had a lot of friends and whenever I had a chance, I'd be at his heels, following him around like a puppy. Roy was bright, lucky, willing to take chances, and wasn't afraid of anyone or anything. Whatever he did seemed to work out well for him. About this time he joined the Civilian Conservation Corps and shortly thereafter enlisted in the military. He'd been a cook in the CCC, and then a chaplain's aid while in the military. Wouldn't you know it; what a place to be! Most everyone else in the Army might be in the mud and dirt or getting shot at, or they might not like the chow or get enough of it, but you can bet Roy was somewhere with a roof over his head, where it wasn't too hot or cold, and where life was good and he had the best. If ever there was a prototype for Sergeant Bilko, the 1950s TV comedy star, it was Roy.

When he left the Army, Roy started an apprenticeship as a printer, and, in a matter of only a few years, he had his own print shop. First, he ran a small office on 2nd Street, but, as his business prospered, he took over most of the sixth floor of the present-day Bon Marche building in downtown Spokane. He had the world by the tail on a downhill pull, but had picked up the habit of drinking when in the Army and he simply couldn't stop. He didn't want to stop. By the time he turned 50, he was dying of cirrhosis of the liver. Over the years I've often thought of Roy. Such a bright, handsome, vibrant young man, and to throw away his life the way he did and so young—what a shame!

★★★

In the 1930s, most of the rest of the world was suffering from economic collapse, too, and some countries also experienced a hemorrhaging of civil liberties, especially in central and eastern Europe. In Germany, Adolf Hitler took office as chancellor in 1933 and in short order made himself dictator (*fuehrer*). Violating international treaty obligations, he secretly began German rearmament, and, to insure immediate control of the German people (and conquered peoples later), he established the *Schutzstaffel*, commonly known as the SS. In 1934, Heinrich Himmler was appointed head of this paramilitary organization, which was given authority above the law—the courts couldn't interfere in its activities.

Almost immediately, concentration camps began springing up across Germany under SS control. Himmler initially was in charge of a few hundred men, but the SS quickly grew by the thousands and struck terror in those who opposed the Nazi party. A special police force, the *Gestapo*, was established as an adjunct of the SS. Thousands, and eventually millions, of unfortunate European men and women, particularly political enemies and Jews, were imprisoned or put to death under the direction of SS henchmen.

Hitler's army, navy, and air force grew by leaps and bounds, as did his international ambitions and demands. First, Austria in 1938, and then Czechoslovakia, were annexed into the German state by coercive means short of war. Armed conflict came in1939 when Germany and the Soviet Union invaded and divided Poland. Then, in the spring of 1940, Norway and Denmark fell, followed shortly by Luxemburg, Holland, and Belgium. Hitler's hard-striking Panzer divisions next defeated the French and English troops in northern France, driving most of the British and many French soldiers into a pocket at Dunkirk on the English Channel. In a heroic effort, Great Britain managed to evacuate nearly 340,000 men by sea, but almost all of the heavy ordnance and other military equipment was left on the beaches.

With the fall of France to the German *Blitzkrieg* in 1940 followed by the conquest of Yugoslavia and Greece in 1941, only the island nation of Great Britain and its overseas Commonwealth stood against Hitler's military juggernaut. Mussolini's Italy, which like a vulture had swooped down on a reeling France, also declared war on the British, hoping to share in the spoils of their defeat.

During the lightning-like events of the summer of 1940, Prime Minister Winston Churchill had rallied his countrymen in a historic speech:

> We shall go on to the end, we shall fight in France, we shall fight on the seas and oceans, we shall fight with growing confidence and growing strength in the air, we shall defend our island, whatever the cost may be, we shall fight on the beaches, we shall fight on the landing grounds, we shall fight in the fields and in the streets, we shall fight in the hills, we shall never surrender—until in God's good time, the new world, with all its power and might, steps forth to the rescue and the liberation of the old.

This appeal for English resolve presented in the British House of Commons was especially aimed at America and, in particular, President Franklin D. Roosevelt. In Roosevelt, Churchill found both a friend and ally. Roosevelt felt that with America's industrial help, England could persevere. He proposed that America become a great arsenal of democracy and supply the nations fighting

Hitler with the weapons and supplies necessary to prevent and even turn back German conquest.

In 1940 and most of 1941, however, a majority of Americans felt secure behind the Atlantic and Pacific ocean barriers. There was a political struggle between the "isolationists," who wanted to stay out of the European conflict, and President Roosevelt and similar minded people, who believed that America's very existence as a democracy ultimately was threatened and that the United States needed to join Britain to defeat the Nazis. Japan's expansion in China and its close ties to Germany, too, had ominous implications. The deep division in public opinion may best be shown by the narrow passage of the extension of the Selective Service Act in August 1941. Approval of continuing the "draft," as it was known, barely passed Congress by a single vote—this occurred only three months before the devastating Japanese attack on Pearl Harbor.

Meanwhile, the American economy was improving and employment was expanding to meet the demand for providing England with military assistance. Despite the debate over isolationism, Roosevelt moved decisively to prepare the country for war. Factories that had been idle for years came to life and buzzed with activity. In Seattle, the economy rebounded with unprecedented vigor, and Boeing expanded bomber production lines, working at a startling pace. The Bremerton shipyards likewise hummed with newfound life.

★★★

With employment opportunities opening up, Mother said she was thinking about moving to find work—and, she was divorcing Joe. We were elated! Mother finally was free from loveless bondage—a plight endured only to allow her to provide for us children. Norma had just married Jerry Dahlgren, a graduate of Eastern Washington College, who was employed by Potlatch Forests as a log scaler. They had moved to Lewiston, Idaho, to be closer to his work.

With jobs becoming more plentiful, I too sought work through an employment office on Trent Avenue—Spokane's "skid row." This was a rough part of town, known for girlie shows, pawnshops, used clothing stores, saloons, and similar establishments. A lot of unemployed men spent their time in the area, many of them "winos." Mother had told me to stay away unless I was with her or Joe. At the time, logging camps, lumber mills, construction outfits, farmers, and other employers were soliciting men from jerk-water employment agencies located on Trent Avenue. These agencies often were located in small, one-room offices—just cubbyholes with a telephone, desk, and chairs, while outside on the sidewalk stood a large chalkboard listing the available jobs and the number of men needed. When someone got work through one of these offices, it was called getting a job "off the boards."

In the summer of 1941, I saw a notice on one of these employment office chalkboards indicating that thirty men were needed at a blister rust camp. I was only fifteen years old, but in a short time would be sixteen, and I was big for my age and husky. Employers weren't concerned with how old you were. They were interested only in knowing if you could handle the job. At the time, the white pine forests of the northern Bitterroot Range were among the most valuable commercial timberlands in the Pacific Northwest. Unfortunately, white-pine blister rust was advancing rapidly through these stands, not only in north Idaho, but also in adjacent parts of Washington and Montana, and actually had reached epidemic proportions in some areas. At the time, it was believed that blister rust eventually would eliminate the white pine forests unless it was controlled.

Congressional delegations from the region worked diligently to obtain federal financial and administrative support for a massive eradication effort, which was conducted in national forests as well as on state and private timberlands. Blister rust was highly contagious, killing certain sugar pines as well as white pine. It didn't spread directly from tree to tree, but spent one stage of its complex life on gooseberry and currant bushes, also known as "ribes." Seeds and spores that spread the disease were carried by the wind between the two different hosts—spores from the diseased white pine afflicting ribes, and then the diseased ribes infecting other white pines. It was thought that the problem could be attacked by removing all of the currant and gooseberry bushes growing within the short, infectious range of white pine. Thus, men were hired by the federal government and sent to temporary forest camps in the mountains to do this job.

Although not known at the time, the blister rust control program proved largely impractical. The disease continued to kill countless millions of seedlings and seriously damaged older trees. This, together with the heavy logging later conducted in the 1940s and 1950s, ultimately eliminated much of the great white pine forests in north Idaho.

Mother gave me permission to work as a blister rust worker and I was hired. Twenty or thirty of us were picked up in front of an employment agency on Trent Avenue and transported in an old, grey, beat-up government bus to Newport, Washington, and thence to Priest Lake in north Idaho, not far from the Canadian border. Some of the men were pretty hung over. A few looked to be winos, and two or three carried bottles in their coat pockets. When hired, we were told to leave all such bottles at the employment office—they'd be catalogued, stored, and could be picked up after the termination of employment.

At hiring time, everyone was supposed to have a pair of boots, an extra pair of socks, and a jacket. The ones that didn't simply went into the alley behind the employment office and temporarily borrowed a coat, boots, and socks from a friend and reported back at the employment desk. For the first few days after the hiring, some of the boozers had the "shakes," or they got the "snakes" during which time they'd hallucinate and imagine seeing all kinds of terrible things.

Sometimes they'd get deathly sick, but by the end of the first week, they usually got over this. It took them longer than the rest of us, however, to get into the good physical condition needed to do the hard labor required. Some never did, and hiked all the way down to the lake to find transportation back to Spokane.

A number of men in our group, such as the winos and some of the older itinerant laborers, pretty much had a day-to-day existence—they lived in a world of temporary employment, flophouses, saloons, soup kitchens, and brothels. They floated from one job to another. You'd often hear the saying: "In camps and sawmills there always were three crews—one coming, one going, and one on the job."

There weren't any roads around Priest Lake on either side at that time. At the south end, we boarded boats and were taken to the upper end where we disembarked and then hiked probably five or six miles to Green Bonnet Mountain. On our arrival, the first thing we did was establish a base camp with support facilities. It was a "rag camp"; in other words, tents served as living quarters, with outdoor toilets, a mess hall, and a radio room where the "head push" of our crew stayed with the radio operator.

With the camp established, we were divided into crews and started eradicating currant and gooseberry plants. This was done as follows: two men with white cord or string marked an area on each side, then the crew advanced between the two borders digging up every currant and gooseberry bush encountered, putting them in a large cloth sack which we carried. Later, the contents of the sacks were burned. The work often was straight up and down steep slopes, between creek bottom and ridge top. It was hot, hard labor, but we mostly were young men and soon were in fine physical condition. We enjoyed trying to outdo crews on each side of us.

The area where we were camped was beautiful. By walking a short distance to a high ridge, a view could be gained of Priest Lake, both Upper and Lower, and of the huge granite monolith known as Chimney Rock. The food was good. All of the young men in camp were friendly and hard working, and the summer was one that I enjoyed thoroughly.

To dispose of trash, we built a large garbage sump by digging a deep hole and covering it over with logs, leaving a two-feet-by-two-feet opening to throw the garbage in. The abundant black bears and grizzly bears in the area soon found the sump hole and came to eat the garbage. Whenever a grizzly was present, black bears gave them wide birth. You could tell they were afraid of the grizzlies. My buddies and I would gather in the evening, sitting on logs that we arranged on a sloping hillside, almost like a small amphitheatre, and watch the bears. They'd get completely into the pit and come out with food scraps and carry them away.

One guy said we should try and trap a bear in the sump. Everyone thought this was a great idea, especially, they thought, if we caught a grizzly. Accordingly, the first thing we did was saw about an eight-foot length out of a large log with about a three to four foot butt. We then laboriously set this piece on its end next to the sump hole opening, kind of like a trap door ready to be dropped.

After dinner, we waited for the bears to appear. In the evening, of course, they'd begin coming into camp near the garbage pit. When grizzlies came down, the black bears moved away. There always were two or three, and, on occasion, as many as four grizzlies. One grizzly seemed to be more or less in charge. When he approached and lowered himself into the garbage pit, the others stood at a respectable distance, waiting for him to come out. When we saw this grizzly enter the sump hole, a few of us ran as fast as we could and knocked the eight-foot stump over, covering the hole, and then we sat on it, holding it down.

The roar of that grizzly was unbelievable. He slashed at the tree trunk with huge claws. The tree trunk didn't completely cover the opening and the bear reached up through a crack, trying to get his head and shoulders out. We were in a serious situation. "We had a tiger by the tail," only in this case it was a grizzly bear, and we couldn't let loose. We looked at each other inquiringly, "What are we going to do?"

The bear was furious and roared like a wounded lion, while three of us sat on the log scared to death. We realized we'd done a foolish thing. We decided the best thing we could do was simply get out of there as quickly as possible. With one mind, we let loose of the log and, thoroughly terrified, ran as fast as we could back to camp. We didn't even turn around to see if the bear came after us.

That one experience was enough. We never tried it again.

★★★

After working at the blister rust camp throughout the summer of 1941, I returned home at the end of August to play football and start the fall term at North Central High School. Mother and I had a long talk about her planned move to Seattle. I told her I was playing football, my friends all were in Spokane, and I could board with one of their families. I'd be one less child for her to worry about. It was a hard sell, but she finally agreed to let me stay if I found a place to live.

To most teenage boys, the truly important things in life are sports and friends. Girls, I believe, come in a poor third. To most boys, even those with only ordinary athletic ability, like myself, the ultimate dream is to be on the varsity, whether it's football, baseball, or some other sport. Being awarded a varsity letter is the crowning achievement. I rationalized then that I was helping Mother by staying in Spokane, but I realize now, that to a certain extent, I was just being selfish. I probably should have moved to Seattle with her and my sister.

It wasn't hard to find a place to live. Football practice had started and we had a turnout of 60 or 70 boys vying for positions on the team. I already had a number of friends among them, and I made several more. One was Garland

DeRoshia, whose family lived on the south side of town. Why it was that he went to North Central, instead of Lewis & Clark High School, I don't know, but he did. When I broached the subject of boarding with him, he said he'd discuss it with his parents and let me know. I told him I could afford to pay board and room. He came back the next day and said that if I paid $25 a month, I could live with his family that year. Mother said she would get the $25 from Dad or she would send it to me herself if that wasn't possible.

I found it necessary to find employment in the afternoons or evenings to earn spending money. My first job was washing dishes at a restaurant in a Greyhound Bus depot. Dishwashers like myself were called "pearl divers," and I spent my time up to my elbows in dirty water and suds, washing each dish, flatware, and utensil. I usually went to work at 6 P.M. after football practice, and worked until after dinnertime around 9:30 or 10:00. The rest of my time was occupied with school, football, and girls, but not necessarily in that order.

When you are sixteen, what's happening in the world around you doesn't seem important. In the fall of 1941, although we didn't know it, an uncertain future lay just over the horizon. The flames of world conflict were moving toward America.

Notes

1. My father-in-law, Dr. Thomas Rex Walenta, told me that in 1924 he and his brother John drove from their father's ranch near Lemon, South Dakota, through Montana, and on to Moscow, Idaho. They were investigating land to purchase and Rex wanted to visit the University of Idaho. In Montana, after driving for many miles over rough, narrow, dirt roads, they reached a stretch of concrete highway extending west from Billings to Laurel, a distance of about ten miles. After driving over it, Rex turned to John and said, "That was the most fun we've had on the whole trip, let's go back and go over it again."

   As late as 1930, there were only 8,148 miles of roadway in Montana, of which less than one-fourth (1,846 miles) were graveled. Fewer than 80 miles had asphalt or concrete surfaces and most of it was located in larger municipalities such Billings and Great Falls. Imagine—less than 80 miles! And, with most roads being dirt, they became impassable during wet weather. See "Highway Statistics," *Montana: The Magazine of Western History* (Autumn 1994), 29.

2. As my children were growing up, my wife and I often took them to Glacier National Park in the summer. We stayed in some of the magnificent lodges built during the pre-Depression years. I've often marveled at the complexity of the construction and wondered about the difficulties that the builders must have encountered.

3. Mother left this artifact to me when she passed on and I still have it in my family room.

President Roosevelt's War Message to Congress

To the Congress of the United States:

Yesterday, December 7, 1941—a date which will live in infamy—the United States of America was suddenly and deliberately attacked by naval and air forces of the empire of Japan.

The United States was at peace with that nation and, at the solicitation of Japan, was still in conversation with its government and its emperor, looking toward the maintenance of peace in the Pacific.

Indeed, one hour after Japanese air squadrons had commenced bombing in Oahu, the Japanese ambassador to the United States and his colleague delivered to the secretary of state a formal reply to a recent American message. While this reply stated that it seemed useless to continue the existing diplomatic negotiations, it contained no threat or hint of war or armed attack.

It will be recorded that the distance of Hawaii from Japan makes it obvious that the attack was deliberately planned many days or even weeks ago. During the intervening time, the Japanese government has deliberately sought to deceive the United States by false statements and expressions of hope for continued peace.

The attack yesterday on the Hawaiian Islands has caused severe damage to American naval and military forces. Very many American lives have been lost. In addition, American ships have been reported torpedoed on the high seas between San Francisco and Honolulu.

Yesterday the Japanese government also launched an attack against Malaya.

Last night Japanese forces attacked Hongkong.

Last night Japanese forces attacked Guam.

Last night Japanese forces attacked the Philippine islands.

Last night Japanese attacked Wake Island.

This morning the Japanese attacked Midway Island.

Japan has, therefore, undertaken a surprise offensive extending throughout the Pacific area. The facts of yesterday speak for themselves. The people of the United States have already formed their opinions and well understand the implications to the very life and safety of our nation.

As commander in chief of the army and navy I have directed that all measures be taken for our Defense.

Always will we remember the character of the onslaught against us.

No matter how long it takes us to overcome this premeditated invasion, the American people in their righteous might will win through to absolute victory.

I believe I interpret the will of the congress and of the people when I assert that we will not only defend ourselves to the uttermost but will make very certain that this form of treachery shall never endanger us again.

Hostilities exist. There is no blinking at the fact that our people, our territory and our interests are in grave danger.

With confidence in our armed forces—with the unbounded determination of our people—we will gain the inevitable triumph—so help us God.

I ask that the congress declare that since the unprovoked and dastardly attack by Japan on Sunday, December 7, a state of war has existed between the United States and the Japanese empire.

FRANKLIN D. ROOSEVELT, The White House, December 8, 1941.

2 WAR COMES TO AMERICA

O N SUNDAY AFTERNOON, December 7, 1941, I was sitting in the DeRoshia living room playing Monopoly with Garland and his mother and father. Suddenly, Mr. DeRoshia raised his hand, saying, "Listen, quiet." A newscaster on the radio was announcing that the Japanese had attacked the U.S. naval base at Pearl Harbor. We looked at each other, unable to comprehend the impact of what we'd heard. We didn't know exactly where Pearl Harbor was, but we knew it was in the Hawaiian Islands, which were off the West Coast and maybe not so far away as we'd thought.

Mr. DeRoshia looked at Garland, saying, "I'm sorry, son, but I believe that you and Mac and all the boys your age are going to end up fighting in this war. I hate to even think about it. It's going to be a terrible thing."

We soon understood the enormity of the disaster from newspaper and radio accounts. In a sneak attack, Japanese planes launched from aircraft carriers had sunk or put out of action eight U.S. battleships in Pearl Harbor's shallow waters, and several other naval vessels were destroyed or heavily damaged. Nearly 200 planes also were destroyed, and thousands of military personnel had been killed and wounded. Fortunately, two U.S. aircraft carriers assigned to Pearl Harbor were out at sea and escaped harm.

On Monday, almost everyone had radios tuned-in to hear President Roosevelt address Congress and the nation: "Yesterday, December 7, 1941—a date which will live in infamy—the United States of America was suddenly and deliberately attacked by naval and air forces of the empire of Japan." The President continued his spellbinding speech, as practically all of America listened. In conclusion, he stated: "I ask that the congress declare that since the unprovoked and dastardly attack by Japan on Sunday, December 7, a state of war has existed between the United States and the Japanese empire."

While listening to the President's solemn words, people became aware of the grave danger that our nation faced. Although we couldn't yet fully realize what it all meant, we knew we'd have to prepare for and fight a "total" war. Everywhere, Americans expressed their unity and support for the President and our armed forces. Although the nation had suffered an appalling defeat, there weren't any signs of panic, but everyone wore expressions of concern. Many feared that there'd be air attacks on the West Coast, and some people even talked about moving east of the Rockies, which they believed would be a natural bulwark to a Japanese ground invasion if it came.

The seriousness of the situation became even more evident and depressing a few days later on December 11, when Hitler declared war on the United States. The "Axis" nations—Germany, Italy, and Japan—having earlier signed mutual assistance pacts, stated their intention of waging a joint war against the United States, Great Britain, and associated countries—i.e., the "Allies."

For myself and everyone I knew, December 7 changed our world forever. Even though Christmas was a couple of weeks away, gloom descended on America. The bright, sparkling Christmas lights in homes, apartments, and department stores—put up in hopeful anticipation of the coming holiday—began to be extinguished during government ordered blackouts. A dark and forbidding shadow settled on the land.

Looking back today, it may be difficult for people to understand the depth of despair that Americans felt in the first months following the Pearl Harbor attack.

U.S. DECLARES WAR

(AP), Dec. 8, 1941.—Congress voted a formal declaration of war against Japan today after President Roosevelt requested immediate action as an answer to Japan's "unprovoked and dastardly attack" on Hawaii.

The senate vote of 82 to 0 and the house vote of 388 to 1 told their own story of unity in the face of common danger. The speed with which the two chambers granted President Roosevelt's request for a declaration was unprecedented.

The single adverse house vote was that of Miss Jeannette Rankin, Republican congresswomen from Montana, who was among the few who voted against the 1917 declaration of war on Germany.

The officially announced loss of two warships and 3000 men dead and wounded in Japan's raid of Hawaii was fresh in the minds of the legislators...

They cheered him enthusiastically and then pushed the resolution through with not a moment's waste of time...

"In this shocking hour words will not express our feelings nor our righteous indignation," said Representative Luther Johnson (Dem., Texas).

He called the Japanese attacks "dastardly treachery characteristic of the totalitarian outlaws who talk peace when they have already drawn the dagger to strike."

Representative Katharine Byron (Dem., Md) said she was "willing to give her sons" and that she was "100 per cent for going into this thing and beating the Japanese."... Representative Martin of Massachusetts, the Republican leader, won thunderous applause as he pledged "unqualified support" to the President... "There can be no peace," Martin shouted, "until the enemy is made to pay in a full way for his dastardly deed. Let us show the world we are a united nation."

Colossus-like, the Japanese Army and Navy strode across East Asia and the vast Pacific archipelagos, shouting "Banzai" and planting rising sun flags in victory after victory. They seized the U.S. possessions of Wake and Guam. They stormed down the Malaya Peninsula defeating British and Indian forces, and continued on to Burma, Borneo, the Celebes, Sumatra, Java, and the rest of the Dutch East Indies, conquering additional, usually outnumbered British, American, Dutch, and Australian units. They attacked the American and Filipino army in the Philippines. They occupied the Solomon and Gilbert Islands and much of New Guinea.

Like a typhoon, they raced southward, winning regions rich in raw materials and food supplies—particularly tin reserves, rubber, rice, and oil—all of which were vital necessities to Japan's protracted war effort. Everywhere, conquered peoples were subjected to ugly brutality and incredible heartlessness.

In early 1942, news on the radio described one depressing Allied defeat after another. The ruthless and arrogant Japanese were subjecting Allied prisoners and captured civilian populations to an unimaginable future of slavery, starvation, and death. Australia and New Zealand feared an invasion and threatened to withdraw their forces from the North African desert where they were engaged against German and Italian troops. This precipitous action was averted when the United States expressed its intention of defending Australia.

President Roosevelt ordered General Douglas MacArthur to vacate his hopeless command in the besieged Philippines and proceed to Australia, where he'd take command of the U.S. build-up. Upon arriving in Australia, MacArthur made his epic promise to the people of the Philippines: "I shall return."

★★★

After the attack on Pearl Harbor, Spokane hurried preparations for defense, which, as I've mentioned, included nightly city-wide blackouts. Rather than causing apprehension among my friends and I, the blackouts were an excuse for turning out the lights and trying to make time with a girlfriend while on a date.

Young men in Spokane began volunteering for military duty by the hundreds, and an Army recruiting office was opened in the Ziegler building. The compelling feeling that I remember most strongly after the Pearl Harbor disaster was one of patriotism and love of country—a willingness to sacrifice for the common good, to join the military, or otherwise contribute in some way to the war effort. Most people considered a man classified as 4F (physically unfit for military service) a shirker. It intimated, often without justification, that one was a slacker and avoiding military service. Patriotism flowed like a tidal wave and most young men felt compelled to enter the Army, Navy, or Marines and make our friends, neighbors, and families proud of us.

As time went by, families having a son, daughter, or father in the armed forces displayed a flag in a window of their home, or, more often, mounted a blue star in a window pane, denoting a family member serving in the military.

Too often, as the war wore on, gold stars took their place, a sad and poignant notice that someone from that household had been killed in the line of duty. "Rolls of Honor," naming employees who were away in the military, were proudly posted in the windows of stores and businesses.

Prepare for Blackout

Spokane Daily Chronicle, Dec. 1941.— Residents of Spokane should be prepared for a blackout at a moment's notice air force officers at Fort George Wright said today.

Whether a blackout will come remained problematical today, but with word received here…that the Puget Sound area would remain blacked out "indefinitely," officials said it appeared obvious that the blackout orders might be extended to Spokane.

As a result of that warning many Spokane firms, particularly those which have offices operating at night, were making blackout preparations today. Many business men pointed out that because it is essential to use lights to conduct their business, windows and doors must be darkened…

Officers here pointed out that London war experience has proved that the blackout is one of the most effective means to prevent needless loss of life in the event of air raids.

Spokane has no alarm system in case of a sudden blackout, but today Commissioner A.B. Colburn is working with J.E.E. Royer of the Washington Water Power company to put into effect a warning system which will reach residents in all parts of the city. The nature of it was not revealed.

…A.T. Amos, Municipal Defense council coordinator, gave out a few pointers.

"In the event of a blackout, people should stay at home or at their places of business to as great extent as possible," he said.

"Don't drive a car unless you absolutely have to. It will mean driving without lights.

"Be sure that all blinds are drawn as tightly as possible.

"Have a flashlight or candles in the house just in case the power is shut off. Small party candles are inexpensive and will serve to light a darkened stairway or some other part of the house.

"Be sure to have plenty of matches in the house. In this day of electric stoves, many residences don't have any great supply of matches.

"Listen for announcements by air-raid wardens and Defense council officials and follow out their instructions as completely as possible."

Amos said business firms are organizing today and each appointing one employee to act officially in event of a blackout to see that lighted signs are off and no light shining onto the street from the interior. Many electric signs were turned off in Spokane last night.

Fog formed an effective blackout for Spokane last night, but army officials pointed out that in event of an actual air raid the "lights out" order would be executed anyhow.

After the first few months, when it became evident that the Japanese wouldn't be mounting an invasion of the West Coast, Spokane's citizens adjusted to life on the home front. There was rationing of gasoline, tires, automobile parts, shoes, household appliances, and many food items, but the people of Spokane largely accepted this as part of the war effort, though there was grumbling about fuel rationing. They volunteered—men, women, and even children—in any way possible to contribute to victory. For example, people collected and refurbished old clothing, household furniture, and jewelry, and resold these items, giving the proceeds to the American Red Cross and other philanthropic associations associated with the war effort. Boy Scouts held neighborhood drives, collecting scrap metal, paper, and aluminum for the war industries, and they also went door to door, distributing posters and leaflets for defense bond drives and savings stamp sales.

As the United States vastly expanded its war economy and so many men entered the armed forces, male workers were in short supply. Consequently, women entered the labor force in great numbers as the conflict continued. In the Pacific Northwest, this was most evident in the Puget Sound and Portland areas, where additional airplane factories, shipyards, production plants, and military facilities sprang up practically overnight. Spokane, located several hundred miles inland and safe from potential Japanese air attack, also became a center for wartime activities. The city was a key rail hub, and had fairly clement weather—several thousand military personnel were stationed at Fort Wright and nearby Geiger and Felts airfields. Huge factory facilities were established or enlarged at both Trentwood and Mead for manufacturing aluminum, used mainly in aircraft construction. These plants employed thousands of people.

Nearby in Idaho on Lake Pend Oreille, the U.S. Navy established the second largest naval training center in the nation. At one time, the Farragut naval base housed approximately 43,000 instructors and trainees. Spokane warmly welcomed the military personnel assigned to Farragut, Geiger Field, and other facilities, and people donated books and other hard-to-get domestic items to soldiers and sailors.

Spokane's streets were filled with men in military uniform seeking recreation and diversion. Young women, in particular, eagerly sought ways of greeting these mostly young and attractive servicemen, who in turn eagerly welcomed female companionship. Several USO clubs were established and became popular places where men in uniform congregated. Young women volunteered as hostesses, serving snacks, playing cards, and dancing with the men to top hits. Lyrics of the popular World War II songs played at the USO clubs often reflected loneliness, the pain of separation, and a longing for the war to end: "I'll Be Home for Christmas," "Don't Sit under the Apple Tree with Anyone Else But Me," "White Christmas," and "The White Cliffs of Dover."

★★★

Sailors from the Farragut training center (Lake Pend Oreille) marching in Spokane, 1943. *Northwest Museum of Arts & Culture/EWSHS, Spokane, WA (L93-18.76)*

One aspect of the war effort, however, that soon caused disgruntlement was gasoline rationing, although everyone understood its necessity. The typical "weekly" gas allotment—four gallons from an A rationing book—allowed a driver to travel only about 35 to 40 miles a week. People driving more than 6 miles a day to and from work qualified for a B book and received more fuel, as did persons in essential types of employment and government occupations, who received C books for even more gas. Farmers and ranchers were allowed to consume all of the fuel they needed for food production, which, of course, led to some surreptitious black marketeering.

Gasoline rationing also was intended to save rubber. The Japanese seizure of the vast Southeast Asia rubber tree plantations led to concerns about wartime tire shortages. In the United States, synthetic rubber wasn't yet being produced in any significant quantity for the civilian market. As a result, the stealing and black marketing of tires became common. A person could register tires at service stations so, if stolen, they might be identified and retrieved.

In addition, beef, chicken, and pork were rationed, as were sugar, butter, and most canned goods. There were fewer restrictions on the purchase of fresh fruits and vegetables. Grocery stores no longer delivered orders, which proved to be an additional hardship for the elderly and people with disabilities. The World War II shortages, however, were different from those of the Great Depression when many millions of people actually faced starvation. Wartime restrictions were more of an inconvenience, rather than actual deprivation. With rationing and purchases on the black-market (if one were willing to pay the high prices), almost anything could be obtained. The truly essential thing—sufficient food—was available to everyone.

Another shortage—of silk stockings—inevitably led to a change in fashion for women. With silk stockings nearly impossible to find, leg paint was introduced that simulated stockings. It was poured from small bottles and rubbed on the legs. A special pencil also could be purchased to draw and simulate the seams of a silk stocking on the back of the calves. Such paint inconveniently lasted only a day or two. As a result, pants came more into fashion. Also, at least in the high schools, white, folded down, bobby socks became prevalent. Most young women, in fact, began wearing short, pleated skirts, argyle sweaters, and bobby socks with brown and white saddle shoes.

★★★

Being a teenager, life for me continued pretty much as it had before. I still attended high school, participated in athletics, dated, and went to dances and parties. Thoughts of the war mostly were pushed into the back corner of my mind. Most of us felt that the conflict wouldn't affect us until after we graduated from high school and joined the armed forces. Only when we read the obituaries did the awful realty of the war make an impression on us—the casualty lists included former classmates, only a year or two older than us.

Early in 1942, I began working as a bus boy at Cooke's Nut Shop, which was both a candy store and restaurant. Aunt Grace was the pastry cook at the shop, and she was good. She made a wonderful red devil's food cake and the best Washington nut and pecan pies that I've ever eaten. The two Cooke brothers owned the restaurant and they were fond of Aunt Grace. Otherwise, I probably wouldn't have been hired. The Cooke brothers' chocolates were hand dipped in a kitchen on the second floor. I worked at Cooke's Nut Shop until the start of summer, when school let out.[1]

I next went to work logging with my cousin, Bud Lofton, in the Mica Peak country near the Washington-Idaho border. Bud had an old logging truck and we cut timber that summer, skidding, loading, and hauling logs to a sawmill in Coeur d'Alene.

Bud was married to my cousin, Gertrude (Aunt Grace's daughter). They were wonderful people, but Bud had one problem—he loved to fight. He'd go into the saloons in or near such towns as Worley, Rockford, or St. Maries on Saturdays with my cousin, Harold Hodges. If he couldn't find someone in the bar to pick a fight with, he'd fight Harold. One of the bars was located at what is now called Fighting Creek. I don't know how it got its name, but I always figured Bud and Harold had something to do with it. The two of them had some of the worst knockdown dragout fights I ever saw. But apparently they enjoyed it.

Harold was a cowboy and later ran a large cattle ranch in the Saddle Mountains locality near Othello, Washington, together with a big game hunting and guiding business. His licensed territory for the latter was the Beaver Meadows country of eastern Idaho, just west of the Montana line in the Lolo Pass region and just north of White Sand Creek. For years Harold also had a large string of stock that he rented out as bucking horses.

Every fall, a rodeo was held at Worley, Idaho, located on the Coeur d'Alene Indian Reservation. There always were a lot of Indian contestants and they could really ride. Whether on bulls or horses, they were exceptional. They had one bad habit, however. The Indian cowboys would go to a fence near the north end of the arena and relieve themselves, urinating in front of the grandstands. They'd been asked many times to stop this, but they continued to do so, right in front of men, women, and children. Finally, Harold, Bud, and some other cowboys decided they knew how to put an end to it. They placed a steel plate underneath the dirt by the fence, covered it with sawdust, and connected it to a long electrical extension cord plugged into the nearest outlet. When the next man went over to urinate on that fence, you never heard such a scream. I don't know whether it had the desired effect, but I didn't see any more urinating on the fence while I was there.

While working for Bud, my job was setting chokers and swamping. Chokers were long steel cables that were attached to horses' rigging. I'd take the other end of the choker cable, pull it through the woods and slash, and fasten it to a log. The horses then dragged the logs to the "landing," a cleared, level area where logs were stacked or "decked." "Swamping" consisted of cutting brush out of the way so that the horses could "skid" the timbers to the landing. Bud had a team of Percherons and it was an experience watching him skid logs with those two big horses.

One day while skidding, a downed branch the size of a man's arm was caught in front by one of the horses, pulled forward, and, when the horse passed, it snapped back and hit Bud, who was riding on the logs as they were being skidded. It struck him right on the nose and knocked him unconscious for several minutes. When he came to, the first thing he said, after wiping blood off his face and shaking his head, was, "Goddamn it, who hit me?"

Poor Bud, his nose was smashed as flat as if he'd been a professional boxer all of his life. He never did anything about it. Actually, I think he took a little pride in having his nose flattened that way.

Bud loaded logs on his truck by "cross hauling." Two small logs were put up against the side of a truck or trailer, like a ramp. Ropes or cables then were looped around a log on one side and passed over to horses on the other side of the truck. Horses then pulled the logs up the ramp and onto the truck or trailer until it was fully loaded.

Bud was a "jypo" logger; that is, he was paid according to how many logs (in thousands of board feet) he hauled to the mill. The faster he worked, the more logs he got out of the woods, and more logs meant more money, so Bud worked at double time. He didn't believe in "coffee breaks," although he'd stop occasionally to get out his Bull Durham pouch and roll a cigarette. Of course, a logger worked as a jypo if he thought he'd make better wages than company men being paid by the hour.

Bud was a good logger, but I was just a green teenage kid. He had to show me how to do things. It slowed him down, but he never lost patience with me. When I drew my first paycheck, he drove me to Spokane to buy a pair of logging boots—not just any boots, but White Loggers. These were hand-manufactured by the White family in Spokane at a small store on Trent Avenue. Bud said I couldn't be "slick shod," but had to have a good pair of caulked boots, or "corks" as he called them, to ride the logs when skidding and to walk on the decks at the landing. Bud also said that if I was going to be a logger, I needed to look like one. In addition to corked boots, I ended up wearing wide red or yellow suspenders, long Johns (flannel underwear), a plaid shirt, and short legged, or "stagged," wool pants. These were expensive and when Bud paid for them, I figured I'd be working most of the summer just to pay him back.

Bud knew that the way to make money was to get as many logs as possible to the landing, and he needed my help to do that. He drove the horse team, skidding the logs through the thick, heavy underbrush, while I kept ahead of him with an axe, cutting and clearing the trail.

"Goddamn it, Mac," he'd say, "clear that brush out of there, get those chokers around those logs. We're jypoing. Anytime I'm waiting on you, it's costing us money."

I was exhausted when summer ended and glad to return for my senior year at North Central.

★★★

I no longer boarded with the DeRoshia family—my friend "Gar," who'd been a year ahead of me in school, had entered the service. Another one of my pals on the football team was Buck Hill, a sophomore at North Central. I made similar living arrangements with Buck's folks as I had with the DeRoshias. Buck had a brother, Wayne, or "Slitz" as we called him, who was one of the best and hardest hitting football players I ever knew. When he hit someone, you'd hear it clear across the field. He'd graduated the year before. Even with Slitz, however, the 1941 team had not done well.

Our 1941 North Central squad did have some other good players—Jack Latta, Tom Biallis, Don Freeman, Pat Haynes, Jack Erlandson, Bob Weeks, Norm Cross, and others—but we didn't have enough depth. We ended up with an overall record of 3-4-1, and 1-4-1 in the city league, tied for last place (our record in 1942 would be about the same, too). We wouldn't have done even that well except for Jerry Williams, our running back in a single wing offense. Jerry was one of the all-time sports heroes of the Spokane area. He only weighed about 155 pounds, but was extremely quick and had the greatest desire to win of anyone I've ever known. It didn't matter whether he

Wayne "Moose" MacGregor, 1941.

played handball, ping pong, anything, he had to win. He earned all-city honors and enrolled at the University of Idaho, intending on playing football, but the U of I coaching staff thought he was too small and didn't encourage him.

Jerry went across the state line to Pullman where he became one of Washington State College's great stars and a member of the school's Athletic Hall of Fame. His football career, however, was interrupted when he enlisted in the U.S. Army Air Force. He served as a P-38 fighter pilot in the South Pacific and didn't play football again until after the war. Returning to Washington State College, he went on to a star-studded National Football League career as an all-pro with the Los Angeles Rams and later the Philadelphia Eagles. He eventually became Philadelphia's head coach, leading them to an NFL championship. Subsequently, he also coached the Calgary Stampeders, taking them to the Gray Cup play-offs for the first time in 19 years.

North Central's coach was Archie Buckley, who'd been quarterback of the Washington State College team that played in the 1931 Rose Bowl. He was a fine, dedicated man, and an inspiring example to his young players. He, too, was called into the military, joining the Navy and serving on an aircraft carrier in the Pacific. He lost his life off Okinawa when a Japanese kamikaze pilot hit the carrier.

Sometime during the fall of 1942, I began going steady for the first time. Betty Campbell was slender and attractive, with beautiful dark brown eyes and a wonderful, intriguing smile. I was a member of the North Central Hi-Y social club, which had a pin similar to what college fraternities had. I "pinned" Betty when we started going steady. A popular thing for people going out together at the time was to have matching sweaters. Betty and I wore the same color of argyle sweaters. She was a lot of fun and I enjoyed being with her.

Until my junior year, I hadn't driven a car because I was boarding with other families and didn't have access to an automobile. I walked or took a city bus wherever I went. You can imagine that this interfered substantially with my social life. There weren't many girls that were anxious to go out on a date on a bus. This all changed when my friend, Dale "Johnny" Johnson, bought a car for $10—a 1925 Oldsmobile. It might've been old, but it ran and we had wheels. Johnny owned the car and, since I was always working, I had money for gas, which wasn't hard to find on the black market. This opened up a whole new world for us.

Johnny, like most of my friends and classmates, later went into the armed forces, enlisting in the U.S. Army Air Force. He eventually was sent to China, becoming a member of the USAAF's "Flying Tigers," and spent the war strafing trains, bombing bridges, and combating the Japanese in other ways to keep them from capturing more Chinese territory.[2]

I'd never had a real date with a girl until my junior year, so going steady with Betty was quite an experience for me. In fact, during my senior year in high school, the word somehow got around that I was a real "operator." I believe the popular expression now is "stud"; however, it was all unearned. There was a saying in those days as to how far you got with a girl on a date. You'd get to "first base" with a kiss, to "second base" with something more, and so on—I'm sure you get the picture. Well, let me say in all honesty that as far as my friends and I were concerned, I don't know anyone that actually—really and truly—scored a "home run." There was a lot of talk about it, usually by those who didn't know anything about what they were saying, but it was just that—talk. But talk can create rumors that blow around a high school like leaves in the wind.

All these years later, however, after visiting with my former classmates, the consensus now is that we were all a bunch of virgins when we entered the service, though some admit this only reluctantly. I don't know how the girls felt, but I believe most boys were somehow afraid of "going all the way."

North Central High School had a student body of more than 2,000 and there were well over 400 in my graduating class. In the four years that I attended North Central, I personally never knew of any girl becoming pregnant. There may have been instances of this occurring, but, if so, it was unusual and kept so secret that few, if any, of the students found out about it. If a girl should become pregnant, she'd immediately be ostracized and expelled from school, and her family would feel shame. Heavy petting occurred, yes, but not much else.

Betty was from Eastport, but she lived on the south side of Spokane with her married sister and attended North Central. Betty was an usherette at the Fox Theater, a gorgeous, opulent movie house with loge boxes, an immense gallery, a large stage, and seating for over 2,000 people. Built in the early 1930s, it was probably the only theater in Spokane that had air conditioning at the time. Usherettes at the Fox and one or two other theaters had special uniforms. At the Fox they wore black, wide-legged pants and white satin blouses with puff sleeves. In those days, dating an usherette was similar in status to dating a girl lifeguard at one of the city swimming pools. It was the ultimate in a boy's fantasy. On

Usherettes standing in front of the Liberty Theatre, summer 1942. *Northwest Museum of Arts & Culture/EWSHS, Spokane, WA (L87-1.18857-40)*

Saturday or Sunday evenings, I'd go to the Fox and Betty would come to the lobby and let me in; it didn't cost me anything. After the movie started and the audience was all seated, Betty and I'd go up to the balcony and we must have steamed up the place some.

In the afternoons after school, a favorite pastime for many North Central students, if they had the time and weren't working, was to walk downtown to the Crescent, an upscale department store. We'd go south on Stevens Street, over the Spokane River bridge to Main Street, and then turn west. Everyone met "under the clock" at the Crescent. What a gathering place! Not just North Central kids went there, but also Lewis & Clark and Gonzaga students. Hardly anyone came from Rogers High School, however, because it was too far away. We'd step down the broad stairway just north of "the clock" to a sandwich counter and soda fountain in the basement. Here, sitting on stools and sipping Cokes, kids spent hours talking about school, weekend plans, who was going out with whom, what the girls were wearing to the prom, and other things that seemed so important then.

Later while in the Army, I often reflected on these days. It seemed strange to think about it when laying in the rain and mud with shells exploding all around,

Looking west down Main Street, with the Crescent department store at left. The Main Street entrance is under the awning. *Northwest Museum of Arts & Culture/EWSHS, Spokane, WA (L87-1.76-31)*

and listening to bleeding buddies sobbing while waiting to die or for evacuation to an aid station. I knew that back in the States my high school classmates, the underclassmen of a couple of years ago, were at the Crescent—safe from harm, and probably unaware of the scores of young men who were dying on distant battlefields at that very moment.

When at the Crescent lunch counter, we'd put coins in the jukebox machines, and tap our fingers in rhythm to the popular songs of the time and silently mouth the words. Betty and I considered "White Christmas" as our song. Whenever we heard those lyrics, we were to think of each other. The concluding verses went as follows:

> I'm dreaming of a white Christmas
> With every Christmas card I write,
> May your days all be merry and bright
> And may all your Christmases be white.

Even today, when I hear "White Christmas," particularly the Bing Crosby version, it still haunts me. It's not entirely about Betty either. We both were too young to get really serious. Rather, it's an emotional link to the past, a time when I was 17 and my friends and I had our hopes, dreams, and whole lives yet ahead of us.

During the winter of 1942–43, when I wasn't working, I tried to get away from the house in my spare time. I didn't want to interfere too much with the normal routine of the family in whose home I was boarding. Consequently, I started boxing at the YMCA. I wasn't any kind of exceptional fighter, but I did have a good

The YMCA building where I spent time playing pool and boxing. *Northwest Museum of Arts & Culture/EWSHS, Spokane, WA (L87-1.18657-20)*

record and spent as much time at the "Y" as I could. I was the best light heavyweight boxer in the "Y" program that attended North Central and was chosen to represent my school in a city-wide boxing tournament held at the Masonic Temple. Eight boxers were selected to represent each high school—North Central, Gonzaga, Rogers, and Lewis & Clark—to vie for city championships in the various weight classes in a three-day, single elimination tournament.

Weight classifications were required in high school competition, but I didn't think they made all that much sense. I thought Bob Parker, who was only a welterweight on our team, probably had a chance of whipping any of us. The whole idea bothered Betty to no end. Only "brutish oafs" fought each other, she exclaimed, and it was "uncivilized and demeaning." If I boxed in the tournament, she'd give back my Hi-Y pin and we'd no longer be going steady. Well, there was nothing I could do, or wanted to do, really. My name already had appeared in the newspapers, and I liked boxing and wanted to fight in the tournament.

In the semi-final, I was paired up with Mel Updike, a short, broad, squat guy, probably four or five inches shorter than I and built like the proverbial "brick shit house." My friends told me that he liked going to Saturday night dances at Newman Lake and beating up anyone he could pick a fight with. I felt that somehow this wasn't really an encouraging thing to tell me.

On the evening of my match with Updike, I arrived at the Masonic Temple and went downstairs to the dressing room, which was cold, damp, and had a table for sitting or reclining. Our trainer was a man by the name of Taylor, whose son was a member of our boxing team. We were told that he'd worked, when much younger, as a trainer for Jack Dempsey, the world heavyweight champion. During each of the proceeding bouts, as my fists were being taped and I waited

School Fights Get Under Way

Spokane Daily Chronicle, Feb. 3, 1942.—Pirate[Rogers]-
Mead and N[orth] C[entral] Hi-Y Teams Split—Last Night's
Results.

120—Lou Baker, Pirate-Mead, decisioned Doug Wirsche.
125—Cy Bare, Hi-Y, decisioned Bob Dakely.
135—Fred Henry, Hi-Y, decisioned Orville Dean
145—Lou Johnson, Pirate-Mead, decisioned Bill Taylor.
155—Bob Parker, Hi-Y, decisioned Brandy Rush.
165—Ken Johnson, Pirate-Mead, decisioned Hal Stern.
175—Mel Updike, Pirate-Mead, decisioned Wayne McGregor.
Heavy—Bob Weeks, Hi-Y, won on forfeit.

Four Rogers Pirate-Mead fighters and four from North
Central's Hi-Y club survived the [first session of the high
school] three day elimination boxing tournament last night,
as the two teams put on a fast, slam-bang seven-bout card for
the well-filled Masonic Temple arena…
Probably the top fight of the evening was the slam-bang
155-pound tussle in which Bob Parker of Hi-Y and Brandy
Rush slugged it out for three blistering rounds, with Parker finally getting a bloody, hard-earned decision. Both boys fell
down twice in the third round, with Rush, the taller of the two
giving no quarter as he punched and crowded his opponent re-
peatedly into the ropes…
The 175-pound tussle between Mel Updike of Pirate-Mead
and Wayne (Moose) McGregor proved to be another excellent
contest…

patiently to go into the ring, I could hear the roar of the crowd. Since the heavyweight contest had been forfeited, my fight was the main event.

"The Auditorium" was a large cavernous room with seating all around the
ring. When my turn came, I walked down the aisle, climbed into my corner, and
looked across the ring at Updike. He was a tough looking guy with a flat nose
that reminded me of my cousin Bud Lofton and he had muscles on top of
muscles. He proved just as tough as he looked. The first round was pretty much
a draw. In the second round, we fiercely fought toe-to-toe, but he caught me
with a good right hand followed by a crushing left hook. It knocked me down,
and my mouthpiece flew out. I took advantage of the full count to nine, and
clearing my head, rose to my feet and actually finished the round strong. Though
completely exhausted, I somehow made it through the last round, but lost a split
decision.

With the boxing tournament over, I thought Betty and I might get back together. Whether it'd been just an excuse on her part or not, we never again dated. You don't forget someone like Betty, though, and I'm sure that on every white Christmas, inadvertently or otherwise, I'll remember her.

★★★

In the first four months of 1942, the Japanese had run wild throughout the Pacific. The only place that our military had slowed them down in any way was in the Philippines. But, with our brave men finally backed up to the sea, hopelessly outnumbered, and reduced to defending only the small island fortress of Corregidor, General Jonathan Wainwright was forced to surrender on May 6, 1942.

During the long, brutal campaign, the Japanese captured tens of thousands of American and Filipino soldiers. Only after several months did the world hear about the savage, pitiless treatment afforded the prisoners. The Japanese military, following the medieval Samurai Code of Bushido, considered surrender an ultimate act of humiliation and dishonor. In their eyes, soldiers should die, even commit suicide, rather than surrender. Men who did give up were to be despised and didn't deserve protection or care from their scornful conquerors.

The most infamous instance of mistreatment occurred in April 1942. During the Bataan Death March, American and Filipino prisoners were forced to walk more than 80 miles in searing tropical heat and humidity. With little or no food and water, and subjected to constant humiliation and severe physical abuse, hundreds of men died. They did so not just from disease, untreated wounds, exhaustion, heat stroke, and physical debilitation, but also from shootings, beheadings, stabbings, beatings, torture, being buried alive, and other brutalities performed by the Japanese guards, who didn't tolerate any straggling or complaints from the prisoners. Japan's military already had practised similar barbarities on a grand scale in China. For other nationalities, the Bataan Death March was a precursor of the inhumane treatment exhibited by the Japanese toward all prisoners in the remaining 3½ years of the Pacific war.

Jubilant Japanese soldiers celebrating yet another victory. *U.S. Army*

With the Pacific battleship fleet savagely blasted at Pearl Harbor, Americans generally thought we were greatly weakened. But in actuality, the U.S. Navy yet retained a formidable fighting force. We still had the valuable aircraft carriers, plus numerous cruisers, destroyers, and other vessels, all ready for action. Importantly, the vast oil tanks, shops, dry docks, and other port facilities at Pearl Harbor had largely escaped destruction. In time, six of the eight battleships sunk and damaged in Hawaii were refloated, repaired, and returned to active duty.

The first American retaliatory blow against the Japanese homeland was of little military consequence, but it had great psychological impact in both Japan and the United States. On April 18, 1942, the carrier USS *Hornet* steamed within 650 miles of Japan and launched sixteen Army B-25 bombers commanded by Lieutenant Colonel Jimmy Doolittle. The Japanese high command, knowing that the U.S. task force was close by, was preparing counter operations, but the American attack came a day earlier than they expected.

During the surprise assault, the Doolittle fliers dropped bombs on Tokyo and two other Nippon cities. Flying on to China, they crash-landed or bailed out at night. One B-25 landed safely in Russian territory. Several airmen were killed in the bailouts and crash landings, and the Japanese captured eight others, who suffered brutal captivity and three of whom were executed. However, the rest of the Doolittle Raiders made their way to safety, living to fly and fight another day in Asia, North Africa, and Europe. Eighty men in all had participated in the raid.

B-25 Mitchell bomber leaving the flight deck of the USS *Hornet*, April 18, 1942. *U.S. Army*

This audacious mission inspired a desperate America—a blow finally had been struck against the enemy! But also of significance, for the first time the Japanese public and military realized that their home islands were vulnerable to attack, and a clamor arose to prevent further assaults. Consequently, Japanese military leaders prepared plans to capture American-held Midway Island, a small atoll located 1,300 miles northwest of Hawaii. In the process, the Nippon high command intended to trap and destroy the American carrier fleet, which they expected would come west from Hawaii to defend Midway. With the final destruction of the American fleet and the occupation of Midway, a Japanese invasion of Hawaii was likely.

At this time, the Japanese Imperial Navy was one of the three strongest naval forces in the world—the other two being the American and British fleets. The

U.S. Navy's units, however, were divided between the Atlantic and Pacific, while the British were largely concentrated off Europe to counter the German submarine campaign and the smaller, yet still dangerous, German and Italian surface fleets.

In early 1942, however, there was no question that the Japanese fleet was the dominant force in the Pacific. Admiral Isoroku Yamamoto held nothing back in gathering a huge armada of battleships, aircraft carriers, cruisers, destroyers, oilers, and troop transports for attacking and invading Midway atoll. The Japanese planned to use Midway as an advanced post in a vast central Pacific defensive perimeter, which was intended to thwart future American assaults on Japanese gains in Southeast Asia and the western Pacific.

Meanwhile, far to the southwest in the Coral Sea between New Guinea and Australia, smaller American and Japanese task forces fought to a draw on May 4–8, 1942. Though the Japanese had a slight tactical advantage, losing only a small carrier compared to America's loss of the big fleet carrier *Lexington*, further Japanese occupation of New Guinea was blocked by this action. Japan's timetable of conquest was disrupted for the very first time.

The Japanese, however, considered the Battle of the Coral Sea of minor concern compared to the upcoming Midway operation. But, unbeknownst to them, the American intelligence service had broken the secret Japanese naval code. The American high command knew when and where the Japanese attack was coming. When the Japanese carriers approached and launched planes to bomb Midway on June 4, an American fleet, including the carriers *Yorktown*, *Hornet*, and *Enterprise*, lurked undetected to the northeast. The Americans launched a perfectly timed surprise attack against the unaware Japanese, who believed the major U.S. naval units still were in Hawaiian waters and wouldn't arrive to try and defend Midway until later. Instead of ambushing the American carriers as they confidently expected, the Japanese themselves were ambushed. American planes destroyed all four of Yamamoto's large fleet carriers that were involved in the operation—the *Kaga*, *Akagi*, *Soryu*, and *Hiryu*. The *Yorktown* was lost, too, but Midway held and the Americans had delivered a crushing blow to the larger Japanese fleet.

This great victory was exhilarating for the American people. In retrospect, historians have determined that the Battle of Midway was the most decisive action of the Pacific war. The Japanese Imperial Navy, though still a formidable force and destined to win further victories, nevertheless was severely weakened and never fully recovered from the loss of the four fleet carriers at Midway. The U.S. Navy had evened the ledger in the Pacific in mid-1942. Shortly, bustling American shipyards began launching the victorious armadas that advanced toward the Japanese homeland in 1943, 1944, and 1945.

After the Midway and Coral Sea battles, the United States by a narrow margin had seized the initiative, and launched the first American ground offensive of the war. On August 7, 1942, U.S. Marines landed in the remote, Japanese-held Solomon Islands, located several hundred miles northeast of Australia. A vicious, six-month-long naval, air, and ground campaign of attrition began for the island of Guadalcanal. Army troops soon attacked in New Guinea, too.

We really didn't know it for sure, but the tide was turning.

★★★

Shortly after school had started in the fall of 1942, I'd begun working as a janitor and stock boy for the Thomas and Gassman's men's clothing store located mid-block on Riverside east of Howard. It was a wonderful store, selling Hart, Schaffner, and Marx clothing, Oxxford suits, and Florsheim shoes. They carried casual clothes, too, and gradually as I worked cleaning up the store and stocking shelves, manager Jerry "Red" Miller sent me out front to greet the public. They began selling more and more merchandise to young people coming into the store. It was the best job I'd ever had. I bought my own clothes at 20 percent off and worked almost any hours I wanted. Needing the money, during holidays I worked as many hours as possible, often leaving the store as late as 10 or 11 P.M.

The late hours, however, disturbed Buck's mother, which resulted in me looking for another place to live. Fortunately, my sister Norma's husband, Jerry Dahlgren, interceded on my behalf. Otherwise, I might have ended up on the streets. He arranged for his parents, Oscar and Hazel Dahlgren, to take me in until I completed high school.

As the end of the school term approached, my friends and I all made plans to go into the military—some to the Army Air Force, some the Marines, others into the Navy or Army. As graduation came and passed in the early summer of 1943, I turned 18 and went down to the induction center and asked to be inducted. I took a physical and they told me to wait for orders. I'd be notified when to report for active service.

Mother was living with Joyce in Seattle and working at the Harborview Medical Center. I still worked at Thomas and Gassman's, but knew I'd be going into the service at any time. I wanted to spend a few weeks with Mother and Joyce. Accordingly, I quit my job and moved to Seattle. Mother was living in an apartment at 825 10th Ave., a block or two off Madison Avenue and west of Seattle University. It was a tough neighborhood, right next to the downtown area. In the few weeks that I was there, a girl was assaulted and raped, and a man was stabbed, all right in front of Mother's apartment house. There wasn't much for me to do with Mother working and Joyce attending summer school. Consequently, I took another job, this time as a guard in the West Seattle shipyards. I joined the night shift so I could spend more time with Mother.

The job didn't require a uniform, but they issued me a badge and a .45 caliber semi-automatic pistol with holster. They said the docks I'd be guarding were filled with military hardware, ordnance, and munitions for shipment to the South Pacific. The port authorities were concerned about sabotage. If I found anyone inside the guard fence, I was to apprehend them, ask for identification, and, if they weren't authorized to be in the area, to take them into custody. If they refused my orders or directions, I was to shoot them.

I said, "What do you mean 'shoot them'? I can't just shoot someone if he doesn't do what I tell him to do."

The supervisor looked at me and poked his finger in my chest, replying, "If they don't have proper identification and they won't submit to custody, or if they run, shoot them."

I asked, "What if they turn and run? You wouldn't want me to shoot them in the back, would you?"

I still remember his answer. "I don't give a good goddamn where you shoot them. If you can't shoot them in the back, shoot them in the asshole. Now, do you want the job or not?"

I took the job.

★★★

I soon was notified to report for active duty on August 16, 1943, at the Union Pacific station in Spokane for transportation to Fort Douglas, Utah. A day or two before leaving for Spokane, Mother sat down beside me in the kitchen.

As I ate breakfast, she took my hand, saying, "Mac, I don't know when we'll see each other again once you leave here. I won't be able to go to Spokane to see you off at the station because I can't get off from work. But, you know I love you and I'm proud of you and I know you'll do well in the service. Remember to be honest in all your dealings with everyone. Say your prayers every morning. It's not cowardly to be afraid and you may be afraid many times before I see you again. But, don't let fear overcome you. Do your duty, do what you know is right in your heart, come home, and I'll be waiting for you."

With that, she handed me a small, pocket-sized King James version of the New Testament. She'd underlined several passages and written the verses on the back page, the first of which was Proverbs 3:5–7: "Trust in the Lord with all thine heart and lean not unto thine own understanding. In all thy ways acknowledge him, and he shall direct thy path. Be not wise in thine own eyes; fear the Lord and depart from evil."

The last paragraph that she'd written in the little missal was Genesis 31:49: "A mizpah, for he said The Lord watch between me and thee, when we are absent from another."

I kept the little Bible with me throughout my entire time in the service. I was never without it. I brought it home and eventually gave it to my son, Kirk, after his confirmation service at Sts. Peter and Paul Church in Grangeville. While these verses were comforting and I kept them in my heart, the prayer I cited most frequently was the 23rd Psalm.

I can't tell you how many times I repeated it: "Yea though I walk through the valley of the shadow of death I shall fear no evil for thou art with me. Thy rod and thy staff comfort me."

Reciting this seemed so appropriate on the many occasions that I lay in a foxhole, or was on patrol and under fire, trying to make myself as small as possible, hoping that somehow I wouldn't get hit by enemy fire. I've heard it said that there are no atheists in foxholes. I'm not sure that is true, but I do know that a lot of people have found God while lying in a foxhole.

Boarding the train in Seattle, I said good-bye to Mother and Joyce, while kissing and hugging them and wiping tears from their eyes. It was nighttime when the train pulled out. I briefly saw Mother and Joyce standing on the railroad platform, and then my coach disappeared into darkness.

★★★

I tried to curl up in the seat and get some sleep, but it was hard to do. The train arrived in Spokane at 4 A.M., and since I'd been ordered to report at 8 A.M., I went into the Union Pacific station and waited. I sat down on one of the wooden benches in the waiting room, which were arranged like church pews. The wait was long and uncomfortable. As dawn came, young men reporting for induction began coming into the station with their families. I watched as they talked. Often a father held an arm around a son's shoulder, or a mother was patting a son on the back, all consoling each other. To me, a railway station was a depressing and foreign place, perhaps because it was where good-byes are said and partings made from loved ones. I'd only been on a train but twice, and very recently—when I went to visit Mother in Seattle, and on this occasion, returning to Spokane to start a new life in the military.

I'd lived by myself for almost three years. In that time I hadn't developed a special closeness with the people I'd boarded with, though, of course, they were good people—but not family for me. Watching the poignant family farewells that morning, I felt a lump forming in my throat. In one way, though, I was sort of glad no one was there to say good-bye to me; I might've broken down emotionally.

For the first time in my life, I was beginning to feel sorry for myself. I'd never before really felt lonely, but I did now. Looking around, I saw that I was the only person in the station with no one to talk to, or to bid good-bye. I realized that although I'd been separated from Mother and my sisters for several years, I'd always felt close to them emotionally. Also, I'd been able to phone them, or get in touch in some other way, when I needed them.

Now I was leaving for God knew where and I missed them. I already was homesick. Nothing could be more lonely than being just 18, sitting unattended in a railroad station on a grey, wet, drizzly morning, with a vacancy in your heart and wishing, hoping, that someone—anyone—would come and put their arms around you, hug you, or whisper comforting words.

Eight o'clock arrived. An army sergeant with a clipboard in his hands stood at the end of the room. In a loud voice, he called us to attention and took roll call, forming us into a line. When ordered to board the train, I picked up my small suitcase, stepped out the doorway, walked across the platform, and climbed up the steps of the passenger car.

I paused momentarily, looking back. I didn't see anyone I knew. I lowered my head and moved into the coach, finding a place to sit down. I settled back in the seat, straightened my shoulders, and looked out the window as the train started up. I promised myself that I'd do what Mother asked of me. I'd be honest, work hard, and do everything I could to make her proud of me. With that, I leaned my head back against the seat and silently said the Lord's Prayer.

NOTES

1. I remember Cooke's Nut Shop for another reason, too. One time when I was six or seven years old, Mother took me to Manito Park for a picnic. As we were stepping off the city bus, a fly flew into my ear. There's no way of describing the fright and panic that I, just a small boy, felt with that fly inside my ear, buzzing incessantly. Evidently it couldn't find a way out and its wings were beating on my eardrum. I began screaming. Mother, finding out what was wrong, took me to the emergency room at Sacred Heart Hospital where the fly was removed. Knowing how upset I was, particularly for missing the picnic, she took me to Cooke's Nut Shop where she bought me a hamburger and a milkshake so thick that I ate it with a spoon. I well remember that day and that milkshake.

2. The famous name, "Flying Tigers," went through an evolution in World War II. Originally, the term Flying Tigers specifically referred to the American Volunteer Group (AVG) of former Army, Navy, and Marine pilots who flew P-40 fighters for the Chinese against the Japanese from December 1941 until July 1942. After that date, the AVG became part of the China Air Task Force and then the U.S. Fourteenth Air Force. This was formed into the Chinese-American Composite Wing of the U.S. Fourteenth Air Force, which was China's only air arm during World War II. Its insignia was a tiger with wings, and consequently all American airmen who served in China during the war were considered Flying Tigers.

Stateside Training

My initial assignment in the infantry was as a machine gunner. However, while training with the 63rd Infantry Division at Camp Van Dorn, Mississippi, a call came through for volunteers to join an understrength division needing additional personnel to go overseas. I immediately volunteered.

I was sent to Camp Pickett, Virginia, where I joined a recon platoon that was attached to the 306th Regimental Combat Team of the 77th Infantry Division. I then underwent reconnaissance and intelligence training. Recon platoons are the eyes and the ears of the infantry. At Camp Pickett, we arduously trained in patrol and reconnaissance techniques, and map and compass reading. We were taken out at night into forested, marshy, or swampy localities and left alone to make our way back through unfamiliar terrain to our camp, and we were expected to do this in a limited period of time.

We also underwent other special preparations for overseas duty and combat. We were taught how to infiltrate enemy lines, attack supply and transportation facilities, and avoid detection by the enemy. Instruction was received in field sanitation, personal hygiene, and first aid, including taking care of wounded personnel, since medics usually didn't accompany squad and platoon sized patrols. The training was tough, rigorous, and exhausting. We also learned how to use and maintain nearly every type of infantry weapon—the .50 caliber machine gun, .30 caliber air-cooled machine gun, .30 caliber water-cooled machine gun, Riesling automatic submachine gun ("grease gun"), Browning Automatic Rifle (BAR), Thompson submachine gun, M1 rifle and carbine, .45 caliber pistol, bazooka, explosives, and hand grenades.

Like a regular infantry platoon, a recon platoon consisted of three squads with 10 to 12 men in each squad. A rifle squad usually included a sergeant as squad leader, a corporal, a BAR man, an ammunition carrier, and six to eight riflemen carrying the M1 Garand rifle, which was loaded with an eight-round ammunition clip. (Over time, however, soldiers tended to select light arms based on their personal preferences and experiences gained in combat.) A platoon normally was commanded by a lieutenant, assisted by a platoon sergeant and tech sergeant, who were armed with M1 carbines. (In combat, the complement of a squad and platoon changed constantly due to casualties, losses from sickness, and with men being assigned to other duties or transferred to different units.)

We also trained diligently in attacking with the bayonet. It's strange how using the bayonet, when it's attached to a rifle muzzle, is somewhat akin to handling a foil or saber. There are certain stylized steps that must be learned. Even now, I can go through the entire routine because it was so thoroughly drilled into us—we could never forget it.

In summary, my main recon training focused on patrolling, gathering intelligence, using high explosives, and destroying enemy ordnance and communication systems. The hard training and physical conditioning at Camp Pickett was even accelerated, because a shipping out date already had been set for our division and time was running out.

Private First Class Wayne C. MacGregor Jr., 1943.

3 EMBARKATION

*M*Y TRUE DEPARTURE FROM ADOLESCENCE began as I boarded the train at Camp Pickett, Virginia, and we left for the West Coast. Our destination was Camp Stoneman, located on the Sacramento River just east of San Francisco Bay. After our arrival, we remained at Camp Stoneman only a short time. Most of us took our last physicals and were given any needed medical treatment prior to shipping out.

I was told to report to the dental lab. After a lieutenant performed a dental examination, he directed me to sit down in an armchair. Immediately, two orderlies approached me in front, one on each side, and reached through my arms and clasped their hands behind me, locking me in an embrace. Hardly saying anything about what was happening, the dentist immediately started working on my teeth. He filled four cavities, without anesthetic or sedative! I'd never been to a dentist before.[1]

After my "dental appointment," I returned to our quarters. We packed our duffel bags, put them on our shoulders, and climbed into trucks. On March 25, 1944, we were driven to the docks at Camp Stoneman, where we unloaded from the vehicles and walked under a large sign proclaiming, "Through these portals pass the best damn soldiers in the world."

It made us feel good, but I'm not sure any of us felt that

Preparing to board river transport at Camp Stoneman. *AP Photo*

we were, at that time, "The best damn soldiers in the world." As we walked up the gangplank onto the river transports, a band on the dock played "Over There." Most of us had lumps in our throats.

After moving down the bay to San Francisco, we disembarked from the river steamers, and boarded a large, gray Navy transport. My platoon was sent three decks down and far forward to our assigned bunks in the hold. The troops dropped duffel bags and equipment in the aisles or on the canvas bunks, which were stacked four or five high. With only about 20 vertical inches between bunks, these canvas cots were attached to pipes bolted to the deck and ceiling. There barely was enough room for a man to crawl into a bunk and lie under the man just above him. With no ventilation and little light, none of us were very comfortable in our crowded quarters. The humid air smelled of stale cigarette smoke, sweat, and vomit.

The ship stayed in port overnight. The next day after moving out of the bay, past Alcatraz Island and under the Golden Gate Bridge, we encountered large ocean swells. With each swell, the ship rose in a long upward movement, then slowly came down into the trough between swells. It wasn't long before practically everyone was seasick. Open gratings of crisscrossed 2 x 4s had been built into the decks, from topside on down through all levels belowships. This allowed for some ventilation in the hold. As seasickness spread, men vomited into garbage cans arranged in each hold—and some of the cans began filling up. As the seas became rougher, garbage cans were knocked over and vomit spilled out on the decks and into the hatch gratings, dripping onto the men in lower decks.

Fresh water wasn't available for showering, only salt water, and the sanitation facilities were poor. Urinals were nothing but "V" shaped steel troughs running the full length of a head. The toilets, situated along the opposite side of a latrine, simply consisted of galvanized sheet metal with holes cut out about every two feet. Underneath, salt water flowed continually over another flatter trough, removing the deposited waste. Seating arrangements were all open—no stalls, no doors, no side panels, no privacy! There weren't any seat covers and when sitting on a hole, a man's genitals sometimes hung down into the flowing salt water.

I can still hear my friend, Junior Cotter, singing a ditty to the sea chantey tune in "The Mikado" as we came out of the head after our first visit:

Do your balls hang low,
do they wobble to and fro,
Can you tie them in a knot,
can you tie them in a bow,
Can you throw them over your shoulder
like a bloody English soldier,
If you can, watch out, if your balls hang low.

The convoy continually zigzagged to avoid submarine attacks. Black out conditions were observed as soon as the sun went down. It was a miserable trip. After almost a week, we were extremely glad to see Oahu in the distance.

★★★

My unit—the 1st Battalion of the 306th Regimental Combat Team of the 77th Infantry Division—together with other attached units, was trucked from the docks to a partially constructed camp on the northeast side of Oahu near Kaneohe. Our quarters were pyramid tents erected on board frame foundations. Six men were assigned to each tent.

Lou Ryman and Wayne MacGregor in camp on Oahu, Hawaii, April 1944.

During the entire time on Oahu, I received but one overnight pass. I hitch-hiked by myself to Honolulu and, strange as it may seem, the governor of the island picked me up in his chauf-feur-driven limousine. He took me as far as the Governor's Palace, where I got out. From there, I walked west along the highway to Waikiki Beach and the Royal Hawaiian Hotel, a large, beautiful pink palace. It'd been requisitioned by the military and was full of servicemen. I checked in for the night; however, there really wasn't much to do in Honolulu. I went downtown, met some other soldiers and became buddies with them, and spent most of the afternoon and evening just drinking beer, going from one tavern to another.

It amazes me now to look at pictures of Honolulu—the huge crowded city is filled with towering buildings and hotels line the shore. In 1944, I don't remember seeing a building much taller than three or four stories, and the Royal Hawaiian, as I recall, was practically the only hotel on the beach.

We were assigned to the jungle-training center on Oahu, learning to live and survive in the tropics, and were taught hand-to-hand combat and how to attack enemy pillboxes, trenches, and blockhouses. We also went through Advanced Amphibious Training and a complete program of weapons firing on the ranges. Special emphasis was given to developing small combat groups (i.e., squads and platoons) into hard hitting, closely coordinated teams.

The Intelligence and Reconnaissance Platoon, of which I was a member, was sent to Waianae on the southwest side of the island for amphibious training. We were instructed in the use of rubber boats, taking them through reefs and rough surf to land on an enemy-held beach. One night we were taken out by an LST (Landing Ship Tank) and let out through the nose of the huge vessel. We paddled our raft in toward shore, simulating a patrol. There were 11 men in the squad, but the rubber raft only had room for 8. Several of us held on to the sides of the raft (I couldn't swim) or swam alongside.

Suddenly a large fin making a fluorescent wake came toward us through the water. Feeling something rub my leg, I felt certain sharks were attacking us. Everyone started yelling!

Finally, someone shouted, "They're dolphins. Don't worry, they won't hurt you."

However, they certainly scared the hell out of us.

★★★

By this time in the Pacific war, U.S. forces had made large gains in New Guinea and the Solomon Islands, and the U.S. Navy's "island hopping" strategy, working in close coordination with Marine and Army troops, had penetrated and eliminated Japan's "outer defensive perimeter" in the Gilberts and Marshalls.

In June, as the American fleet pushed relentlessly westward, we began hearing about the hard fighting on Saipan in the Mariana Islands. It was obvious that our unit was being prepared for a combat operation, and the rumor was that we'd be invading Guam, located not far from Saipan. We loaded aboard APA (Army Personnel Assault) attack ships, and in bright, warm, beautiful weather, left for the Marianas during the first week in July.

Our Intelligence and Reconnaissance Platoon was a small, close-knit group. Even when we started our training, we never had more than about 30 men.

GIs on our troopship en route to Guam, reading, shooting dice, playing poker, and getting fresh air. *U.S. Army*

Friendships had formed fast. Our leadership was good and we were a well-trained, competent outfit. The men were selected for above average intelligence and a willingness to take part in the tough, dangerous patrol work that was assigned to them. We kept pretty much to ourselves. Not that we were loners, but somehow we exercised a certain amount of independence from the rest of the company. I never met a better bunch of guys to depend on in any circumstances.

NOTE

1. After leaving the military, I remember my first visit to a dentist in 1947. I was working as a logger for Potlatch Forests out of Headquarters, Idaho, at Camp 54. Mac Barnes, the camp boss, seeing that I was having dental problems, told me to go to a dentist in Orofino. When the dentist inspected my mouth, he said my wisdom teeth were impacted and needed removal. From my experience with the military dentist, I assumed that pain killer was given for extractions, but not fillings.

    Consequently, I told the dentist how relieved I was that my teeth were being pulled rather than filled.

    With a blank look on his face, he said, "What do you mean, relieved. Why does that make you feel good?"

    "Well," I replied, "now you can give me some type of pain killer."

    "Sure I can give you painkiller," he said. "Why wouldn't you think I'd do that?"

    I then related the incident in which my teeth had been filled without "anesthetic" before going overseas. He thought that was quite humorous!

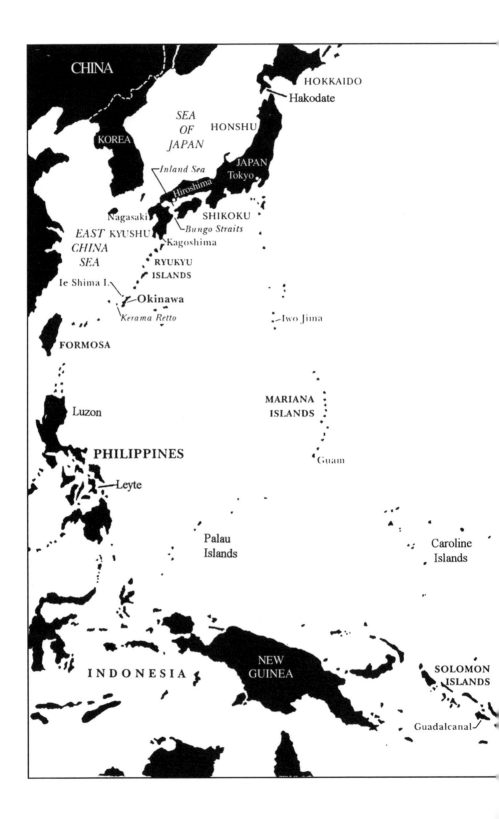

CHINA

HOKKAIDO

Hakodate

SEA OF JAPAN

KOREA

HONSHU

Inland Sea

JAPAN

Tokyo

Hiroshima

Nagasaki

SHIKOKU

EAST CHINA SEA

KYUSHU

Bungo Straits

Kagoshima

RYUKYU ISLANDS

Ie Shima I.

Okinawa

Kerama Retto

Iwo Jima

FORMOSA

Luzon

MARIANA ISLANDS

PHILIPPINES

Guam

Leyte

Palau Islands

Caroline Islands

INDONESIA

NEW GUINEA

SOLOMON ISLANDS

Guadalcanal

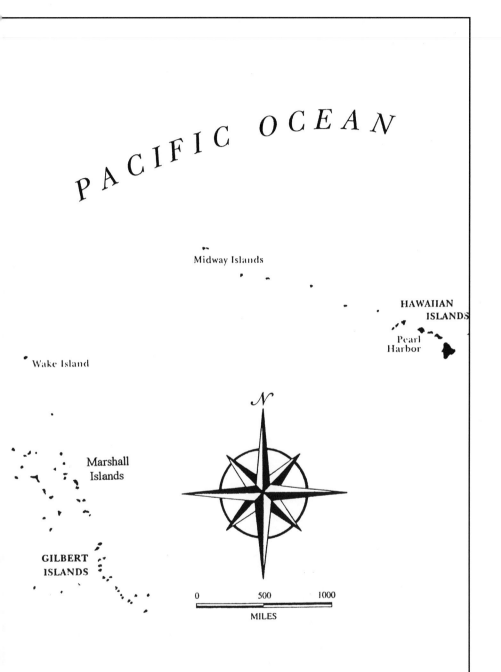

PACIFIC OCEAN

Midway Islands

HAWAIIAN
ISLANDS

Pearl
Harbor

Wake Island

N

Marshall
Islands

GILBERT
ISLANDS

0   500   1000

MILES

Prologue to My War Years, 1944–45

For more than five decades, I thought little about the war, seldom bringing it up with friends and hardly ever discussing it with my children. It wasn't that I wanted to avoid talking about it, rather I felt that people just couldn't fathom or were incapable of understanding the confounding and appalling actuality of being a combat infantryman in World War II. As time went on, the war drifted further and further into the recesses of my memory. I believe, too, in retrospect, that we tend to forget and try to blot out the terrible things that happen to us in our lifetime—to a great extent, we are successful at doing this. Our best memories remain and over time they crowd out the sorrowful and shocking things that we'd rather forget.

Consequently, when I started writing this memoir, I realized that a number of my recollections from the past had faded into dim memories. Thus, I've had to exert considerable effort to recall some events. I've reviewed appropriate historical works, magazines, and periodicals, as well as old 77th Division newspapers published during the Pacific conflict. Also, the unit operation reports from the Department of Army's Historical Records Section, once designated as "Secret" and "Restricted," contained a wealth of information recorded at the time of action.

During and after the war, I fortunately acquired what I now realize is an exceptional collection of photographs documenting my time in the Pacific. My platoon was fortunate to frequently have a U.S. Army photographer close by. I also went over the correspondence between my mother and I during the war, which she saved in her dresser drawer. She also cut out and saved pertinent articles from newspapers. Excerpts from my mother's extensive collection of newspaper clippings provide a fine running commentary on the course of the war, often focusing specifically on operations in which I was involved. A number of them are reproduced in *Through These Portals*. From all of these sources, I tried to recall and refresh memories of that distant time more than a half-century ago.

If one has read William Manchester's excellent memoir, *Goodbye, Darkness*, and sees similarities to my experiences on Okinawa, it should be noted that he fought with the 6th Marine Division in comparable circumstances. Like myself, he was in a reconnaissance platoon. Our duties were the same—serving as a rifleman, scout, and "runner." Until he was wounded and evacuated, we probably never were more than a few thousand yards or a mile or two apart. My division, the 77th, moved into the line on the Maeda Escarpment on April 29, 1945. The 6th Marine Division, of which Manchester was a member, relieved troops on the western, or far right, flank of the U.S. line during early May, taking over an area that had been occupied by the 1st Marine Division on bluffs above the Asa River. Shortly thereafter they ran into the enemy's terrible defenses entrenched on Sugar Loaf Hill to the south.

While the 6th Marines were taking Sugar Loaf, we were in the process of attacking Chocolate Drop Hill, also to the southward. In the small space between the 77th Division and the 6th Marines, the 1st Marine Division was fighting to seize Wana Draw, Dakeschi Ridge, and Shuri heights. Okinawa was a horrible killing ground, with the 77th, 1st and 6th Marines, and several other Army divisions, the 7th, 27th, and 96th, all fed into a maelstrom of hell, frontally assaulting increasingly difficult objectives and fortified positions.

I consider Eugene B. Sledge's eloquent *With the Old Breed, at Peleliu and Okinawa* to be the finest written account of World War II combat that I've read. Sledge was with the 1st Marines directly on my division's right flank. Both of us fought our way up the Maeda Escarpment. We faced the same Japanese resistance and lived in the same mud, filth, and death during April, May, and June in 1945, until the island finally was secured.

I have, in my writing, sometimes used the pronoun "we" when I might not have actually been involved in a specific action. In this manner, however, I'm referring to my squad or platoon, and, on occasion, even my company or a larger combat unit. However, I directly participated in most of the events described in *Through These Portals*.

I served over 27 months in the military, of which 21 months were spent overseas. I contracted malaria, dengue fever, and dysentery, was wounded and awarded the Purple Heart, and earned two Bronze Stars with a V as well as the Bronze Arrowhead (for beachhead assault), five campaign battle stars, and the Combat Infantryman Badge. I fought at Guam, Leyte, the Kerama Retto, Ie Shima, and Okinawa, and participated in the occupation of Japan.

After the war ended, my friend Lou Ryman and I were standing at the railing of the ship taking us from Cebu in the Philippines to serve in occupation duty in Japan. We both had difficulty understanding why we'd managed to survive when so many others had died.

I remember commenting to Lou, "You know, some day we won't even be able to remember what it was like out here in the Pacific. We'll have forgotten about it and no one else will give a damn."

And then I said to myself,

> But the one thing I'll always remember, and will hold it in my heart, is that there is nothing as terrible, as gross, as the horror of what happened here when we were fighting in the Pacific. No matter how bad things may get as I grow older, nothing will ever even remotely approach the terror and ugliness that I saw, particularly on Okinawa. If the time comes that I've forgotten just how bad it was, when my memories of individual circumstances and events have faded, I'll always remember to say to myself that it was the worst possible thing that could happen to a human being, and nothing, nothing, can ever be that bad again.

And so, while I'm still able to write down some recollections of those long-ago years, I have attempted to do so. I hope I convey in some small way the pitiless savagery of those times—tempered, however, by the courage, daring, and sacrifice exhibited by thousands of young men, some actually still only youngsters, who fought and died on those strange foreign shores.

★

PATI POINT

MT SANTA ROSA

TUMON BAY

YIGO

AGANA BAY

BARRIGADA

PITI ASAN AGANA

OROTE PENINSULA

SUMAY

MT TENGO

AGAT

PAGO BAY

AGAT BAY

YLIG BAY

MT ALIFAN

TALOFOFO BAY

UMATAC

INARAJAN

GUAM

Modified from *Ours to Hold It High.*

4 Guam (Mariana Islands)

*F*OR TWO DAYS, we watched the fighting on Guam from the deck of our APA, wondering what was happening on the beaches. Guam had been a U.S. possession before the war, but was seized by the Japanese shortly after the Pearl Harbor attack. Now we were taking it back.

We waited impatiently for orders to clamber into the LCVPs (Landing Craft Vehicle and Personnel), also known as Higgins boats, and head to shore, joining the Marines and our sister unit, the 305th Regimental Combat Team. Lou Ryman and I had found a place on the forward deck that was sheltered from the sun for most of the day. We managed to sleep there, rather than below in the suffocating, smelly, humid belly of the ship.

One of us always remained at the spot to keep our place, while the other went to eat or to the head. The tropical sun beating down on the steel decks turned the troop compartments below into ovens. Sleeping was almost impossible. Those of us who were able—with or without permission—found places on the top deck to spend the evenings and enjoy the night air.

We'd been aboard the APA for over two weeks since leaving Honolulu. The monotony, sweaty conditions, and endless lines at the latrines and mess hall made us anxious to get off. Each day, we had performed calisthenics and were briefed about the upcoming operation. Our duties and responsibilities when landing on the beaches and heading inland were outlined to us over and over again. Most of us had never heard of Guam before, or hardly had any idea where it was located in the vast Pacific Ocean.

★★★

The timing of the Guam invasion actually was behind schedule, primarily due to the heavy casualties our forces suffered during the invasion of Saipan that began five weeks earlier on June 15. Saipan is situated more in the central part of the Mariana Islands, whereas Guam stands about 100 miles southwest near the

Performing calisthenics aboard our APA on the voyage to Guam— temporary relief from the stifling conditions below decks. Note the landing craft on the davits at the ship's rail. *U.S. Army*

south end of the chain. During the early days of the invasion, June 20–21, huge U.S. and Japanese fleets clashed in the Philippine Sea west of the Marianas in the climactic aircraft carrier battle of the war. Popularly known as the "Great Marianas turkey shoot," the Japanese lost over 400 naval aircraft and three carriers. The U.S. Navy didn't yet fully realize it, but the back of the Japanese naval air arm had been permanently broken.

On Saipan, the Army's 27th Infantry Division had been ordered in to assist the 2nd and 4th Marine divisions in the fierce, drawn-out struggle. The fanaticism of the Japanese defenders and their willingness to die had taken a high toll on our units on that island. Saipan finally was secured on July 9, 1944.

Originally, Guam was to be assaulted only by the 3rd Marine Division and the 1st Marine Provisional Brigade. Given the example of Jap resistance on Saipan, however, Major General Roy S. Geiger of the U.S. Marine Corps, the ground commander for the Guam invasion, requested additional troops and was given the 77th Infantry Division. The initial invasion date for Guam was set back, since two weeks were required to move our division from Hawaii. The delay proved to be a blessing. During this time, our naval aircraft and warships bombarded Guam extensively—the heaviest pre-invasion operation up to that time in the Pacific theater.

The assault on Guam's beaches had begun at dawn on July 21, 1944, under nearly perfect conditions. The sunny sky was only slightly overcast, and the sea was calm, almost as flat as a tabletop. The initial attack was directed at the west side of the 35-mile-long island. The 3rd Marine Division landed in the mid-part of Guam, near the village of Asan on Agana Bay, while the 1st Marine Provisional Brigade stormed ashore further south near Agat. The five-mile-long Orote Peninsula, jutting westward, divided the two beachheads.

Before the landing, battleships, cruisers, destroyers, and other vessels provided fire support for the assault troops. Carrier planes also swept in, strafing and bombing Japanese positions on the coastline. Minutes before the Marines landed on the beachheads, the naval gunfire intensified. When the assault waves were about a thousand yards from shore, rocket launchers on LCIs (Landing Craft Infantry) fired volleys of rockets at the Japanese lines. Shortly, the naval bombardment lifted. Smoke and haze covered almost the entire area as the Marines landed.

The Marine assault below the village of Agat suffered heavy losses from Japanese artillery. Twenty-four out of 40 of our Amtracks (amphibian tractors) were knocked out before reaching the beach. Casualties continued mounting. Soon, however, Sherman medium tanks, brought in by landing craft, secured the beachhead, which by nightfall was almost a mile deep.

Troops from our sister unit, the 305th Regimental Combat Team, also had embarked in landing craft on the morning of the assault, but they had circled, waiting for orders to go in. They landed at Agat Bay early in the afternoon.

On the second day of the invasion, men from the 305th and the 1st Marine Provisional Brigade pushed inland to attempt to take Mt. Alifan. At 858 feet, this was the highest point behind the beaches where our forces were attacking on Agat Bay.

★★★

For two days, as Lou and I lay on the forward bulkhead trying to avoid the sun, we talked about what we might expect when entering the front lines. We were apprehensive, but eager for combat, and mainly concerned about not letting our buddies down. No matter what happened, we said, we wouldn't turn our backs and run. We could see shells exploding on the beaches and the slopes of Mt. Alifan. We wondered what it was like to be under fire—whether our courage would hold up.

On the 23rd, the Marines had solidified the Agat beachhead. Approximately at noon, our commander, Colonel Aubrey D. Smith, received orders to send the 306th Infantry ashore. Each man had an M1 Garand rifle or other personal weapon, a steel helmet, two bandoleers of ammunition, a full backpack with rations, two to four grenades, an inflatable life belt, a waist-belt full of ammunition, two canteens of water, and a gas mask (the latter, however, would prove unnecessary and was discarded soon after we hit the beaches). In addition, men carried machetes, ammunition tins and boxes, parts of mortars and machine guns, phone line reels, and other equipment.

These heavy loads were burdensome and awkward for us when stepping over the railing and climbing down the cargo nets to the waiting 36-feet-long LCVPs. With the rising and dropping of the waves, precise timing was required when letting go of the netting and stepping safely aboard. If care wasn't taken, a man could be injured by taking a long fall into the bottom of an LCVP or landing on top of a soldier waiting below. Worse yet, a man might be crushed or drowned if

Climbing down a cargo net into an LCVP (Higgins boat) to assault the beachhead. The soldier at the bottom is carrying a bolt, single-action rifle, indicating that he's probably a sniper. Other men have standard semi-automatic M1s with eight-round clips. *U.S. Army*

caught between the converging hulls of a landing craft and the troopship in choppy seas.

Each landing craft carried about 20 to 30 men. The recon platoon, of which I was a member, was sent in on crowded LCVPs toward White Beach on Agat Bay. Our approach was unopposed, other than occasional splashes from Jap mortar shells and small arms fire. After a time, we encountered Guam's broad barrier reef—one of the great coral reefs of the Pacific Ocean. Since the landing craft couldn't negotiate through or over the reef, the front ramps went down and we began unloading into the water, still hundreds of yards from shore.

It seemed to take hours to wade through the reef in mostly waist- to chest-deep water. It was a "helluva" long distance to go. Sometimes a man dropped into a hole up to his neck or entirely over his head, and he'd struggle to the surface gasping and trying to hold onto his equipment, while always moving toward the beach. Some men didn't have enough strength and had to discard their gear in order to get ashore. Others stepped into depressions and just disappeared—one minute they were there; the next minute they were gone!

We staggered out of the water and walked up the beach late in the afternoon. Everyone was sent to assigned positions where we began digging foxholes. On the troop transport, we'd been instructed to pair off with someone from our squad who'd be a foxhole buddy when reaching the shore. I paired off with Lou Ryman. My God, what luck! We first became good friends while on the transport sailing from San Francisco to Hawaii. Lou was a big, strong, handsome young man from Canton, Ohio, who'd attended college there and played football. Quiet and soft-spoken, Lou always was there when you needed him. Steady as a rock, he never got excited even when everyone and everything else was falling apart. We became the closest of friends and I considered him one of the finest, most courageous men I'd ever met. Foxhole buddies were responsible for each other. They protected and looked after each other regardless of the consequences. I know if it'd been necessary, I'd have died for Lou.

Our section of the perimeter was situated several hundred yards in from the beach in a small, fairly open clearing surrounded by a heavy growth of jungle. The ground was broken up and pockmarked by naval bombardment. We could see damage to the nearby trees, too. A disturbing smell permeated the area and none of us wanted to stay here, but Sergeant Phillip Ames ordered us to dig two-man foxholes about every 10 yards along the perimeter.

I put down my pack and, taking the spade from it and with Lou standing by, I chose a place to start digging. The ground felt spongy and soft. I stomped one foot on a spot where I intended to thrust in my spade. As my foot sank into the ground, the rotten decaying elbow of a human body emerged—it was a dead Japanese soldier. As it oozed to the surface, dozens of maggots came with it, together with a foul, putrid odor. Startled, I straightened up, moved sideways, and stepped onto more of the soggy, damp fill that lay over the body. My foot sank into the dirt up to my ankle and the oily, gaseous contents of the internment spewed out on my boot. I backed up with a gasp, hardly able to keep from vomiting.

Lou, also edging away, looked at me and said, "Throw some dirt on that goddamn hole and let's get away from here."

We informed Sergeant Ames about our problem and he said to pick out another position, keeping the same spacing if possible, and dig there. I looked down at my feet and saw little white maggots crawling on my pant legs. Feeling nauseated, I shook my legs and feet as hard as I could. I then walked to the edge of the jungle and broke off several large leaves to wipe off the rotting moisture and maggots. Even though a lack of drinking water might be a problem later, I used the contents of one of my canteens to wash my hands and the legs of my fatigues as best I could.

Lou, who occupied the same foxhole, of course, had to remain there with me. When dawn broke the next morning, however, it became apparent that no one else particularly wanted to be in my close proximity, until the hot jungle sun finally dried my uniform and the stench disappeared. With the thousands and even tens of thousands of Japanese casualties hurriedly buried in unmarked graves during the Pacific war, I've sometimes wondered how often internment sites were unknowingly dug into by soldiers like myself.

Though situated several hundred yards behind the front lines, our company's first night on shore was a fearful occasion. Machine gun and rifle fire whistled overhead. We could hear the crump of artillery explosions in the forward areas on Mt. Alifan, along with the cries and screams of men in pain. Our foxholes were dug in a V shape, with the apex pointing toward the enemy lines. In each foxhole, one man remained on guard for four hours while the other slept, trading off until dawn came. Rain fell the first night, as it did every day and night that we were on Guam. There never was a day without rain, and some days it rained harder than usual. We always were wet and miserable in the foxholes, often sitting in several inches of water. After our men arose at dawn on July 24, our division consolidated its lines and made preparations for further action.

★★★

The next day, July 25, Sergeant Ames called my squad together and said, "Men, we're going to move up to Mt. Alifan. The 1st Marines took the mountain yesterday, but we're going up to scout the forward positions and escort one of our artillery observation men. So lock and load, be sure you've got ammunition and combat rations for two days, and let's move out."

In a short time, eight of us—most of the squad—started up a trail that we were told led to the summit. We'd hardly left our company area when we began receiving hostile fire. Bullets snapped overhead—whistling, popping, and in some instances making ripping sounds like canvas being torn. None of us had

Men dug in along our company's perimeter. Two soldiers manning a .30 caliber "air-cooled" machine gun occupy the nearest foxhole. The next two men have fixed bayonets on their M1s. *U.S. Army*

faced enemy fire before. We all fell to the ground, not knowing what to do or where to go.

Sergeant Ames, although as inexperienced as any of us, yelled, "Damn it, get up off the goddamn ground and let's move out. We can't stay here. We've got to get to the top of that mountain."

With that, we rose up. Although continuing to receive some enemy fire, none of which harmed anyone, we moved up the trail and entered the heavy jungle, at which point the enemy shooting stopped.

The enemy infantry usually were equipped with the Arisaka Model 38, .25 caliber rifle. A bolt action, single-shot repeater, it was a fairly long weapon to which a bayonet almost always was attached. Because of the small caliber, it had a peculiar sound when fired, different from any American weapon.

In a short time, we began passing through the forward elements of the 1st Provisional Marine Brigade. A number of wounded men were lying in the vicinity. They told us they'd received heavy fire that night and suffered casualties. After passing through the Marine positions, we continued up the trail, guided by a Marine who'd been to the top of Mt. Alifan. Our guide didn't look any older than 17 or 18. In a short time we reached the summit.

Here, the artillery observer that we were escorting set up a "flash" observation post. This actually wasn't too effective because the heavy rain and mist hindered visibility. Our Marine guide now left us to go "hunt Japs" by himself.[1] From a huge rock outcrop on the peak, we could see a vast area beneath us as well as the five-mile-long Orote Peninsula to the northwest, jutting out to sea.

The Marines planned on cutting off the Japanese on the peninsula by sending a strong force north from Agat across the rice paddies to Apra Harbor on the peninsula's other side. This soon was accomplished. Supported by Sherman tanks, they fought their way across the base of the peninsula, while seizing a road that allowed the tanks to move through the rice paddies. A counterattack by Jap tanks hit the Marines, but all were quickly destroyed by the Shermans.

In just four days of fierce fighting, the 1st Marine Provisional Brigade already had suffered in excess of 1,000 casualties with almost 200 killed in action. The weather since the beginning of the invasion worked against our forces. Rain, rain, and more rain. On Mt. Alifan, observation became even more difficult as the cloudy, misty conditions increased.

In the early morning darkness of July 26, Joe "Junior" Cotter from our squad shook me awake, saying something was happening and I should take a look. Joe was a slight, almost delicate looking young man. He had a baby face, which is why we called him Junior, but he had the heart of a lion. Before the war ended, he earned two Bronze Stars with Vs, the Silver Star, and a Purple Heart. I believe he was the most decorated man in our platoon.

We probably were 3,000 or 4,000 yards from the base of the Orote Peninsula, but even so we could hear the Japanese screaming, yelling, and firing their weapons. While their tracer bullets etched the dark sky, they drank themselves to drunkenness to raise their courage for a banzai charge.[2] Then we saw and heard a holocaust of weaponry down in the valley.

The next morning, we were told that the Japs had struck the Marine lines in a desperate attack, shouting, "Fuck Babe Ruth," "Eleanor Roosevelt is a bitch," "The Emperor draws much blood tonight," and similar phrases. Running, shooting, and throwing hand grenades, the desperate, alcohol-sodden Japanese ran headlong into the Marine lines. They were hit by Marine rifle and machine gunfire, as well as by our divisional artillery, which was being directed from our position on Mt. Alifan. Most of the Japanese were blown to bits. With the attack broken up, the survivors tried to retreat, but were trapped in surrounding mangrove swamps. For at least two hours, artillery fire was directed down from our observation post, killing in excess of 500 of them.

★★★

The next day, with the Orote Peninsula battle nearing an end, my squad was sent down the mountain to our regimental command post. As an Intelligence and Reconnaissance Platoon, we'd be called on frequently to conduct patrols while on Guam. Our commanders believed that by sending out reconnaissance platoons on repeated aggressive missions, we'd keep the Japs on edge and off balance, and gather useful information about their probable intentions.

The .30 caliber "water-cooled" machine gun was considerably heavier than the "air-cooled" model. The man closest in the foreground holds an M1 Garand rifle. *U.S. Army*

Accordingly, Lieutenant Wright Powers called our squad leaders in and briefed them. We'd been ordered to conduct a reconnaissance across the entire eight-mile-wide island—from the west to the east side—to a small village located on Pago Bay.

The distance across the island wasn't far, but we thought we'd have to stay out at least one and possibly two nights, so we took the necessary supplies and equipment. From a point north of Agat, our route would take us in an easterly direction along the base of Mt. Tenjo, which still was in enemy hands, as was the area we'd be patrolling further east.

After setting out, the going at times was really tough because of the steep, slippery terrain and extremely hot weather. All of us perspired extensively. Each man was alert, eyes constantly probing the jungle to the sides, front, and back. No Japs were seen on the way across the mountain, but we began noticing signs of enemy activity as we got closer to Pago Bay.

We entered a canyon that led down toward a stream flowing to Pago Bay, where the village was located. At a point where we could look down the ill-defined trail that we were following, we were surprised when four Jap soldiers broke out of the thick jungle underbrush and ran across the trail directly in front of us, not more than 20 yards away. We were so startled that none of us got off a shot. Following on down the canyon of the Pago River, we soon saw Pago village in the distance. Sergeant Ames told me to take the "point," while Lou Ryman and Joe Geiger were sent out as flankers, one on each side of the platoon and about 50 to 75 yards behind me.

★★★

Whenever a sergeant yelled "Scouts out," and you were one of them, or when individually told to "Take the point," I always felt queasy. My heart beat harder, my instincts seemed to take over, and my every sense became sharper. The scouts out in front or flanking a patrol, of course, were extremely vulnerable. You worried that each step might be your last, and you kind of hunched your shoulders forward, bracing for a bullet that you feared was coming. A scout getting hit usually was the first warning that a patrol was under attack. By being shot at, you'd found the enemy's location, which usually was the purpose of a patrol.

Normally, the point man and flankers were too far in advance or distanced from the rest of the patrol to get much assistance when the action started. Being a rifleman, I often was put out on point. Men carrying the Browning Automatic Rifle (BAR) and Thompson submachine gun always were kept back with the main body. Their firepower was too valuable to chance being lost at the start of an ambush.

Because of the thick jungle foliage, patrols generally had to advance in single file along trails, and consequently the enemy often set up ambushes along these jungle tracks. Sometimes the Japs let the point man and flankers pass by, and then opened up on the main body, leaving the scouts to be finished off later.

Combat could erupt at any moment and usually at close quarters—10, 20, 40, or 50 feet away. Our early campaigns in the Pacific mostly consisted of small unit actions. Often we didn't even know where our flanking companies were. Thus, the members of your squad and platoon were the most important friends you had. We normally didn't even associate with anyone else.

When fighting erupted, it usually was sudden and intense, and happened so fast that you really weren't ready for it. Everyone was shooting, grenades were being thrown, and people were screaming, and then the shooting would stop—the Japs had disappeared and the firefight was over.

★★★

We came out of the canyon and moved into the outskirts of the village. Suddenly there was a flurry of movement, and two or three rifle shots were fired at us. Out of the corner of my eye, I saw three or four Jap soldiers scurrying out of a house built on stilts and running toward the jungle. Tex Barnes, a BAR man in our squad, opened fire, knocking two of the Japs down, one of whom got up and continued to run away. We received little return fire.

Barnes was a husky, blonde, crewcut kid from Texas. You had to be strong to handle the Browning Automatic Rifle. It was an excellent weapon—fully automatic and capable of long range use. However, like our platoon's pair of .30 caliber machine guns, BARs were heavy (nearly 20 pounds) and you could get a hernia carrying one of the goddamn things around. BAR ammunition was carried in detachable 20-round magazines (but only filled with 18 or 19 bullets to prevent jamming in the magazine). A large batch of these could be weighty—too much for a single BAR man to haul around. Consequently, sergeants usually handed out several loaded magazines to other squad members, increasing their already cumbersome loads. No one complained, however, because this provided a squad with much additional firepower.

Arriving in the village, we noticed holes or dugouts under several of the buildings. Sergeant Ames and Junior Cotter systematically dropped hand grenades into each opening as they walked by. Suddenly I heard two or three shots coming from across the road; it recognizably was the sound of a Jap rifle. A man in our platoon turned around and fired. A figure on the other side of the road crumpled to the ground. The soldier who shot him studied the body for a moment, then walked across the road, weapon at the ready.

Approaching the figure, he turned it over with the toe of his boot, and said, "Oh, shit," for there lay what appeared to be an old Chamorro. Guam's natives, the Chamorros, were particularly friendly toward Americans. Everyone in the squad felt badly, especially the rifleman who fired. We tried to console him.

Our assignment at Pago Bay, besides harassing the enemy and determining his local strength, was to find an artillery emplacement previously spotted by aerial reconnaissance and put it out of action. At the edge of the village we found

A Note to My Children

During the long months of the Pacific war, death was a constant reality. Unfortunately, not only enemy soldiers, but sometimes non-military personnel, even women and childen, were killed or wounded by our men. On no occasion did it happen intentionally, but I noticed that as the war dragged on, particularly in sustained combat, men became more tired, nervous, edgy, and prone to make mistakes.

Every time they went into enemy territory, they were at peril. When engaged in a firefight—receiving fire from and shooting at the enemy—a soldier doesn't pay a lot of attention to extraneous details. He's primarily concerned with staying alive, and sometimes that means shooting at anything in front of him, and occasionally it isn't the enemy that's out there. As the war continued and we engaged in one campaign after another, there were a number of instances where non-combatants were fired upon. I never blamed the men doing the shooting, although I felt sorry for them, as I did for the people they injured or killed.

Often, troopers were sick, hungry, dirty, sleepless for 24 or more hours, scared and stressed by the continuous danger, and primarily concerned with trying to stay alive. In combat, you never know what's going to happen. Fear is not just an emotional state of mind, it affects and orchestrates the way you operate. Under these conditions, soldiers occasionally made mistakes. Unless you've been under fire and understand the terrible confusion, turmoil, and uncertainty that confronted us, it's hard to appreciate how this occurs. When coming face to face with the enemy—fanatical, determined, resolute foes who, in most instances, would rather die than surrender—we learned that the man who shot first was the one who lived.

The idea of killing a person was entirely foreign to us before we entered the military. In normal society, of course, it's unheard of—people just don't do things like that. It's immoral, it's unChristian, and you don't even want to talk about it. Consequently, it's hard for the ordinary person to actually realize and understand that the whole purpose of war is to destroy the enemy, and the infantryman is a main means of accomplishing this task. War is bloodshed. War is death.

As we were told in jungle warfare training in Hawaii, "You have just one purpose—kill Japs, kill Japs, kill more Japs."

Men who fought on the front lines often are asked by people who weren't there, "What does it feel like to kill someone?"

It's hard for them to understand and believe that a father, brother, cousin, uncle, neighbor, or the guy they drink coffee with at a cafe every morning could do such a thing. To adequately answer this question, you have to understand that the whole purpose of war is to eliminate the enemy. It's easy to say, "destroy." It's harder to say "kill," but that's the purpose of war. Soldiers are recruited, trained, and transported to battlefronts with but one purpose—to kill the enemy.

No one likes to talk about killing, and I've never really answered the question about it until now. Over the years, some of you children have asked about it, and I'd try to adroitly turn the conversation in another direction. It's not something that one likes to discuss or dwell upon. However, one purpose I have in writing this memoir is to tell you what happened in 1944–45 when your father—a teenage boy—was sent to the Pacific to fight the Japanese.

I was just 18, wanting to serve my country, eager to get into combat, but apprehensive of the unknown. I was trained as a machine gunner, rifleman, and scout in the infantry to kill the enemy. In the Pacific, most men who served in infantry line companies, reconnaissance platoons, tank units, and other combat units had to have killed or wounded enemy soldiers. If they hadn't killed the Japanese, they would've been killed themselves.

Basically, that's the elementary answer to the question as to whether one has "fought" for his country. If he was an infantryman or served in a combat unit for any extended period of time, you almost can be assured that he killed or injured some of the enemy during the fighting.

There are reports and studies claiming that some American soldiers in combat never fired their weapons, and I'm sure that's true. I don't believe, however, that the percentage is nearly as high as some of the investigations might claim. Certainly for some soldiers in their initial confrontation with the enemy, when the moment came to make a decision to fire their weapon, they couldn't bring themselves to do so—to kill another human being. A few simply weren't able to overcome their moral upbringing. Sometimes, too, it was because they'd forgot to do what they'd been trained to do—to stand their ground, aim their rifle, and squeeze the trigger. These are fundamental combat actions, however, and these functions had to be done. If not, it could result in the death of yourself or your buddies.

Most of us prefer not to admit that we've killed another human being. Many veterans, in explaining their conduct during the war, also have tended to be modest about their accomplishments as an infantryman or Marine. They didn't want people to believe they were bragging or "making up" stories. However, you have to understand that the only way the war was won in the Pacific was by killing the enemy, and we had to kill more of them than they killed of us. If we didn't do that, then we wouldn't win the war. We sought the enemy, searched him out, and then killed him. Killed him in every way possible and at every opportunity, without compassion or sorrow.

So how does a person feel in combat when firing his rifle and seeing an enemy fall and knowing you've hit him? Again, it's something that most of us would rather not dwell upon. You children know that I haven't talked about it. I will now say, that in the excitement of battle—knowing it was either them or us—we had a feeling of accomplishment, exhilaration, even jubilation when killing our foes.

I've read accounts of soldiers or Marines who, after killing one of the enemy, became sick, sometimes even to the point of vomiting. This also is a fairly common scene in Hollywood movies made since the war. However, I never saw this happen to any of the soldiers I served with. First of all, there wasn't time to get sick in a firefight. You had to keep your wits about you and be prepared to continue fighting—finding the enemy and getting him before he got you. If anyone did get sick, perhaps it would've been after a battle, not during it.

I don't mean to trivialize this, but by way of example, all of you children have been bird hunting with me at one time or another. While out in the stubble of a wheat field and hunting pheasants, if a big rooster flushes out in front of you and you knock it down with a good shot, you're excited and feel good about it. Well, this may not be a good comparison, but it's the best I can come up with.

When a soldier moved up on patrol or a mission and saw the Japs in front of him, and fired at them and knew he'd hit one, he felt good. And, why shouldn't he? He'd done what he'd spent months, perhaps years, learning to do. All the training as an infantryman was directed at this one defining moment. This was his purpose. This is what he was supposed to do. And, he felt like he'd saved himself or his buddies from getting wounded or killed.

So, in answering this question and explaining how I felt about it, I'd have to say that I'm not apologetic for what we did in the war. We didn't start the war, and we believed we were defending our country from a terrible, despotic, and cruel foe. As the war dragged on, hatred of the enemy grew. To the troops fighting in the Pacific, the Japanese were those "Dirty little yellow bastards" and we hated them with a passion. While in the tropical jungles or on Okinawa, we had but one thought, and that was to kill the Japs before they killed us, and to kill as many as we could. There was no feeling of remorse after we'd done what we were trained to do.

Remember, the Japanese had, without warning and while still in peace negotiations with our government, deliberately attacked us. At that time, the tide of world conquest seemed heavily in favor of Germany and Japan. The fate of our country—of the world—was very much in doubt. The Nazis had swept across all of mainland Europe to the gates of Moscow and Leningrad, while the Japanese had conquered most of East Asia and the western Pacific. The Japanese also had attacked Dutch Harbor, Alaska, and occupied Attu and Kiska in the Aleutian Islands. To Americans, an invasion of Hawaii (and even California and the Pacific Northwest, in the minds of some) seemed imminent. We felt violated and our very existence was threatened.

It was against this background that your father, and millions like him, went to war. The attitude of our nation, the military, and myself, may now, in looking back at that time, appear racist and bigoted, but it was the attitude that then existed. Just note my repeated use of the term "Jap" in my memoir. Except perhaps for some old veterans of the Pacific conflict, our nation and people now have dropped this usage as being disrespectful. During the war years, however, such words were a part of our daily life, and as such, are a part of our history.

two huge howitzers, possibly in excess of 200 millimeters, overlooking the bay and pointing out to sea. The emplacement was unmanned. First, we dropped thermite grenades down the barrels, causing destructive, heat-intensive explosions. Then we removed the hinged breach blocks from the guns and laboriously carried them down to the shore and threw them in the sea. We weren't going to allow the Japs to ever use these guns against our troops.

Having accomplished our mission, we returned via the Pago River canyon again, but by an alternate route so as to avoid a possible Jap ambush. The next day we arrived at our regimental area.

The following several days were physically wearying. Rain fell solidly almost all of the time. The wet, muddy jungle seemed to grab at us and hold us as we struggled forward along our division's general advance. During the day the heat was intolerable and we sweated continually. Because of the sweat, rain, and humidity, our uniforms constantly were wet. At night, after we dug in, rain filled our foxholes to within three or four inches of the top. While sitting there with water up over our waists, the evening grew cold and our teeth chattered. Mosquitoes came out in swarms, retreating only as the dawn approached, when black flies took over.

Gradually, the 306th moved to the right flank of the 77th Division and, after a grueling march northeast across the island, we moved into the line. The 1st Battalion was hit hard by an ambush on the Finegayan-Yigo Road. The Japanese pressed forward with heavy machine gun and grenade attacks. We'd learned special tank tactics for times like this. We never let armor advance unassisted in the jungle because Jap infantrymen would throw satchel charges underneath the treads, disabling the tanks, and then dispose of them.

Consequently, our attached regimental tank platoon normally only advanced with infantry support. One tank would proceed just off a road or trail on the right, another just off to the left, and the remaining two or three tanks would be spaced off the road 50 or 100 yards to the rear. A squad of infantry guarded each tank. This kept satchel carrying Jap soldiers at a distance. The dispersed formation also allowed tanks to aid one another when engaging enemy armor or anti-tank weapons. It also kept the leading tank out of the center of a road, where it otherwise would be a clear target for the enemy's deadly 47 mm anti-tank gun. The latter was an extremely effective weapon firing a 3.6 pound armor-piercing shell at a muzzle velocity of 2,700 feet per second.

As the division proceeded north along the Finegayan Road approaching Barrigada, small, fierce firefights erupted all along our advance. When we were just beyond Barrigada, Colonel Smith sent word to our platoon leader, Sergeant Harry Sall, informing him that the regimental headquarters was receiving sniper fire and several men had been wounded. We were ordered to come back and secure the area before the command post dug in for the night.

When arriving at 306th headquarters, we talked to the company commander, who pointed toward a thick patch of jungle, indicating the general direction from which the sniper fire was coming. Our platoon was ordered to clear it out, making sure that we didn't leave any Japs in there to shoot at the command post as it was set up. Sergeant Sall led one squad into the jungle,

Two of our Sherman tanks destroyed by the Japanese on the Finegayan-Yigo road. *U.S. Army*

while ordering Sergeant Howard Crawford to take the squad that I was in and go around on the flank. We hardly reached the forest edge when six Japs broke out of a heavy, wooded patch near a small native hut and ran down into a creek bottom. Two of them carried machine guns.

Crawford shouted for three of us to follow him and we broke into a run. We rapidly closed on the Japs. They turned and fired several bursts, but none of us were hit. We returned fire and thought we'd hit one, but they disappeared into a patch of jungle and we lost them momentarily. Then three of them broke out again in the creek bottom at a hard run. Crawford, a dead shot, who was a little in advance of the rest of us, raised his rifle and fired three times. All three fell dead.

We couldn't find the other three Japs and returned to the regimental command area. We learned that earlier that afternoon, the divisional Chief of Staff, Colonel Douglas McNair, had been fatally shot by one of the snipers that we'd been pursuing. We also were told that his father, Lieutenant General Lesley J. McNair, the former commander of all Army ground forces in France, had been killed on the Normandy front in France only a week or two earlier.[3]

Later in the evening on August 6, our division was attacked by enemy armor for the first time when four Japanese medium tanks protected by infantry assaulted the 305th Regiment. Jap crewmen threw hand grenades from the tank turrets and fired machine guns as they raced through the regimental perimeter. Some Company A soldiers were killed when the tanks ran over their foxholes, grinding the men into the ground under the heavy treads. The 1st Battalion suffered approximately 50 casualties and the tanks escaped.

That night I dug in with Sergeant Ames. I'd been assigned a bazooka and Ames wanted me in the foxhole with him in case of another tank attack. As soon as darkness fell, which in the tropics was around 6:30 or 7:00 p.m., no one left their foxhole or trench.

★★★

It was doctrine to shoot at anyone moving around in the dark. Each night, our artillery and mortars laid a protective ring of fire around our perimeters to discourage Japs from infiltrating into our positions. We couldn't leave our foxholes for any reason once the sun went down. Anyone seen walking, standing, or crawling was considered to be Japanese and shot at without warning.

At night, we defecated and urinated in our foxholes, usually into our steel helmets after removing the helmet liner. Then we threw the contents over the edge of the parapet that'd been built up with entrenching tools. Often, because of the rain and our dysentery, the human waste was loose and slimy, and it fell or slid back into the foxholes. We sat on it and rubbed it into our clothes when moving about on our knees.

All combat units in the Pacific established perimeters—normally a circle of foxholes occupied by a squad, platoon, or company. In most instances, there really wasn't any "forward line" in the jungle; rather, our many small-unit perimeters actually were the "front." Men dug in each afternoon as night approached, usually spacing foxholes about 15 or 20 feet apart.

7,419 JAPS, 1,022 YANKS KILLED IN FIGHTING ON GUAM

[AP] Aug. 2.—Killing seven Japanese for every Yank slain, American conquerors of the south half of Guam have seized a second airfield—seventh won in the Marianas—in a mile gain made against stiffening resistance.

Adm. Chester W. Nimitz [chief U.S. Pacific naval commander] reported in a communique tonight that Tiyan airfield, believed to be a fighter strip, was overrun yesterday by marines and soldiers who in 13 days of invasion action have killed 7,419 Japanese at a cost of 1,022 Americans...

Nimitz said that Lt. Gen. Holland M. Smith, commander of fleet marine forces in the Pacific, has congratulated Maj. Gen. A.D. Bruce of the army for the excellence of 77th Division troops in the Guam operation...

Smith congratulated Bruce for the cooperation of the 77th (Statue of Liberty) soldiers "with other fighting elements" (Third Marine Division and First Provisional Brigade Marines). Smith said the 77th has "shown marked tactical ability in moving its forces into position over unfavorable terrain and in the face of great difficulties."

It was the 77th's capture of 1,020 foot Mt. Tenjo [on] July 27 which paved the way for the drive to the east coast of Guam, splitting Japanese forces.

In addition to the 1,022 American dead, as counted through yesterday, Nimitz said 4,946 have been wounded and 305 are missing in action.

On Guam the Yanks on both coasts are about 12 miles from the north end with 10,000 Japanese, minus air and naval support doomed to slaughter.

How deep you dug depended on the composition of the ground—whether it was hard coral or clay, soft sand, or just plain dirt. The depth also depended on whether you were receiving or expecting artillery and mortar fire, or on "just how damned scared you were!" One thing that we all learned was to dig it deep enough to get yourself completely below ground level. Usually we tried to excavate a hole about 6 feet long and 1½ feet deep. Any exposed part of the body could, and often did, get hit.

If we weren't exposed to enemy fire and time allowed for it, we'd set up trip wires around the perimeters. Stakes were driven into the ground every 10 or 20 feet, and string or twine was strung between them about a foot or so above the ground. Then we'd tie empty C ration cans to the lines and put small pebbles in them. Any contact with the trip wires would cause the cans to rattle, alerting us to nighttime intruders.

I was told that some soldiers took the pins out of grenades, straightened the ends, and then shoved them back into the holes of the ignition mechanisms. A grenade's arming lever remained depressed, tied down with a slipknot of string that was intricately attached to the pin and a trip wire. A Jap infiltrator, who entered the perimeter in the dark and made contact with the trip wire, unknowingly would pull the pin out and then the slipknot, releasing the lever and causing the grenade to explode. They said it worked well. The trouble came in disarming the damn things in the morning. There were too many accidents, and finally they quit doing this.

When night fell, fear came with it. Your heart pounded and your imagination worked up all sorts of terrible images. We knew the Japs were out there and could occasionally hear them. Now and then they'd throw a grenade or a satchel charge at us. Although none ever crawled into my foxhole to attack me as they did other GIs, this was another reason to dread the night. We squatted in wet, muddy foxholes, listening to bullets whistling overhead and praying for dawn to come. Even after all these years, I'm still afraid of the dark and don't like being out alone once the sun goes down.

★★★

Word was passed along to expect a tank attack coming down a small dirt road—really not much more than a trail—on a slight hill off to the left of the company perimeter. As usual, we arranged for watches, four-hours-on and four-hours-off. Sergeant Ames and myself, having the bazooka, were prepared to engage the tanks.

Rain had fallen in sheets all that afternoon and into the evening, pounding on the ground and filling the bottoms of our foxholes. I'd been sick for at least two days. My temperature was over 100°, but in the front lines they wouldn't send you back to a medical station unless it exceeded 102°. A lot of our boys were contracting dengue fever and malaria, and dysentery was rampant.

Dengue also was called "breakbone fever." The pain was excruciating; you hurt all over and even your teeth ached. Dysentery caused extreme fatigue and weight loss. If you had it bad, you weren't worth a damn for anything. You'd keep trying to defecate, but after emptying yourself over and over, all that came out was blood.

In addition to the bazooka, I was armed with my rifle and had been given a flare gun to light up the area in front of our perimeter if we were attacked by armor. Near the end of my first watch, I began hearing heavy vehicles moving about not too far beyond the road and the hill in front of us. I shook Sergeant Ames awake and said I thought we were going to be attacked by tanks, and soon.

There were many things in combat that frightened me, possibly the worst being artillery. But, there was something absolutely terrifying about sitting in a shallow foxhole in the dark and fearing an assault by enemy tanks while armed solely with a bazooka, which I'd only had a small amount of practice in operating.

As the sound of the tanks grew louder, Ames said, "Set off a flare. We've got to be able to see 'em."

I reached into my pack lying beside the foxhole parapet, took out the flare gun, and inserted a flare into the barrel. This type of flare gun operated by striking a triggering mechanism on its bottom against something hard, such as the ground. This sent the flare up out of the barrel, like a mortar. The parachute flare then would slowly float down, providing quite exceptional visibility. This was how the flare gun was supposed to function—in my case, it didn't!

My stomach churned—diarrhea from dysentery had taken over. Crouching in the foxhole, I was shitting in my helmet, vomiting over the side of the parapet, and trying to operate the flare gun. I'd never been so sick and miserable in my entire life. I moved onto my knees in at least three inches of water. Rain fell so hard that I could hardly see, and, of course, wearing glasses made it all the worse. When I slammed the flare gun against the ground, the flare ignited, but it remained stuck in the barrel. This definitely "lit up" the foxhole that Ames and I were crouching in. Getting more scared, I threw the blazing flare gun as far away as I could.

I looked for tanks. Through the heavy pounding rain, I dimly saw them on the hillside coming down the road toward us. Before reaching the bottom, however, they suddenly turned left when about 50 to 75 yards from our foxhole. Ames and I had loaded the bazooka and were prepared, but because of the heavy mist and driving rain, we didn't feel the tanks presented a good enough target to fire at.

Later that night, however, we were attacked twice by small groups of Japs. Yelling, screaming, and throwing grenades, they charged forward with bayoneted rifles, trying to break through our perimeter. The flanking company had strung up wire on the edge of our lines. Most of the Japanese ran into it and were stopped there, and were blown to pieces by our rifle and machine gun fire.

Watching men caught in barbed wire, trying desperately to extricate themselves, was a harrowing experience. You knew they were suffering and in some small way you almost hoped they'd get away. But then our training took over, and we fired round after round into them until they quit struggling and were left hanging limply on the wire, like thrown-away rag dolls. We were fortunate; our defending units suffered only three wounded during the evening.

I was shaking the next morning with what later was diagnosed as malaria and dengue fever. My temperature had climbed to 104° and I was sent back to the regimental hospital, where I was treated for two days. The best thing about being evacuated was that I could wash the excrement off my boots, get new socks and underwear, and have my dungarees laundered.

★★★

Perhaps I could've stayed longer, lying safely on a canvas cot in the hospital tent, but I kept thinking about my buddies. I knew they were moving forward, and

SPEEDY AMERICAN DRIVE CORNERS JAPS ON GUAM

[AP] Aug 5.—Quickening American advances on both flanks of Northern Guam's jungle fighting line Friday pressed the Japanese defenders back into a sector covering about a fourth of Guam's 225 square miles Adm. Chester W. Nimitz announced today.

While the tough jungle-clearing drive to complete the island's conquest progressed into its third week, Nimitz reported the surprising total of 22,000 civilians had found refuge within American lines.

Only a small number of Chamorro natives can now remain in the northern area still held by the Japanese. The 1940 census of Guam's population listed a total of 23,067 inhabitants.

A three-mile American advance on the east coast by the 77th Army Division brought the right anchor of the line to Lumuna Point, two miles north of Sassayan Point.

A mile and a half push by marines on the west coast reached Amantes Point, gaining full control of Tumon Bay.

The Japanese were cornered in a 56 square mile area at the island's northern tip.

John Henry, a war correspondent at the scene, said, "it is evident that a decisive finish is imminent. Guam for all practical purposes, is ours."

American cruisers, destroyers, and gunboats, which have poured more than 4,400 tons of hot shells on Japanese defense positions since marines and soldiers first landed July 21, were operating on both sides of the island. The naval guns were not only exacting great toll but were blocking any possible Japanese escape attempt by sea.

we'd probably be engaging the enemy's main line of resistance sometime soon. I didn't want that to happen without me being with the platoon.

It's hard to explain, but there is closeness among men who face death together every day, and you're relying on the man next to you to step up and do his part. You're sure that he will, and you hope that you can. Once you get into combat, you realize that you're not mainly fighting, as was so often expressed in the newspapers and on radio, for "Liberty, country, and mother's apple pie." That's mostly bullshit. You're fighting for the guy next to you in the foxhole and your buddies in the platoon. They're your family, your brothers. You depend on them to fight beside you, to protect you, and to lay down their lives if necessary. You knew you'd do the same for them. The trust you have in each other is stronger than anything you've ever known. Your lives are in each other's hands and that's the most valuable thing that you have.

Actually, this dependence and trust is what makes small units—squads and platoons—work in combat. This utter reliance on others largely determines a soldier's willingness to risk death in pressing forward an attack and exerts a tremendous pressure on each to do his duty. Remember, we were very young—some only 18 or 19 years old. Everyone wanted the respect of his comrades. Even if you were killed, the way you wanted your buddies to remember you was, "He had guts!"

The military system worked upon and encouraged this. When on a patrol, or assigned mission, or an attack, if everyone did his job, the squad or platoon had a good chance of succeeding, but if even one man screwed up, if he didn't do his part, the unit and every man in it was at risk. Combat is a desperately lonely place and the 8 or 10 men in your squad, and the 20 or 30 in your platoon, are your family and the most important thing in your life.

At the aid station, every time I could, I told the lieutenant taking care of me along with the other sick patients that I was better—that there really wasn't anything wrong with me. I said my temperature had gone down enough and I wanted to go back. I wonder sometimes if he really believed me. Before my temperature was really reduced, I was allowed to rejoin my outfit and was grateful when I saw my squad.

Of course, everyone kidded me, saying that if I was only sick enough to stay away for two days, why'd they send me to the hospital in the first place. They also wanted to know if I'd laid any nurses. While the bantering went on, I knew they were glad to see me, and I was glad to be back.

The good feelings, however, were tempered by the fact that our company and a company of the 307th had accidentally started a firefight between themselves while I was gone. Quickly, both regiments became involved, with each thinking they were shooting at the Japanese. Even tanks began firing before the mistake was realized. About 10 men were injured. Fortunately, no one was killed, but one of the wounded was my buddy, Junior Cotter.

★★★

During the second week of August, squads from our recon platoon were assigned as killing teams in ambushes. A squad would be sent out to find a trail with indications of Japanese foot traffic. The enemy traveled extensively along the jungle tracks in the northern end of Guam. This part of the island was quite porous and the rain quickly sank into the ground, consequently there was little available drinking water. Japs took trails leading to coconut plantations, where they gathered coconuts and broke them open to quench their thirst by drinking the milk.

My squad, when scouting a section of trail bordered by thick vegetation, would pick a spot where the trail made an elbow- or "L"-shaped turn. Four or five men concealed themselves above the turn and about the same number below. In the middle, where the trail turned, we'd set up Tex Barnes, who carried a BAR. The rest of us were armed with M1 rifles, hand grenades, and Thompson submachine guns. The squad would wait, watching for the enemy to come down the trail. We'd let them enter the turn. At that moment, Tex's BAR opened up first, followed by the rest of the men hidden along the path. Squads from our platoon took turns going out to the killing ground, and conducted several successful ambushes, probably killing a total of 25 to 30 Japs.

I vividly remember the last of these ambushes that my squad conducted. I was situated at the lower part of the bend, along with a couple of men between Tex and I. We were near the edge of a clearing and I lay facing up the trail toward where Tex was stationed with his BAR at the bend. At my shoulder on the left was a palm tree. Several palm fronds had fallen off it and I'd arranged them for camouflage. I was prone with my rifle pointing up the trail ready for the Japs. We'd been there possibly 1½ to 2 hours under the blazing hot sun. The mosquitoes and flies were thick and eating us alive, but we couldn't make any movement or sound that might alert the enemy.

Having been looking up the trail continually, I momentarily happened to glance toward the small clearing on my left. Three Jap soldiers were advancing out of the jungle directly toward me, no more than 40 or 50 feet away. All were armed, with the one in the lead carrying a rifle in one hand and a hand grenade in the other. They were walking directly toward me.

I was in a serious predicament because I hadn't expected any Japs to come from that direction. I realized that by lying on the ground with the palm tree immediately to the left of my shoulder, I couldn't shoot unless I moved forward and turned toward the Japs. If I rose to my knees or feet and twisted left to fire at them, I'd cause my cover of dry palm fronds, which now had become brittle, to move or make a rustling noise. Thus, I'd expose myself to the Japs before I could get my rifle around the tree to shoot.

I lay there hoping that one of my buddies would see the enemy soldiers and open fire. As the leading Jap approached, I knew I couldn't let him get any closer than 10 or 15 feet before I'd have to take a chance, jump up, and shoot. I was waiting for him to approach within that distance, when suddenly there was a burst of fire on the upper end of the trail. The Japs all stopped, startled. With them momentarily distracted, I rose up, moved forward, lifted my rifle, aimed, and fired. I remembered what Uncle Pete had said, "Don't pull the trigger, squeeze it."

I hit the first Jap squarely in the chest. He stumbled backward, falling to his knees. Looking directly at me, he tapped the hand grenade on his helmet to activate it and tried to throw it in my direction, while at the same time shouting in a hoarse, weak voice, "Banzai." The grenade exploded in his hand. The other two were hit by rifle fire from other members of my squad as well as by myself.

Suddenly, we began receiving heavy fire from the jungle where the three men had come out toward us. We fired back as fast as we could. In addition to the loud reports of our .30 caliber M1 rifles, you continually heard the metallic "pwang" of empty M1 ammunition clips being automatically ejected. We were in a heavily overgrown area and the enemy was moving forward through the brush, trying to close with us. One of our men was hit, went down, and got up. Two of my buddies grabbed and pulled him away, and we started retreating.

Sergeant Ames said, "Let's pull back, we've gotta get out'a here. They must be at least company strength."

As the shooting continued, we withdrew back down the trail toward our company perimeter. The firing finally stopped as we gained distance from the ambush area. Our squad arrived back at our lines with no further problems.

★★★

The next afternoon, my squad again was ordered out on patrol. Our mission was to proceed all the way to the ocean cliffs at the north end of Guam, and see whether or not there were substantial numbers of Japanese in that area still capable of resisting and if they had tanks. We started late and the going was extremely tiring and hot.

We took the same trail along which we'd encountered the Japs on the previous day. Since ambushes had been set up along this trail during the previous two or three days, we thought the enemy probably had learned to avoid this area. We figured we'd get through here without running into any opposition.

As darkness approached, we dug in, it being our intention to stay out overnight. My buddy, Lou, wasn't along on this patrol. A new man shared my foxhole who'd only recently joined the outfit and with whom I was unacquainted.

We dug in that night as usual, with foxholes more or less arranged in a circle to form a perimeter, from which we could fire in all directions if the Japanese approached. I took the first watch, and nothing happened. During the second watch, my foxhole buddy, who heard noises in the jungle and thought the Japs were coming, awakened me. Listening, I heard what seemed like Japanese being spoken and sounds of movement in the jungle. The guys in the other foxholes heard it, too, and were alert.

In a few minutes, shooting erupted from one of the foxholes off to my right and then pandemonium broke loose. The Japs returned fire and threw hand grenades. A flare and explosions brightened the nighttime scene into day, as tracer fire blazed back and forth between our contesting sides.

Three, four, five, or more Japanese grenades fell within our perimeter and exploded. Some of our men were in anguish and shouting. I felt a terrible, sharp pain in my face—I knew I'd been hit. Suddenly everything was black—I couldn't see and couldn't hear! The long firefight continued until the Japs broke off the action and moved back before dawn.

Our squad lay there, with several wounded men moaning and crying. Atkinson was hit the worst, with a leg nearly blown off and the bottom of his foxhole covered with blood. The concussion from an exploding grenade had broken both of my eardrums and drove metal fragments into my face, arms, and hands. I was blinded and deaf. Two other men received less serious wounds.

In the morning, the squad started back down the trail toward our lines. The unwounded men helped the injured, until we finally arrived at company headquarters. Atkinson and I were put on stretchers and taken by a jeep ambulance to the division hospital and then transferred to an airstrip near the beach.

A jeep ambulance transporting wounded men to the rear lines. *U.S. Army*

We'd hardly more than arrived and received emergency treatment, before we were loaded into a plane along with a number of other stretcher cases. The next thing we knew, we were on our way to the Kaneohe Naval Air Force Hospital in Hawaii.

I still remember the hospital ward in Hawaii that first night. Atkinson kept crying hysterically, "Don't take my leg off, don't let 'em take my leg off, whatever you do, don't take my leg off." Unfortunately, his leg already had been amputated earlier that day.

My wounds proved less serious than originally thought. My eyesight came back very quickly, and pieces of metal were removed from my hands and face. (For several years after the war ended, however, small steel slivers continued to work their way out of my face and hands. I'd pull them out like wood slivers. A piece even came out of my left cornea in the spring of 1953. It hurt terribly every time I blinked, as my eyelid moved over the steel sliver. I learned that we blink hundreds of times a day; the pain was excruciating. I was courting my future wife Nancy at the time. She and her father Rex took me to a hospital in Moscow, Idaho, where a doctor surgically removed the metal fragment.)

In another several days, my hearing was fully restored. But before then, a hospital lieutenant who'd been friendly toward me said: "Mac, I understand that your division is leaving Guam shortly and going to a rest camp in New Caledonia. If you want to rejoin your outfit, I'll do whatever I can to see that you're sent back, if transportation can be arranged. If you stay here, you're simply going to be put into a replacement depot and sent to another infantry outfit. No one knows what that unit will be, and you might be going right back into combat."

I told him that the thing I most wanted was to rejoin my outfit, if he could arrange transportation and I was able to get on the plane. Two days later, I landed

VICTORY!

Aug. 9.—(I.N.S.)—United States forces have completed occupation of Guam, ending a furious 20-day land, sea and air campaign to reconquer the strategic island from the Japanese, a Pacific Fleet Headquarters communique announced today.

With the exception of a small inland pocket of Japanese, who were hopelessly surrounded and being pounded to pieces, Guam's 227 square miles were back in American hands...

...Continuing their relentless onward rush yesterday, the Americans apparently surged to coastal points all along the line, encircling the remaining battered Japs inland from Pati Point.

The ground struggle to retake the island began July [21] when assault troops of the Third [Marine Division and the

1st Marine Provisional Brigade] and the 77th Infantry Division landed at two points on the western coast in the wake of blistering aerial and naval bombardments.

The pocketed Japs on the northern part of the island, today's communique stated, were "under heavy pressure" and were expected to be wiped out in short order, if indeed they have not already been slain or captured.

Headquarters also stated that it was now believed the tight U.S. naval blockade around the northern end of the island has prevented virtually all attempts by the doomed Japs to escape by sea during the Americans' northward push...

Meanwhile, it was announced, renewed aerial strikes against other Jap bases in the Central Pacific have been carried out.

on Guam, and in a short time arrived at Camp McNair, a large divisional camp set up just east of Agat village. It was named after Colonel McNair who'd been killed in early August.

Rejoining my outfit was a feeling hard to describe. Practically no one wants to return to combat, of course, but for now, at least, the 77th was being sched-

77th infantrymen carrying supplies. *U.S. Army*

uled for a rest. No one knew when we'd go into action again. The mere fact that I'd returned to my platoon and was with friends made everything seem right.

★★★

During my time at Camp McNair, Guam's rainy season was at its height and there was little rest or recreation for any of us. Many sections of roadway were washed out by the heavy rain—even the ones newly constructed by our naval construction crews, the Seabees—and we had to live on combat rations. The impassable road conditions made vehicular travel impossible in many places, consequently we were utilized as pack animals. Vehicles bringing supplies to Camp McNair stopped a half-mile from camp. We'd walk out and pick up the equipment and provisions, and carry it all back to camp in our arms or on our backs.

This was hard, exhausting work, particularly for men who'd been living on limited rations for several weeks, and many of whom were sick and some even recovering from wounds. However, the generation of young men fighting this war was tough. They'd been raised during the Great Depression and nothing had been easy for most of them.

In those days, you didn't go to the grocery store and buy a chicken for dinner already cleaned, cut in pieces, and wrapped in plastic. No, you'd go into a chicken pen or farmyard, catch a squawking chicken, cut its head and legs off, clean the guts out, dip it in boiling water, pulled out the feathers, cut it up, and take it into the kitchen for your mother to cook.

It was the same way with other meat. I remember helping my uncle by shooting a steer between the eyes with a .22 short rifle shell. As the steer immediately dropped to its knees, stunned, Uncle Pete slit its throat. We quickly pulled it by a rope pulley to the top of a scaffolding, disemboweled and skinned it, and then let it hang for a few days before quartering and putting it up in the icehouse.

Everyone worked. As soon as you were able to do chores, you did them. Most families had wood stoves for heating and cooking. Kindling and wood had to be cut every night and set by the stove, ready for the morning. Kids sold and delivered newspapers. You found work sweeping the floors of a local tavern or splitting cordwood.

Physical labor was common both on the job and in most households. People worked until calluses were thick on their hands and dirt was under the fingernails. Trucks, cars, and farm machinery were kept running by their owners, and usually weren't taken to service stations or commercial garages for repairs. Relatively few young men, as a percentage of the population, attended college. Instead, they went to work right out of high school, or, for half of all youths, after completing just the eighth grade. They contemplated a future consisting mostly of continuous hardship and hard labor. So, to many, when the war came it was a way out.

Patriotism ran high, the flag was revered, and most everyone had faith in our government and leaders. Welded by a lifetime of adversity and deprivation, and shocked by the treacherous Pearl Harbor attack, my generation was ready for the war when it came.

★★★

One morning, Sergeant Sall came up to our pup tents and said, "Listen, we've got to get some decent food. These C rations and K rations are killing me. I'm told that on the beach, the Seabees and other rear units have set up kitchens. They even have bakeries down there, and they're cooking fresh bread. They have beef and even some vegetables. We all have souvenirs—Jap samurai swords, bayonets, helmets, rifles, pistols, letters, photographs, uniforms, and flags. There

Battle souvenirs taken from the enemy. *U.S. Army*

aren't any of us who don't have something. We can take them down to the beach and trade for food. Get back to your tents, pick up what you have, bring it up here, and we're going to the beach and coming back with some food."

Sergeant Sall, Junior Cotter, Joe Geiger, Lou Ryman, and I took two jeeps loaded with souvenirs and headed for the beach area. It was an amazing sight when we broke over the ridgelines and could see the beach around Agat, where we'd first landed. Whereas before there'd been huge craters partially filled with water, shattered palm trees, overturned Alligators and Higgins boats, knocked out tanks, and other flotsam of war, now there was this huge hub of activity—row upon row of tents, trucks and tanks parked in long lines, and ships stretching endlessly out to sea. We could hardly believe it.

When driving down to the beach area, we noticed some rear echelon troops staring at us, almost as if we were some strange type of animals. Looking at each other, we realized just how bad we appeared. Our uniforms and boots were bloody, soiled, torn, and worn. A couple of us had taken off our leggings once we left Camp McNair (though the 77th's Major General Andrew D. Bruce insisted on men wearing them in camp), and being sick, thin, and foul smelling, we must've been a dreadful sight.

The smell of cooking wafted up on the breeze from the beach. We finally pulled up in front of an open tent with a long fly stretched over a number of tables—it appeared to be a dining area. We asked what unit this was and were informed they were Seabees. This was their kitchen.

We showed them the souvenirs we'd brought along and said we'd like to trade for food. You can't imagine the excitement that this caused. Possibly, there weren't any officers in the area at the time who might've prevented the swap. At any rate, Seabees came from everywhere with cans of pineapple and corned beef, fresh bread, canned bacon, and other delicacies that we hadn't even thought about for the past couple of months. The Seabees were so eager to trade food for souvenirs that we hardly had room in the jeeps to carry it all back.

After elatedly sitting down and eating some fresh, warm bread covered with jam and washing it down with hot coffee, we crawled into the filled-up jeeps and headed back into the hills. We even had to carry some of the food on our laps and in our arms. When arriving at Camp McNair, our buddies greeted us with unbelievable excitement and enthusiasm. For the next day or two, we enjoyed feasting, but it didn't last long because, of course, we shared everything with our platoon.

Rumors now began circulating that we'd be pulling out soon, and, as always, there were different stories as to where we were going. The one predominant theme seemed to be that we'd be going somewhere for a rest before being sent back into combat. Camp conditions were gradually improving, though we still essentially lived on C and K rations (food in small cans, plus candy, cigarettes, gum, and toilet paper). We received new green fatigues, underwear, and socks, and began to feel more civilized as toilets were dug—latrines with actual holes to sit on. Showers also were made from large tin cans, and barrels were set up where we could wash ourselves. Gradually we began to look more human again.

About the beginning of November 1944, we were told to be prepared to move to the beach where we'd board transports. We'd be heading for New Caledonia, a large island located 600 miles east of Australia, for rest and rehabilitation.

★★★

The cost of the three-week struggle for Guam was high. The combined casualty count for the U.S. Marine Corps and the U.S. Army was 1,800 men killed and 6,000 wounded, but the capture of Guam, and the rest of the Marianas, would have a devastating effect upon Japan. From rapidly constructed airfields on Guam, Saipan, and Tinian, new B29s of the U.S. Army Air Force began bombing Japan. The commander of the Japanese home forces on Kyushu reportedly said, "Hell is now upon us."

The 77th Division casualties totaled approximately 1,200 dead and wounded. Another final statistic, as turned in by our divisional intelligence staff, stated that there'd been a body count of almost 3,000 Japanese killed by our division and we took 36 prisoners. In addition, the Marines killed over 14,000 Japanese, making a total casualty list for the enemy of 18,000 lost during this campaign. Some isolated pockets of Japanese resistance remained on Guam until the end of the war.

It seems strange now, when reading historical accounts of the fighting in the Pacific, that the Guam campaign usually is glossed over as having been a comparatively easy victory, while the fighting on Peleliu (invaded September 15, 1944) is often called a blood bath—so horrendous that it's sometimes compared to the extreme slaughter on Iwo Jima and Okinawa. The fighting on Peleliu, located east of the Philippines, was savage, of course. The 1st Marines were bled white, losing nearly 60 percent of authorized strength and having one of the highest casualty rates of any Marine invasion in the war.

On Guam, however, the 3rd Marines also were decimated, and the American casualties on Guam and Peleliu were nearly identical—almost exactly the same number of troops were killed and wounded on each island.

On Peleliu, the 1st Marine Division lost 1,252 dead and 5,224 wounded, and the U.S. Army's 81st Infantry Regiment had 277 dead and 1,000 wounded, for 7,753 total casualties. This is slightly less than the 7,800 casualties—2,124 dead and 5,676 wounded—suffered on Guam by the 3rd Marine Division, 1st Provisional Marine Brigade, and the 77th Infantry Division.[4] Furthermore, the number of Japanese killed was considerably greater on Guam.

The views of many authors and historians as to the supposed "differences" in the ferocity of the fighting on the two islands is somewhat puzzling if one considers just the battle statistics. Perhaps this attitude is due to the fact that many military experts believe the loss of life for capturing Peleliu, which had doubtful strategic importance, was too great—that the assault on the island was unnecessary. Regretfully, there were few, if any, positive consequences emanating from the taking of Peleliu.

In contrast, the benefits from capturing the Marianas were almost immediately apparent. Within months, it became a center for strategic Navy and Army Air Force command units, and most of the terrible bombing devastation wrought on Japan was launched from the Marianas.

There were many circumstances that contributed to the success of the Guam operation. The 1st Provisional Marine Brigade and the 3rd Marine Division were both veteran combat units and performed with the excellence and elan expected of them. The 77th Infantry Division experienced its first combat in Operation Forager, of which the Guam invasion was a part. Obviously, the training our division received prior to its departure from the mainland, and while in Hawaii, was sound in concept and had produced an aggressive, coordinated fighting force.

The speed of the 77th's offensive execution and constant forward pressure prevented the Japs from effectively setting up defenses, or organizing synchronized counterattacks. Everywhere, we hit the Japanese before they were ready.

Our division had its baptism of fire in the life and death world of combat. We'd survived and joined what some have called "a deadly brotherhood." We'd learned to kill.

NOTES

1. When we talked to some of the young Marine's buddies a few days later, they said our guide probably did get "a couple of Japs." He was a proficient hunter. During the war, each platoon seemed to have a couple of men like this Marine who were more adept killers than everybody else. At the other extreme, there always appeared to be a few men who never, or hardly ever, fired their weapons or inflicted casualites on the enemy.

2. Americans originated the term "banzai attack." The Japanese themselves never described their frontal assaults in this manner, though their soldiers certainly did shout the traditional battle cry, "Banzai!" when attacking. Banzai meant, in effect, "May the Emperor live 10,000 years."

3. General McNair's death by friendly fire was a particularly tragic error. In late July 1944, the U.S. Army was stalemated by the Germans in the hedgerow country of Normandy, France. The terrain was a patchwork of small farm plots bordered by thick, nearly impenetrable hedgerows, consisting of built-up rows of earth and stone standing several feet high, and held together by a mass of trees, brush, and tangled roots. Each hedgerow formed a defensive position that had to be individually assaulted. Tactical air support was called upon and 1,800 heavy bombers were sent over the lines to bomb the Germans. The massive attack seriously weakened enemy positions, but unfortunately some bomb loads fell short, killing and wounding more than 600 American soldiers, among them General McNair, the chief of Army Ground Forces.

4. Bernard C. Nalty, *War in the Pacific: Pearl Harbor to Tokyo Bay* (Norman: University of Oklahoma Press, 1999), 177, 191.

5 LEYTE (PHILIPPINE ISLANDS)

*U*PON LEAVING GUAM, the 77th Division was loaded into APA transports and proceeded in a southeasterly direction toward Noumea, New Caledonia, where we were scheduled for rest and rehabilitation. We now had plenty of good food and the men began to regain their strength and feel fit once more. Lou Ryman and I again avoided the stinking bowels of the ship by finding a spot on deck. At night we laid there, enjoying the balmy, equatorial climate and watching the bright stars above us. I saw the Southern Cross for the first time as the convoy sailed south of the equator.

While approaching the New Caledonia area, however, a special message came over the ship's communication system. "Now hear this, now hear this! Due to heavy losses by American forces on the island of Leyte in the Philippines and the request of General MacArthur for additional troops, our destination has been changed. We will not be going to a rest area in New Caledonia, but the convoy is turning around and we will be headed to the Philippines."

We learned that the Japanese were putting up a tremendous resistance in the Philippines under the leadership of General Tomoyuki Yamashita, the "Tiger of Malaysia," who early in the war had led troops in the spectacular conquest of the British bastion at Singapore. The Japanese high command had informed the Japanese people that they intended to make the Philippine archipelago campaign, and particularly the fight for 125-mile-long Leyte, the decisive battle of the Pacific war.[1]

★★★

On Thanksgiving Day, November 23, 1944, the convoy bearing the 77th Infantry Division approached Dulag on Leyte's east coast. Our arrival in the Philippines was met by pounding rain. As with Guam, we'd get drenched for weeks on Leyte. For once we were grateful for the rain, mist, and fog, however, as this kept Jap planes from operating against our transports.

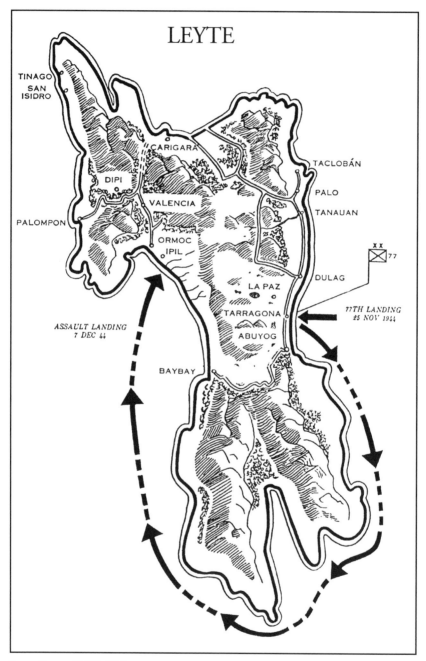

From *Ours to Hold It High*.

A month earlier, our forces had landed on Leyte's northeast coast, between Tarragona and Dulag in the south and Tacloban to the north. At that time, the invading U.S. Sixth Army included the 1st Cavalry Division and the 7th, 24th, 32nd, and 96th infantry divisions. Other divisions soon were added to the Sixth Army in its campaign in this part of the east central Philippines.

In the early morning hours, with mist and fog filling the bay, our regiments began landing at Tarragona during a driving rainstorm. The 307th moved inland to the middle of the island and set up security to protect supply installations and airfields on eastern Leyte. The 305th moved across the island to relieve portions of the 7th Division. Part of our 306th Regimental Combat Team was attached to the 11th Airborne Division, which had arrived on the island following the initial invasion and had moved into the line. The airborne division was to attack across the central mountains of Leyte to the west coast and relieve the 7th Division. The mid part of Leyte opposite Tarragona was about 15 to 20 miles wide.

The 1st Battalion of the 306th Regimental Combat Team, to which my platoon was attached, was held in reserve. We set up positions on the beach somewhat south of where we landed. While there, we observed the war's first instances of organized "kamikaze" attacks by the Japanese against our ships. I remember watching one lone Japanese suicide plane flying down the beach, causing some of our men to run for .50 caliber machine guns mounted on trucks and jeeps, while other men sprawled out flat on the sand. When overhead, the kamikaze turned offshore and dove at a transport, crashing into it amidships just below the bridge.

Kamikaze attacks (which would reach a peak during the Okinawa campaign) were something most of us couldn't understand. We realized that any of us could die on any day, but for a pilot to deliberately set about killing himself, although doing it to further a cause, seemed totally out of human character. But then, we didn't yet fully understand the true nature of the Japanese combatant.

When General Douglas MacArthur's forces first landed on Leyte on October 20, Japanese soldiers, sailors, and airmen were told by their leaders that the battle here was crucial and would determine the future course of the war. Accordingly, the enemy fought with an even greater ferocity and tenacity. To bolster their single division on Leyte, within a few days they began funneling ship after ship of reinforcements from other Philippine islands through the port of Ormoc in western Leyte. Almost 50,000 Japanese troops from five divisions had landed there since our initial assault. These troops were committed to the so-called "Yamashita Line" in the central mountains and the defense of the Ormoc corridor.

The continuous tropical rain had aided them by limiting American air strikes. More than 40 inches of rain had fallen in 30 days. MacArthur, recognizing that the flood of reinforcements had to be stopped, decided to "slam the door" on the Japanese by ordering the 77th Division to capture Ormoc.

★★★

Word shortly came that we'd be loaded onto 160-feet-long LCIs (Landing Craft Infantry) for an assault near Ormoc, which in peacetime had a population of 77,000. We also learned that after the Navy landed us behind Jap lines, the convoy would quickly pull out because enemy planes and small warships still controlled the area. The 77th would be miles from the nearest American units, i.e., the 11th Airborne to the north and the 7th Division to the south. Entirely surrounded by the Japanese, we'd have to fight our way forward through enemy lines to make contact with the nearest friendly troops.

We spent the early days of December preparing for the assault. While many ships of all types were involved in the operation, there were only 25 LCIs provided to land troops during the initial beachhead assault. We were assigned to one of the LCIs.

The flotilla sailed south, rounded the southern end of Leyte, then continued north into Ormoc Bay. Our assault was scheduled to come ashore near Ipil, about three miles below Ormoc. We were instructed to then drive north to Ormoc, which was the main supply base for the Japanese Army. In the interior, the 11th Airborne and the 96th and 7th infantry divisions were engaged in hard fighting, battering the Japs from three sides, but the enemy was resisting fiercely, sustained by supplies and troops funneled through Ormoc. It was our duty to hit them from behind, cutting them off, and causing their troops to wither on the vine.

It's easy now to look back at the audacity of this assault and realize that it was a brilliant military maneuver, but at the time every one of us had doubts as to whether we'd come out alive. The assault force consisted of only seven battalions from our three infantry combat teams—considerably less than a full division. And, we'd be sailing through seas controlled by the Japanese and be landing within a short distance of the main enemy base on the island.

We arrived off the beaches below Ipil on December 7, the anniversary of Pearl Harbor. In addition to our operation, another large air and sea battle also erupted nearby between American forces and the enemy. Almost simultaneously with our landing, the Japanese were intent that same day on bringing in a 13-ship convoy of transports and destroyer escorts, carrying reinforcements to Ormoc. Our planes sank all 13 vessels, 4 of which were large troop transports. An estimated 4,000 soldiers were lost.

While this was happening, our naval escort was only able to provide a limited pre-invasion bombardment. Only four destroyers and two LCI rocket boats were available to shell the Japanese-held beaches. One of these vessels, the destroyer-transport USS *Ward*, was lost while supporting our landing. Ironically, three years earlier to the day—at Pearl Harbor on December 7, 1941—the *Ward* had fired the first shots at the enemy by any of our military forces when sinking a Jap midget submarine at about 6:45 a.m. on that momentous day. Captain William O. Outerbridge, skipper of the *Ward* when it was destroyed at Ormoc, also had commanded the vessel at Pearl Harbor.

The fighting in Ormoc Bay—in the air, sea, and on land—was fierce, substantiating enemy rhetoric that the struggle to retain Leyte was vital to maintaining their Pacific empire. We were concerned about the nearly continuous presence of Jap planes overhead. On this day, they fatally wounded the *Ward* and another destroyer, and conducted other fierce attacks on our shipping.

We hit the beach at about 7:00 a.m. My unit, the 1st Battalion of the 306th, was attached to the 307th. Just as we'd been told, as soon as the ships discharged

U.S. ROCKETSHIP SWEEPS JAPS FROM LEYTE'S SHORE

By Murlin Spencer…(AP)—Rocketship 71, as lethal a weapon for her size as any in Uncle Sam's navy, pointed her stubby green prow toward the Japanese ashore and shook violently as streams of red flame swept back along both sides.

There was a crashing swish unlike anything you ever heard before as over two score rockets flashed towards the beach. Here was war at its deadliest—for the Japanese.

Twelve times this little craft shuddered as salvo after salvo leaped from their green steel launchers. Twelve times streams of fire swept backward. And ashore an ammunition dump exploded with a solid sheet of flame.

Rocketship 71 was on a mission of death and destruction along the sloping green beach four miles south of Ormoc town on Leyte's west coast. She was paving the way with high explosives for the landing of the 77th Infantry Division in the very center of the Jap stronghold in Ormoc Valley, which Gen. Douglas MacArthur has been trying for weeks to crack.

Then, after achieving complete tactical surprise, the amphibious force of more than 80 ships under command of Rear Adm. Arthur A.D. Struble, Portland, Ore., who participated in the Normandy invasion, withdrew under a ferocious nine-hour assault by Japanese planes. American army fighter planes gave magnificent support…

Both sides suffered losses, Japanese pilots flying with the reckless abandon of buzz bombs, left the eastern fringe of the Camotes Sea strewn with the wreckage of at least 42 fighters and bombers. American forces lost one converted destroyer-transport [USS *Ward*]…and one picket duty destroyer. Both were sunk by American guns after they had been set afire and floated dead in the water from repeated enemy hits.

The landing phase of the operation caught the enemy flat-footed. Shortly after dawn destroyers sealed off Ormoc Bay on two sides from Ponson Island and then proceeded with a 20-minute bombardment as assault waves formed off-shore. Five minutes before troops went ashore rocket boats loosed their deadly barrage, clearing away all vestige of life along a thousand yard front.

Maj. Richard Bong, Poplar Wis., the army's top fighter pilot, dashed through American flak to ride enemy planes into the sea. There were at least 20 furious dogfights during which the P-38s bagged 34 Japanese planes.

At times there were two or three Japanese "flamers" in the air simultaneously. In an attack at 9:45 a.m. three Tojos and five bombers were downed by the Americans in six minutes.

It was during this attack that the destroyer-transport was hit twice, bursting into flames. A minesweeper stood by to pick up survivors when the ship was abandoned…

the troops and unloaded the supplies and equipment on the beach, they upped anchor and headed for the east side of Leyte. I think most of us had a sinking feeling as we watched the convoy pull out, leaving us alone behind enemy lines.

As soon as our beach positions were consolidated, we moved inland toward a north-south highway running along the coastline. We set out toward Ipil. Resistance increased as we moved inland, but it was overcome and we continued our progress north up the highway.

My platoon came under heavy Jap mortar fire while we were in a rice paddy. Water covered the paddy to a depth of four or five inches. As the mortar shells fell, we dug foxholes in the mud below the water's surface. Our foxholes were entirely submerged, but we could crouch down below the metal shards buzzing around overhead.

This action behind enemy lines was extraordinary and risky. The usual procedure after a successful assault was to expand a beachhead into a large enough area so that the Japs couldn't bear artillery down on our all-important supply depots on the beaches. However, Major General Andrew D. Bruce, the 77th's commander, decided to quickly move out with our two combat regiments and attempt to capture Ormoc and bring the Leyte campaign to a speedy conclusion. Consequently, only a limited number of troops were left to protect the supply operation on the beach.

Moving forward the next day, we stopped just short of a place called Camp Downes, where we met heavy resistance. It was decided to dig in and prepare for a co-ordinated attack by both regiments on the following day. At this time, and for the next few days, Jap planes strafed us. My unit had been under enemy air assault on several occasions at sea, but this was the first time that we were attacked by Jap planes while on land.

Ormoc Bay Landing on Beach Used by Japs

By Howard Handleman...Dec. 7.— (I.N.S.)—The whole 77th Division, operating with minimum naval support, landed behind elements of a Jap division this morning, cut the Japanese supply line in a matter of minutes and landed guns that will deny the whole Ormoc Bay beach to enemy shipping which until now has been running heavy reinforcements into Ormoc...

The landing was bloodless for the doughboys, who hit a soft spot on the Ormoc beach while the Seventh Division on the south, the 32nd and the 96th on the [east] and the First Calvary on the north continued to apply the pressure which split the Jap forces...

The attack by Bruce's Statue of Liberty Division was even more ticklish than the original Leyte landing. There are more Jap fighting troops on the island now than on October 20 when the Americans first landed.

General Tomoyuki Yamashita . . . has thousands of troops massed in the narrow valley in defenses, which combined with knee-deep mud, held up the doughboys for three weeks ...

Two mortar crews moving forward carrying dismantled equipment and ammunition. *U.S. Army*

Early on the morning of December 9, another U.S. Navy convoy brought in reinforcements, landing them at Ipil. Once again, the convoy pulled out as soon as the troops disembarked. As the ships disappeared over the horizon, we still could see their masts for a time. Again we felt isolated, with a sinking feeling in the pits of our stomachs.

★★★

On the morning of December 10, enemy planes strafed us and dropped bombs in our regimental area. We were told that the objective for the day would be Ormoc and there'd be heavy artillery preparation.

I was called in to company headquarters and ordered to deliver a message to the commander of the 307th Regiment, which was advancing at that time toward Ormoc. Taking one of my buddies with me, I left to locate the 307th command post. A lieutenant always picked at least two of us to act as runners whenever possible. That way, if one runner was killed or injured, hopefully the other man could complete the mission. If a man was hit, we were under strict orders not to stop and help him, but to continue on and deliver the message. It didn't matter how badly he was wounded or suffering, or whatever the circumstances were, delivering the dispatch was the top priority and had to be done regardless of consequences.

Our artillery barrage was in progress as the two of us headed up the roadway toward Ormoc. When passing over the brow of a hill and starting down a slight slope, we could see Ormoc ahead, smoking and burning. The Japanese ammunition and gasoline storage areas were exploding, throwing flame and smoke high into the sky, and causing buildings in town to catch fire. My buddy and I received rifle fire, so we advanced in short sprints of maybe 30 or 40 yards at a time, then threw ourselves on the ground. We waited until the shooting stopped, then jumped up and ran again toward Ormoc, where we intended to make contact with the 307th.

As we neared a small bridge on the outskirts of Ormoc, I happened to see two Japs with a Nambu .25 caliber machine gun on a hillside about 50 yards away. They opened fire on us. I immediately ran toward the bridge intending—for some reason I still don't understand—to run across and throw myself down on the other side in a defilade and out of sight of the machine gunner. I don't know why I didn't just run directly to the edge of the stream and jump down the bank!

The machine gunner aimed at me as I ran. Bullets threw up dirt clods in the road as he followed my movement toward the bridge. Just as I crossed the bridge, I felt a sharp pain in my hand. I knew I'd been hit. Diving down the riverbank out of sight of the machine gunner, I saw blood running down my hand. A medic from the 307th was crouching near the bridge as I ran across and he'd seen me get hit. He came over and immediately provided first aid, using a swab stick to make a splint for my finger, sprinkling sulfa powder on it, and applying a dressing. After "carding," or tagging me with information about my wound, he turned to leave.

I started feeling myself over and realized I also was hit in the groin. I yelled at the medic to come back, but he continued moving away, crouching to avoid enemy fire. I shouted once more and waved at him to return, and he finally did.

Looking at me again, he put a gauze pad and bandage on the crotch wound, taped it over, and gave me a morphine shot from a syrette taken from his first aid kit. When getting hit, I remember seeing bullets striking the road and moving toward me, and even hitting between my legs, as I ran. Evidently, a bullet hit the bridge decking, shattered, and ricocheted upward, tearing off the fingernail and grazing the upper end of my finger from the tip to the second knuckle. A portion of the bullet also flew into my pelvic area, lodging just below the skin. I could actually see its outline underneath my skin, like a large black tick.

By late evening, Ormoc had been mopped up by our troops in a house-to-house advance and we were ready to move toward Valencia. My wound was pretty insignificant and, after delivering the dispatch to the 307th commander, we made our way back to our company CP (command post) south of Ormoc. Upon returning, I was sent to the regimental aid station. Medics removed the small portion of bullet from my groin, again using sulfa powder, and put a proper metallic splint on my finger. I spent less than half an hour away from my company while at the medical tent.

Although the enemy fire our troops received as we bore into Ormoc was heavy, fortunately casualties were light. That evening, General Bruce sent a message to the 7th infantry and 11th Airborne divisions, saying in the parlance of a gambler, "Have rolled two sevens into Ormoc. Come seven, come eleven," referring, of course, to the 77th, 7th, and 11th division numbers.

★★★

77th Infantry Division troops moving through the port of Ormoc after its capture. *U.S. Army*

YANK NUTCRACKER DESTROYS TRAPPED FOE BY THOUSANDS

Dec. 12 (Tuesday).—(AP)—Annihilation of the entire defending garrison at Ormoc, Yank-captured port on Leyte Island, and destruction of thousands of Japanese trapped in a pocket to the south were announced by Gen. Douglas MacArthur today.

MacArthur reported that the veteran 77th Division which landed last week four miles below Ormoc, had been joined by the Seventh Division, closing the southern jaw of a nutcracker vise, and "enemy forces which were trapped between the two have been destroyed." ...

Great quantities of equipment and supplies were seized.

Fierce fighting preceded final destruction of the Ormoc garrison. Fall of Ormoc, Japan's last big port of the reinforcement for her troops to the north in the Ormoc corridor, was a sharp blow to the enemy...

"The fighting in Ormoc itself before its fall was of the most desperate character," MacArthur reported.

The general reported yesterday that "many thousands" of Japanese were in the narrow pocket between the 77th and Seventh Divisions coming together just below Ormoc...

The next day our regiment stayed in perimeter defenses, sending out reconnaissance patrols, while we prepared to attack north up the highway toward Valencia. All of our regimental artillery was moved into the area to provide support for the advance. That evening, troops guarding the Ormoc waterfront sighted Japanese vessels moving into the bay and determined that the enemy intended to land on the beaches just north of Ormoc.

When a barge carrying hundreds of Japanese approached the shore in the dark, it was met by all of the weapons of the protecting units—not only rifle and machine gun fire, but also tank and artillery fire at point blank range. A huge fireball rose from the barge. Apparently, about 750 men on the vessel were killed. One lone survivor was found about a week later aboard the derelict and was taken captive. By the light of the exploding ammunition and shells, two other Japanese vessels were seen approaching. Again, artillery, machine gun, and rifle fire were brought to bear, literally blowing the Japanese out of the water. They evidently thought that their forces still were in control of Ormoc.

As our lieutenant said, "There's always someone who doesn't get the word."

On the morning of December 16, we moved out, less our vehicles. We were leading the division's advance and we'd be by ourselves, without contact with other units. We had to carry all of the equipment, ammunition, and food needed to sustain us for several days. It was hard enough carrying one's own ammo and supplies, but we also had to carry the regiment's extra equipment and ammunition. This included mortar rounds, machine gun and small arms ammunition, bangalore torpedoes, cases of hand grenades, blood plasma, radio batteries, stretchers, and the other miscellaneous items needed for an attack, and which normally were brought up by supply troops.

We set out across the rice paddies north of Ormoc under a broiling sun. The rice paddies were water-covered and at every step we sank at least ankle deep in mud. Men often hit deep spots where they went in up to the waist or shoulders, and they'd have to be pulled out by other soldiers. Each step required considerable effort and, as the afternoon wore on and the hot sun beat down on us, we became exhausted. Only our good physical conditioning and toughness from our days in training and combat kept us going.

Rice paddies and marshland of Leyte. *U.S. Army*

As we moved north toward a main highway coming from the west, we began encountering more Japanese troops and heavier resistance. By late afternoon, we reached a roadway and established a position across it, digging foxholes in a perimeter on both sides.

Earlier that afternoon while out on patrol, my platoon had captured two Jap soldiers. When we dug in that night, we bound their hands and legs, and laid them out on the ground in front of the foxholes. We began our four-hour-on and four-hour-off watches.

That night, we suddenly heard a vehicle driving at high speed down the highway towards us. As the vehicle approached, the .30 caliber machine gun in Sergeant Crawford's squad opened up, as did the riflemen in adjoining foxholes. Shortly, a huge explosion engulfed a heavy truck loaded with enemy troops and it burst into flames. The Japs screamed as we fired into them and as they were torn apart by explosions.

The following morning we untied our Jap prisoners' limbs and set a guard over them. We almost felt sorry for them because mosquitoes had attacked them savagely during the night, biting them until their eyes were practically swollen shut. Being out on our own and with no rear lines, we'd have to march the prisoners along with us and tie them up at night.

We also had to take along our wounded. There were a number of walking injured, of which I was one. Other wounded men had to be carried on litters. It was extremely tiring for men ordered to be litter bearers. Four men carried each litter and, of course, they had to have guards to protect them from enemy attack. At all times during our campaigns in the Pacific, the Japanese never relaxed their efforts to kill our wounded at every opportunity.

For several days, we fought doggedly up the highway in the attempt to contact the 1st Cavalry. Our supplies were a serious concern. However, a large band of Filipino guerrillas, moving west across Leyte's mountains, had made contact with us as we advanced up the highway. They brought supplies and acted as litter bearers for the wounded.

In combat, every round of ammunition is precious, especially for rapid firing weapons like machine guns. Everything had to be

JAP POCKETS CLEANED OUT

Dec. 14 (Thursday).—(AP)—Troops of the U.S. Seventh Division in Ormoc, on the Leyte Island west coast, are cleaning out pockets of Japanese resistance to the east of American positions, while the 77th Division maintains pressure to the north, Gen. Douglas MacArthur said today.

The 77th Division, which captured Ormoc Sunday and later was joined by the Seventh coming up from the south, has been regrouping its units and sending patrols north to probe enemy strength to the rear of the Yamashita defense line.

Deprived of Ormoc, port through which the Japanese received most of their supplies, the Nipponese are being pressed into the mountains to the northwest also under attack by the 32d U.S. Division coming down from the Carigara Bay coast and the First Calvary Division driving in from the northeast.

MacArthur said the Japanese caught by the juncture of the Seventh and 77th Divisions were suffering "extraordinarily heavy" losses in the desperate effort to escape over mountain trails.

Three small Japanese transports loaded with troops were sunk in Ormoc Harbor Tuesday night by American shore guns. The Nipponese apparently were unaware the Yanks held the town when the craft slipped into the harbor...

carried by the advancing soldiers or brought up by men supplying the front line companies. Grenades were packed in wooden boxes, with each box weighing approximately 40 pounds—"the stupid sons of bitches" who manufactured the boxes often forgot to put rope handles on them.

Machine gun ammunition was carried in a green, rectangular metal container (larger than a typical lunchbox), with a metal handle on top. When carrying one in each hand, with a rifle slung over the back, a backpack filled with personal items, and carrying additional rifle ammunition and hand grenades, a man was weighted down. You became exhausted even when walking on level ground, let alone trudging through a muddy rice paddy or fording a swamp up to the waist. Your arms felt like they were being pulled out of the sockets. You got so tired that you were afraid to put anything down because you might not be able to pick it up again. Obviously, the guerrillas who joined us and brought supplies were welcomed with open arms.

The third day out, we encountered heavy fighting. On that day, our battalion estimated that we killed over 1,000 enemy soldiers, breaking the back of their resistance. Among the numerous Japanese bodies along the highway, we saw Samurai swords, rifles, pistols, and other items that we normally took as souvenirs, but under our present circumstances most of this was left where we found it.

We continued our advance through terrain impassable to vehicles, and we still had the two prisoners with us, whom we'd nicknamed Alphonse and

Typical squad action—BAR man up front followed by riflemen, one of whom carries an anti-tank bazooka. *U.S. Army*

BAR man and a pair of riflemen alertly approach the same native hut depicted in the previous photo. *U.S. Army*

Garscon. We didn't ever discuss killing them, though it was difficult to drag them along, keep them under guard, and feed them. However, I have my doubts now as to whether we'd have taken prisoners under the same circumstances in the future. I know it sounds cruel and inhuman, but the likelihood is that we probably would've shot them. I am not saying it would've been right. I'm just telling you what probably would've happened.

Surrounded as we were by enemy forces, there wasn't anywhere to send our two prisoners for interrogation and confinement. They were a burden. Someone always had to be guarding them, which under the circumstances was a serious safety factor regarding our own platoon. Everyone by now wished they'd been killed when we'd first captured them. They were just too damn much trouble!

But now that we had them, we were determined to take care of them and see that they were safely delivered to an intelligence officer after we established contact with the 7th division or the 1st Cavalry.

★★★

It's true that the percentage of Japanese prisoners taken in World War II was extremely small compared to the numbers that were killed. The most obvious causes for this, of course, were their fanatical style of fighting, their refusal to surrender, and their willingness to commit suicide.

Following the sneak attack on Pearl Harbor, movies, literature, and radio began cultivating in the American public a deep loathing and contempt for the enemy—an attitude that was, unfortunately, of a racist nature. For the front line soldier, another reason for our passionate, almost visceral hatred of the enemy was the fact that buddies and fellow soldiers had been maimed and killed by them. Also, we'd heard about, and some had witnessed, instances where the Japs brutally executed Americans.

On Guam, the young Marine that led my patrol up Mt. Alifan said that earlier in the campaign his squad had found two dead Marines that'd been captured and murdered by Japs. When their bodies were discovered, their hands and feet were bound behind their backs, their throats slit, and their cut-off penises stuck in their mouths. On the island of Ie Shima near Okinawa—which the 77th Division attacked later in the war—several instances of Japanese barbarity were documented for war crimes prosecution. After several American airmen were shot down and captured there, two were beheaded by a Jap officer and a third was tied to a stake and used for bayonet practice by a squad of infantry.[2]

The disdainful loathing of the enemy was practically universal among our front line infantry. No doubt the stories of atrocities grew more lurid as they were retold, but, as the war went on, our growing familiarity with the brutal character of the enemy caused an animosity and bitterness toward them that was indigenous throughout the Pacific theater. Enemy soldiers tended to be small in stature, some even dwarfish-like, but they were tough and mean; their own officers constantly slapped and beat them. When the fighting was going against him, rather than surrender, the Japanese soldier was indoctrinated to commit suicide. He'd shoot himself or hold a grenade to his chest and blow himself apart, or two soldiers would play catch with an activated grenade until it exploded, killing them both.

When Japs did offer to surrender, it frequently was a trick to get close to our men in an effort to kill them. One might hide a grenade in his loincloth and take it out when least expected, throwing it at the men taking him prisoner. They'd often pretend to be dead and after GIs walked past, they'd open up fire from behind, shooting our men in the back. Their actions often caused a matching malevolence and barbarity on the part of our soldiers and Marines.

We all learned to approach any surrendering Japanese with extreme caution. We'd make them completely strip naked, even taking off loincloths. Because the risk was so great and the enmity so bitter, many Japanese attempting to surrender were shot by our men under these perplexing and difficult circumstances.

Searching prisoners for weapons—even their clothing seemed alien to us. Beginning with the Leyte campaign, 77th Division troops had the outline of the division's "Statue of Liberty" patch stenciled on their helmets. *U.S. Army*

I'm personally not aware of any captured Americans being held alive by the Japanese during any of the actions in which I participated. It's obvious that there must have been instances where our men were cornered and captured, or were rendered unconscious, or were so severely wounded that they couldn't resist and, accordingly, were taken prisoner. I personally know of occasions when American C and K rations were found in possession of Jap soldiers that we killed, and I was told of other dead Japs being clothed in American uniforms. During all of the time I was in action, there wasn't one instance that I know of when an infantryman or Marine was rescued by us after being held alive in enemy hands. Undoubtedly, the enemy killed all captured Americans in the island campaigns that I was involved in.

★★★

77th troops carrying their personal gear plus dismantled mortars, machine guns, tripods, ammunition containers, and other equipment while proceeding toward Valencia. *U.S. Army*

After we took Valencia and when moving forward just north of that town, Colonel Aubrey D. Smith, our regimental commander, happened to be with my squad when we suddenly were targeted by heavy artillery. This barrage was unlike anything I'd been subjected to before. The shrill, terrible roar of the incoming rounds was absolutely terrifying, almost unbearable, and the resulting explosions were ear-splitting and deafening.

There was the awful knowledge that you couldn't do anything about it, and the next shell might land right on top of you, tearing your body to pieces and scattering it all over the landscape. As the explosions ripped into us, we immediately began taking casualties, not just a few men, but three, four, and five being hit at a time.

Everyone was screaming. I could hear Colonel Smith shouting into the telephone, "Find someone to stop that goddamn artillery."

It was friendly fire! He knew that our Long Toms (155 mm heavy artillery) were firing from across the mountains and were tearing us apart. I don't know how many rounds fell into the regimental area. Totally frightened and laying on the ground with my face in the turf, I was shaking from the sound of each explosion and praying that it would stop. After what seemed like an eternity, it finally did.

I heard Sergeant Ames yelling for our squad to get up and start helping the wounded. I counted nine casualties myself. How many more there were, I don't know, but it was a hell of a mistake to be hit and torn apart like that by our own artillery.

Unfortunately, friendly fire wasn't uncommon. I wouldn't be surprised if it caused as much as ten percent of our casualties. It could happen in many forms—short rounds, for example. When artillery or mortar shells fell short, hitting our troops, it could be due to defective powder, mistakes during firing, or errors in range finding and computing distances to targets. Also, injury might be caused by a rifle discharging when dropped; or, the pin on a grenade might accidentally be pulled out; or, American troops might be mistaken for the enemy and fired upon; or a pilot might incorrectly read the target panels and fire rockets into our own positions. There are many other examples too numerous to fully document. In any event, it occurred often and was terribly demoralizing.

The next morning, having recovered from the friendly fire incident, we crawled out of our foxholes and were informed that the 1st Battalion's next objective was to take a bridge on

155 mm "Long Toms" in action on Leyte. *U.S. Army*

the Tagbong River, about a quarter mile north of our position. The assault would proceed in the usual way, beginning with artillery concentration, followed by an infantry attack.

★★★

The structural and administrative organization of the infantry was as follows in ascending order—squad, platoon, company, battalion, regiment, division.

An infantry "squad" consisted of about 12 men usually led by a sergeant (also known as an NCO, or non-commissioned officer). If a rifle squad had been in action for any length of time, however, it likely was decimated by sickness and casualties, and its numbers were reduced to perhaps eight or nine men.

Three squads comprised a rifle "platoon," which was led by a lieutenant and platoon sergeant, assisted by a buck sergeant (a lesser-ranked three-striped NCO) and a corporal.

At the next organizational level, a "company" was comprised of three rifle platoons, a headquarters platoon, and a weapons platoon armed with three 60 mm mortars and three .30 caliber air-cooled light-weight machine guns. The weapons platoon's 20 to 30 men were divided into mortar men, machine gunners, and ammunition carriers. Altogether, an infantry company consisted of about 200 to 210 men.

An infantry "battalion" included three infantry companies, a heavy weapons company, plus a headquarters company with heavy .30 caliber water-cooled machine guns, headquarters personnel and staff, an Intelligence and Reconnaissance Platoon, and three or four 37 mm anti-tank guns. The battalion's heavy weapons company had

Mortar crew supporting attacking infantry. *U.S. Army*

six to eight 81 mm mortars and eight to ten .30 caliber air- and water-cooled machine guns, and included about 150 men.

An infantry "regiment" was made up of three infantry battalions, a service company, a headquarters company, and a cannon company usually consisting of about five or six short-barreled 105 mm howitzers.

Three infantry regiments or combat teams were included in an infantry "division." In addition to the three infantry regiments, each division also had its own artillery consisting of 105 and 155 mm cannons, probably numbering about 50 altogether. Each infantry division likewise had one reconnaissance company with armored cars, plus heavy mortars and machine guns. Also integrally attached to the infantry division was an engineering battalion armed with infantry weapons, plus a medical battalion to handle casualties.

A full complement of personnel in an infantry division was approximately 12,000 to 14,000 men. In my experience with the 77th Division, we rarely had more than 9,000 to 10,000 infantrymen available at any one time when we were on the line. It was the infantry regiments that did most of the hard fighting and bore the brunt of the casualties. Ninety to 95 percent of an infantry division's killed and wounded were in rifle line companies. (My I&R platoon, with more varied duties, suffered a lesser percentage of casualties.)

An infantry company's assault on an objective normally was proceeded by a mortar (and often artillery) barrage. Once the shelling lifted, machine guns fired into the enemy line at the designated attack point. Meanwhile, two rifle platoons usually moved out, with the third rifle platoon held in reserve.

Ordinarily, the two platoons didn't advance simultaneously. Rather, platoons took turns moving forward, with one platoon providing covering fire as the other maneuvered. Leapfrogging in this manner, the assault continued. Men might run in bursts at the objective if the situation and terrain allowed for it. Usually, however, we just walked in the general direction of the objective to save our strength, because we were too tired and worn down, the weather was too hot and humid, and the ground was too rough for running. We usually only ran when fired upon or when finally arriving at the enemy positions. Even if a man wasn't burdened by a heavy BAR, a flamethrower, or a satchel charge, he still had a rifle and bayonet, helmet, two canteens, one or two ammo bandoleers, cartridge belt, rolled up rubber poncho, backpack, and two or three hand grenades. Any running, crawling, or jumping was done only with considerable effort. Often, we intentionally dropped our packs and other unneeded equipment so we could move more freely in an attack.

Riflemen were the basis of most attacks on enemy positions. Generally speaking, the only way to get the Japs out of their entrenched positions was for a rifleman to go after them with a rifle, grenade, flamethrower, bayonet, or sometimes even his bare hands. If the objective proved to be too tough and we were stopped short, our company and platoon leaders generally called in mortar and artillery support, and, if a naval observer was available, naval gunfire from off shore. By taking objectives systematically while working our way forward, we usually seized several hundred to a thousand or more yards of ground in a day.

If resistance still held us up and tanks were available, they were brought forward. We proceeded with the tanks, guarding them from attack by enemy infantrymen and pointing out the Jap positions that were holding up the advance. The tankers in their Shermans then would open the way for us with their 75 mm cannons. By late afternoon, we'd stop and dig in for the night.

Sherman tank moving forward while being protected by an infantry squad. *U.S. Army*

When we moved out of our foxholes and went forward, sooner or later we were going to run into the enemy. They had but one purpose, and that was to try and kill us. Sometimes we came close enough to throw hand grenades at them, perhaps 20 or 30 yards away. Other times we had only distant glimpses of them in our rifle sights. The few hundred or a thousand yards that we took from them each day wasn't given to us; we had to take it. That's the way the war was won, by taking ground from the enemy and holding onto it. For the "poor damn foot soldier," it always was "one more hill." Then, when that was taken, you were told there was another.

★★★

On December 20 after the opening artillery barrage, the 1st Battalion started the attack on the bridge. Company A attempted to cross the Tagbong River, and one squad did reach the other side, but all were killed or wounded. The enemy fire was too heavy to attempt another crossing.

On the morning of December 21, a heavy Japanese mortar and artillery barrage fell on our battalion and about 500 Japanese launched an attack against us, howling obscenities and curses, and screaming "Banzai." Intense machine gun and rifle fire and an artillery concentration met them. Later, we counted more than 400 dead in front of our positions.

Sergeant Harry Sall, Fred Chippiga, and Danny Carpellotti with "Alphonse" and "Garscon." *U.S. Army*

Our attack resumed the next day with the intention of capturing the intersection of Highway 2 and the Palompon Road. We were anxious to take the junction because once that was done, we were told, an American armored column led by tanks would bring in Alligators and ambulances to evacuate our wounded. We also were running short of ammunition and provisions, and it was imperative to be resupplied. For several days, all that we'd received in air drops were plasma, medical supplies, and some ammunition, mostly dropped from small artillery observation planes. Nothing else got through to us.

When reaching and taking the junction, our medical personnel brought up the wounded and set them down by the roadway for evacuation. However, an armored column still needed to break through to us in order to haul the wounded out. While at the junction I remember watching units from our battalion attacking north of the highway. Mortar shells burst all around us and machine gun bullets cut the tall grass.

Finally, we saw tanks leading Alligators down the highway toward us. We knew that the column had breached the enemy lines, and our wounded soon would be evacuated.

Ames and I had just started to walk toward a tank to talk with the crew and find out what was happening up the highway when we heard several rifle shots, causing both of us to drop to the ground. Two or three bullets struck the dirt right between us and whined off into the jungle.

"Shit," yelled Ames looking around, "where is he?"

We lay as close to the ground as we could, but the sniper had us in his sights. He kept us there for five or ten minutes, shooting two or three rounds every time we tried to move.

After a pause in the firing, Ames said, "Mac, take your helmet, hold it up in the air, and see if he shoots at it, and I'll try to tell where the shots came from."

Eyeing him quizzically, I replied, "Hell, Sarge, I've got a better idea. You hold your helmet in your hand, stick it up there, and I'll try to see if I can tell where the shots are coming from."

We looked at each other for a few seconds, hugging the ground with bullets whistling overhead, and then broke out laughing.

It wasn't long afterward that we were able to get the tankers' attention and they fired a burst of machine gun fire into the jungle where we thought the sniper was located. When the shooting stopped, we moved on over to the tanks. In talking to one of the tank men, we learned that other units of the 1st Cavalry Division were just a few hundred yards behind them. Contact had been established not more than an hour or two before. By now, the rest of our platoon had moved up, bringing with them our two prisoners.

Two or three ambulances of an attached medical battalion accompanied by several Alligators came up the road through the mortar fire and stopped near us. Wounded men still were being carried up on stretchers and set alongside the road in a line awaiting evacuation. My squad brought forward Alphonse and Garscon. I walked over to the nearest Alligator and asked a sergeant standing there if he could arrange transportation for our prisoners.

Before he could answer, I heard two shots, not more than 10 or 15 feet away and felt something hit my helmet and the back of my jacket—I'd soon discover that it was blood and brains. Turning around, I saw that Alphonse and Garscon had been shot. They were lying beside one of the Alligators, twitching and kicking, and obviously mortally wounded.

Three or four of our men were holding another man from our outfit who was yelling and screaming that he hated Japs, all Japs, and they should all be killed. He blurted that they'd just killed his buddy that morning and he wasn't going to let any of them be taken prisoner—he'd kill every one of them that he saw. Gradually the screaming man began settling down as several men pulled him away and out of sight.

To this day, I don't know if charges were brought against this man, but I doubt they were. The feelings of almost every infantryman in the line were clear—the concern, friendship, and caring that they had for their fellow soldiers went hand in glove with a loathing for those who shot and killed them. There was a detestation of everything Japanese. Most of those present at the time of the shooting had seen some of their closest friends and buddies die, their bodies torn apart, arms or legs blown off, and their faces disfigured by ugly wounds. When a squad or platoon was reduced day after day, by one casualty after another, the

77th Division troops crossing the Tagbong River. *U.S. Army*

hatred built up and could explode, as it did in this instance. Most infantrymen who actually faced fire and were in the lines—who experienced the terrible stress and strain—had no mercy for any Jap that wanted to surrender.

Those present at this incident had seen so much death inflicted in so many ways that they didn't spend a great deal of time thinking about the two Japs who'd been shot. This act was terribly brutal, it was wrong, and, other than what I've attempted to set down here, there wasn't any excuse for it. I will say that these were the only prisoners that I personally ever saw shot by our side after they'd been captured.

One of my buddies said, however, as he turned and walked away, "After you've shot and killed one of those yellow bastards, it's a lot easier to kill the next one."

The 1st Battalion next attacked a line of small hills located directly northeast of where we'd made juncture with the tanks. We discovered that most of the Japanese had pulled out during the night and the hills were only lightly defended. After taking these positions, we consolidated, dug in, and awaited further orders.

Christmas was simply another day of action—no different from the day before or the day after—except we received an unusual number of artillery rounds. On December 26, for the first time ever in combat, we were given warm food for dinner. During our entire time on Guam and up to now on Leyte, my platoon had never received a hot cooked meal. We'd eaten practically nothing but K and C rations, but on the day after Christmas, cooks brought kettles of warm food up to our company. It included turkey with all the trimmings—cranberry sauce, mashed potatoes and gravy, and pumpkin pie.

Everything looked so good and we were tense with anticipation, but we'd momentarily forgotten about the competition—the ever present swarms of flies.

They were big, green-black, and absolutely fearless. They'd fed on numerous dead Japanese and Americans, as well as excrement left by troops in both armies, until they were bloated, but they still had an insatiable appetite. In the hot Philippine climate, flies multiplied exponentially even when feeding mostly on native night soil, but now, feasting on the rotting, decaying corpses lying everywhere, they'd become astronomically sized swarms of biting, nauseating vermin.

When served and expectantly sitting down on the ground with our meal, the flies attacked. The food was dumped into our deep canteen cups, which seemed to offer more protection against the insects than a food plate. Besides, we hadn't used plates for weeks and most of us had thrown them away. Flies, however, still stuck in the mashed potatoes and gravy, and swarmed on the lips of our coffee cups. If one saw a bite size portion of food in his canteen cup that the flies hadn't settled on yet, by the time it was spooned to your mouth, it crawled with them. For most of us it was simply too much and we gave up, throwing the food away and creating more breeding ground for these pests.

Undoubtedly, flies were a cause of the almost universal dysentery afflicting our troops. It resulted in many of us messing our pants, causing further physical

Leyte Victory Sure with New Landing

Dec. 26.—(Tuesday)—(AP) —Gen. Douglas MacArthur declared today the Leyte-Samar campaign "was closed except for mopping up" yesterday after American doughboys had captured Palompon in a water-borne assault which sealed the fate of the Japanese and closed their last escape port on northwestern Leyte Island.

Asserting that Gen. Tomoyuki Yamashita... "has sustained perhaps the greatest defeat in the military annals of the Japanese army," MacArthur's communique said the Japanese had lost an estimated 112,728 killed and 493 captured in the 67-day campaign...

"The completeness of this destruction," said MacArthur, "has seldom been paralleled in the history of warfare."

The magnitude of the American victory in the first phase of the campaign to liberate the Philippines was further borne out by General MacArthur's assertion that 2,748 enemy planes were destroyed in the islands since the landing on Leyte by the Third and Seventh Fleet Carrier planes, the Army's Fifth Air Force, Marine units, and American

shore and ship anti-aircraft guns.

A total of 27 warships and 41 transports sunk during destruction of 10 Leyte-bound Japanese convoys does not include enemy losses in naval battles in Leyte Gulf October 25. The American casualties of 2,623 killed, 8,422 wounded and 172 missing covered only the American ground force losses...

The coup de grace was given the Nipponese on Leyte Christmas morning (Philippine time) when a 77th Division force entered Palompon Bay and stormed ashore while escorting U.S. Seventh Fleet PT boats beat a tattoo against the beach and the division's own artillery laid down a heavy bombardment from advanced positions inland from Palompon.

The enemy had little with which to reply to the two-way barrage. By the time the 155-millimeter "Long Toms" had lifted their barrage, Japanese survivors of the blasting were doomed just as their comrades were on December 7 when the 77th landed just below Ormoc, on Leyte's western coast, to provide the anvil on which the Seventh U.S. Infantry Division smashed the Japanese 26th Division...

weakness and deterioration. To this day, I have a hatred of flies. I can't stand them. They are an abomination. Every time I see one, it reminds me of the Pacific war—how they crawled all over our dead and those of the enemy, into nostrils, across vacant blind eyeballs, and into mouths, laying eggs and hatching maggots. When I find one in our house or at a restaurant, I can hardly rest until I've hunted it down and killed it.

Our battalion and the remainder of the 306th stayed in position covering the Tagbong River bridge, which had been in our hands for some time now. On several occasions in the next few days, our platoon went out on patrol looking for the enemy, but we only found stragglers and succeeded in killing 12 of them.

Bodies of Japanese soldiers in the path of 96th Division Sherman tanks. *Sylvan R. Thompson collection*

We also observed several hundred Filipino natives that'd been released from Japanese custody. They marched along the highway toward Valencia, carrying their possessions on their heads or in their arms, with the lucky ones having a buffalo and cart, or a wheelbarrow, for hauling. Men, women, old people, babies, children, even a group of Catholic nuns—all with smiles on their faces—waved at us as they walked by.

The island had been declared "secure" by General MacArthur, but as always after such announcements, we continued to take some casualties. If a man was killed or wounded after an island was "secured," he was just as dead and injured as if it'd happened before the proclamation. I wondered if people back in the States realized this.

We continued to send out patrols, and still encountered isolated groups of the enemy. We found more and more Japanese, too, who'd killed themselves by putting a gun in their mouth and discharging it, or by blowing themselves up with grenades. Organized resistance had disappeared for all practical purposes, and the only Japanese left that we ran into were small disorganized bands that were just trying to get away from us.

Finally, about the middle of January, our battalion was assembled near the Valencia-Palompon road. After waiting several hours, we were loaded into trucks

Refugees moving into the safety of our 77th Division lines. *U.S. Army*

Nuns escorting young children, who probably are orphans or have been separated from their parents. *U.S. Army*

and transported back over the central mountains to Tarragona on Leyte's east coast. Later, most of the remaining units of our division were relieved by the Americal Division, and we all were reunited near Tarragona.

★★★

Our struggles in the Philippines not only were against the Japanese, but also the forbidding climate and the brutal, primitive terrain. Leyte is about the same distance north from the equator as Guadalcanal is south of it. The fierce equatorial sun and warm Pacific waters create high humidity and almost constant rain. November through March is the "wet season," and rain falls almost continuously every day. This has created a remarkably fertile environment that teems with impenetrable equatorial forests and head-high, razor-sharp growths of kunai grass.

Much of the island is a wilderness of jagged ridges and mountains and vaporous coastal and interior jungles. Fetid, dank, and foul smelling swamps are breeding grounds for snakes, crocodiles, leeches, centipedes, flies, and other flying and crawling insects that bite and dig into people causing malaria and other fevers and persistent running sores, which contribute to heat exhaustion.

Disease was a major cause of casualties in the Pacific war. Malaria was endemic; in fact, half of all American casualties were due to malaria. While it normally didn't cause death, it was debilitating and our military took stringent measures to combat it. Quinine, if taken daily, usually was effective, but many of the troops considered the side effects to be as bad as the disease itself. Atabrine was more effective, but it gave the skin an unhealthy yellowish tint. Also, someone started a rumor that it caused sterility and impotency. Most military personnel simply refused to take it. Malaria and the other tropical diseases took an even greater toll on the enemy than on us.

The weather, terrain, and distances involved created difficult logistical problems; thus our conquest of the Japanese and overcoming the harsh natural environment of Leyte was indeed a gargantuan task. The assault on Leyte—the initial effort by Douglas MacArthur and his troops in a long campaign to free the Philippine archipelago—was accomplished in the face of Japanese proclamations to fight the decisive battle in the Pacific here. It was a hard-fought campaign, and the audacious landing by the 77th's combat battalions behind enemy lines near Ormoc was a decisive factor.

The 77th's bitter fight up the Ormoc Valley cut Japanese supply lines, annihilated the bulk of their reserves, and turned a bloody stalemate on the island into a complete route. Our losses were substantial—approximately 600 killed, 1,500 wounded, and thousands afflicted with dengue fever, malaria, and other tropical diseases. However, we killed almost 20,000 Japanese. It's believed that the 77th achieved here the greatest kill ratio of any division, Army or Marine, in any major campaign during the Pacific war. For every 77th Division fatality, we killed 33 Japanese.

Our fighting skills obviously were improving. Not only had we learned how to stay alive, but we also were learning a variety of ways to take out the enemy. Bunker by bunker, yard by yard, we were what our instructors in basic training had said we'd become—lean, mean, killing machines.

✧

NOTES

1. In the massive and far-ranging Battle of Leyte Gulf on October 22–27, 1944, the U.S. Navy inflicted the final decisive defeat on the Japanese Imperial Navy at sea. The enemy lost 4 carriers, 3 battleships, 10 cruisers, and 11 destroyers, as opposed to the Americans losing 1 light carrier, 2 escort carriers, 2 destroyers, and 1 destroyer escort. This overwhelming U.S. victory eliminated Japan's ability to initiate any future major naval action. The struggle against the Japanese Army in the Philippines, however, would grind on to the end of the war.

2. Atrocities of these types were common in the Pacific conflict. In prosecuting Japanese war criminals after the war, 5,700 were tried, 4,405 convicted, and 984 executed.

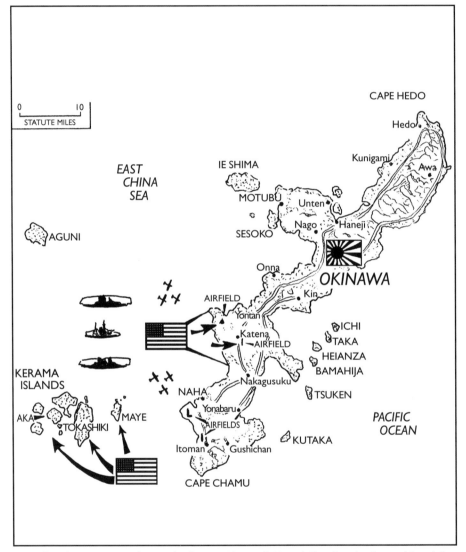

Map of Ryukyu campaign, showing landing on Okinawa's Hagushi beaches, April 1, 1945, and the assault on the Kerama Islands, begun March 26. Sun-rayed pennant is the Japanese Imperial Navy battle flag. Modified from *Associated Press Wirephoto Map*

6 KERAMA RETTO (RYUKYU ISLANDS)

*A*FTER MOVING INTO A BIVOUAC near Tarragona, my platoon along with the rest of our regimental combat team began the operational structuring and other preparations required for our next assignment. Although we didn't know it, battle clouds were moving in again, and our future prospects would be darkened in the most terrible campaign of the Pacific war—the bloody and savage battle for Okinawa.

According to the eminent military historian Hanson W. Baldwin:

> In retrospect, the battle for Okinawa can be described only in the grim superlatives of war. In size, scope and ferocity, it dwarfed the Battle of Britain. Never before had there been, probably never again will there be, such a vicious scrawling struggle of planes against planes, of ships against planes. Never before, in so short a space, had the Navy lost so many ships; never before in land fighting had so much American blood been shed in so short a time in so small an area: probably never before in any three months of the war had the enemy suffered so hugely, and the final toll of American casualties was the highest experienced in any campaign against the Japanese. There have been larger land battles, more protracted air campaigns, but Okinawa was the largest combined operation, a "no quarter" struggle fought on, under and over the sea and land.[1]

After 2½ months of hard campaigning on Leyte, the 77th needed rehabilitation and refitting. We were given new clothing, lost and damaged equipment was replaced, and innovative weapons and devices were issued. Men were given new sniper and secret snooper scopes and were trained in their use. A sniper scope was mounted on a rifle, allowing a soldier to see and shoot in the dark by means of infrared radiation. The snooper scope was used solely for night observation. Our artillery received new 57 and 75 mm recoilless rifles as well as sound locating sets for detecting enemy mortar and artillery positions.

Tactics also had to be worked out with supporting tank units, which for the first time would be mounting flamethrowers. A flamethrower installed in a

Sherman tank's 75 mm gun had an effective range of about 75 to 100 yards. Its fuel consisted of gasoline and napalm—the latter being a soapy granular material, which when combined with gasoline gave weight and consistency to the mixture, allowing for a concentration of the flame when discharged under pressure.

After the war ended, some people criticized our use of napalm as being inhumane. However, knowing the extent of the Japanese fortifications on Okinawa, it might be doubtful as to whether we could've taken the island without napalm. At the least, the battle certainly would've been more difficult for us without it. Although the public generally doesn't know it, the Japanese also used flamethrowers against us. These were portable in nature, carried by infantry teams, and on occasion were quite effective.

Because of the U.S. Army's ongoing operations on Luzon and other islands during the prolonged Philippines campaign, replacements were hard to come by to fill the 77th's depleted ranks. Again, our line companies would be understrength when going into combat.

Plans were being prepared for invading the small islands of the Kerama Retto group, located about 25 miles west of the southern end of Okinawa. This would involve battalion landings, with the 1st Battalion of the 306th being assigned to first assault Geruma Shima, and then Tokashika Shima.

In addition to continued training, including hard calisthenics, marching, and running to stay fit, we also served as stevedores and loaded ships, and we built our camp, even though we'd be leaving soon. There really was no time for rest and relaxation. The assault on the large island of Luzon and the capital, Manila, in the northern Philippines was proceeding at this time and the 1st Battalion loaded 300-foot-long LSTs (Landing Ship Tank), sailed on them as working parties, and did the unloading. We worked 10 to 12 hours a day, and seven days a week, without rest.

The timetable for the Kerama Retto invasion had been set. All units had to be aboard ship and ready to depart no later than the third week of March. The infantry units in which I was included, however, left earlier on LSTs. Again, the 77th would be landing without support from other Army or Marine units. The capture of the Kerama Retto would provide the Navy with an anchorage for a fueling, ammunition, and supply station during the Ryukyu campaign.

Okinawa and its nearby island groups were considered part of the Japanese homeland—the 77th would be the first significant American unit to step foot on Japanese soil in the Pacific war.

★★★

The assaults in the Kerama Retto were proceeded by air and naval bombardment. We landed at Beach Yellow on Geruma Shima early on the morning of March 26. After attacking and killing all of the Japs that we could find on the island, we re-embarked. On March 27, the 306th's 1st and 2nd battalions next

77th infantrymen taking cover behind a stone wall during the Kerama Retto assault. Note the amphibious assault vehicle with cannon and .50 caliber machine gun in the background *U.S. Army*

assaulted Tokashika Shima. After destroying the main Japanese resistance, the 1st Battalion remained on Tokashika Shima until March 31.

On both Geruma and Tokashika, we found hundreds of suicide boats hidden in caves. Many of the Jap crews, rather than surrender, went into the caves where the boats were located and killed themselves. Sixty boats also were found on the adjoining small island of Aka Shima. The capture of the Kerama Retto was swift and done with slight casualties.

Something else captured on Tokashika Shima were several cases of sake, a Japanese rice wine. We'd received shots from a hut about 250 to 300 yards in from the beach and we laid covering fire on it with our M1s and BARs, while two or three men from the squad went around one flank and came at the building from behind. As soon as they were close enough, they lobbed grenades inside, and we all rushed in.

I was as surprised as anyone—nobody was there! Where the shooting came from—I don't know—but it wasn't from the hut. Inside were several straw mats evidently used for sleeping, some kitchen furniture that'd been blown to pieces by the grenade blasts, and several cases, which one member of our squad immediately broke open with a bayonet. With a cry of elation, he raised several bottles of sake in the air. I wasn't much of a drinker, so it made no impression on me, but several of the fellas rushed forward and grabbed two or three bottles of the Japanese rice wine and stuffed them in their packs or carried them in their hands as we left the hut.

Liberating rice wine on Tokashika Shima. *U.S. Army*

Later that afternoon, when we'd settled down and dug in for the evening, the bottles were broken out and passed around. Squad member Governor Bryant said he'd read somewhere that the proper way of drinking sake was to warm it up and serve it in small saucers. We didn't have any saucers, of course, but no one seemed to care. Before long, most of the bottles were empty and several men were lying flat in their foxholes.

During the night, we could hear distant firing, a few flares went up, and there were four or five incoming mortar rounds, but other than that it was real quiet. It probably was a good thing. While several members of the squad seemed to be sleeping, I actually think they were pretty much in a drunken stupor. The night passed without any unusual circumstances and by morning the sake episode was forgotten.

Although we eliminated approximately 600 Japanese and captured 121, our total casualties amounted to only about 250. In addition to the enemy soldiers killed by our men in the attack, however, the Japanese nearby engaged in an unbelievable orgy of self-destruction. In a small valley in the north-central part of Tokashika, nearly 200 Japanese, mostly civilians, killed themselves and each other, rather than face capture. Afraid that the Americans would torture the men and rape the women, fathers had strangled their wives and children, and then blew themselves apart with grenades.

★★★

Having completed our mission, we were loaded again into Higgins boats and transferred to transports waiting at anchorage.[2] We then moved out into the East China Sea.

Our intention upon leaving the Kerama Retto was to put distance between us and those localities where the enemy intensive air attacks were occurring. Unfortunately, the exact opposite happened. As the convoy left the anchorage and within a relatively short period of time, a dozen kamikazes attacked our ships. A destroyer escorting us was sunk and two others were damaged.

That night, our division suffered casualties when suicide planes hit two APAs. A two engine Japanese bomber struck the *Henrico* in the bridge area, starting fires in the superstructure. Almost the entire top echelon of 305th commanders were killed or wounded. Among the dead was Colonel Tanzola, the regimental executive officer. Also quite seriously injured was Winthrop Rockefeller, who later became governor of the State of Arkansas.

This wouldn't be the only time our division suffered casualties from kamikazes during the Okinawa campaign. The troop ships *Monrovia* and *Telefare*, while carrying 77th troops, also were attacked and struck by suicide planes,

JAP MASS SUICIDES APPALL AMERICANS

By Grant MacDonald, Seattle War Correspondent, Ashore on Tokashiki Jima, Ryukyu Islands, March 29... [AP] An appalling pile of civilian Japanese dead and dying, who preferred suicide rather than to face American "barbarians," greeted Yank landing forces on this island today.

Cpl. Alexander Roberts, army photographer whose home is in New York City, was with the first scouting patrol to reach the scene which he described as "the most horrible I ever witnessed."

"We had climbed over tortuous trails leading to the northern end of the island and had bivouacked for the night," he said. "I heard terrible screaming, crying and wailing which lasted into early morning.

"Two scouts went out when it was light to check on the screams. They were both shot. Just before, I had seen six or eight grenade bursts up ahead. Finally we came into the clearing which was littered with dead and dying Japanese, so close together I couldn't walk between them without stepping on them.

"I saw at least 40 women and children strangled with strips of cloth torn from their tattered clothing. The only sounds came from little children who were wounded but not dead. In all there were nearly 200 individuals.

"There was one women who had strangled herself by tying a thin rope around her neck, with the other end tied to a small tree. She had leaned forward with her feet on the ground, pulling the rope tight about her neck until she strangled. What appeared to be her whole family was lying on the ground in front of her, all strangled, and each covered with a dirty blanket.

"Farther on there were dozens of people who had killed themselves with grenades and the ground littered with other unexploded grenades. There were six dead Japanese soldiers and two others, badly wounded.

"Medics took the wounded soldiers back to the beach. I saw one little boy with a big V-shaped gash in the back of his head who was walking around. A doctor told me the child couldn't possibly live and would die any minute of shock. It was terrible."

Roberts said doctors were giving morphine syrettes to the dying to ease the pain.

American litter bearers trying to evacuate wounded Japanese to an aid station on the beach were machine-gunned by a Nipponese soldier hidden in a cave on the trail. Infantrymen put him out of action and the aid work continued.

Japanese who had recovered sufficiently to answer questions told interpreters that Japanese soldiers told them the Americans would violate and torture the women and kill the men. They were amazed when Americans gave them medical aid, food and shelter. One old man who had strangled his daughter was filled with remorse when he saw other women unharmed and well-treated.

Convoy of LSTs under kamikaze air attack off Ie Shima. *U.S. Army*

resulting in additional casualties. These attacks were not as devastating, however, as the losses suffered on the *Henrico*. Colonel Tanzola was an outstanding officer and greatly respected by his men. The 305th Regiment missed him during the remainder of the Okinawa campaign.

In attempting to avoid further kamikaze attacks, our convoy moved further south. We spent each day doing calisthenics and preparing our weapons and equipment for the next action. Everyone spent a great deal of time sharpening bayonets and knives to a razor edge.

At this time, we received word that President Franklin Delano Roosevelt had died on April 12 and Harry Truman now was president. This sent a shock wave through the men aboard ship. Most of us were young, actually not much more than kids. One doesn't think about it much, but many in the Army and Marine infantry were only 18 or 19 years old, and few just 17. A number of us had only recently graduated from high school or quit school to enlist. For us, and even for many men in their 20s, Roosevelt was the only President that we'd ever really known.

We couldn't think of anyone else leading the country. It was startling news. But since we were anxiously anticipating combat, readying weapons, and preparing our harnesses and other accoutrements, the shock soon wore off.

Young we may have been and barely out of childhood, scared, and worried, but still, we were determined to do our best to fight and win. Many of us were too young to vote, too young to legally drink alcohol, but old enough to fight and die for our country.

It was these American boys, many with too large of a helmet hanging down over their ears, and wearing drooping, oversized green fatigues, that gave all they had. They'd measured up when needed, battled their way across the Pacific, and, at the cost of thousands of their lives, bought victory and preserved a way of life that we still enjoy today.

NOTES

1. Hanson W. Baldwin, *Battles Lost and Won: Great Campaigns of World War II* (New York: Harper and Row, 1966), 380.
2. After the Ryukyu campaign was concluded, negotiations concerning the surrender of the surviving enemy forces on Tokashika proved to be an unusual and humorous occurrence. Many Jap soldiers and civilians hadn't been killed by our troops nor had they committed suicide, but rather they'd hidden out in the rugged terrain. For months, the Americans tried to get the Japanese commander to surrender—he led an armed force of about 300 men holed up in the north half of the island. They weren't attacking our troops, but efforts to have them surrender had failed. The Japanese commander, however, offered to allow the Americans to continue to "swim on the beaches" if they stayed away from his encampment in the hills. Eventually he was given a copy of the Imperial transcript announcing Japan's surrender on August 15, 1945. Even then, when capitulating, he brazenly informed his American captors that he could've "held out for another ten years."

Intelligence and Reconnaissance Platoon
306th Infantry Regiment, 77th Division
April 1945, Ie Shima

Harry Sall, Lt. Compton, "I&R" Breuders, Sam Inkeles, "Governor" Bryant
"Moose" MacGregor, "Tater" Ames, Ernie Schaer, "Tex" Barnes, "Chippy" Chippiga
"Lucky" Last, Joe Geiger, "Killer" Funk, "Junior" Cotter, "Knuckles" Crawford, "The Brain" Singer

Eleven of these men trained together at Camp Pickett, Virginia, in the spring of 1944. Lou Ryman also trained at Camp Pickett, but isn't included in this picture. Ernie Schaer joined the platoon as a replacement on Ie Shima. Compton, Breuders, Last, and Funk also were replacements. Nearly everyone had a nickname.

7 IE SHIMA (RYUKYU ISLANDS)

*M*EANWHILE, THE MAIN INVASION of Okinawa had begun two weeks earlier on April 1. Word came that the 77th's next objective, however, would be Ie Shima, a five-mile-long island lying just west off Okinawa's central coast. The island's terrain was quite level, except for the southeast part where an abrupt rocky outcrop known as Iegusugu Mountain, or "The Pinnacle," rose up almost 600 feet. The Japs had three airstrips on Ie Shima, and a primary reason that we were invading was to capture them for use by our planes.

For three days, we watched our ships pound the island with heavy naval artillery. Unknown to our intelligence units, the Japanese had constructed massive defenses on Ie Shima. The entire island was a virtual fortress. It'd been extensively mined, especially the airfields, and Iegusugu Yama was honeycombed by caves, gun emplacements, and other heavily protected defenses.

The Japs, however, had done everything they could to give the appearance that the island had been largely evacuated and was only lightly defended. Our reconnaissance flights failed to show evidence of heavy troop concentrations or any activity on the airfields. The Japs, too, had tried to instill the appearance that the southeast beaches were less heavily fortified than those to the north.

After a careful study of the overall situation, the 77th Division high command decided that the island probably was significantly fortified. My regiment, the 306th, would assault the northwest portion of the island, while the 305th was assigned to the southeast part. The 307th would be held in reserve. Though division headquarters had, for the most part, correctly interpreted the intelligence assessments, they greatly underestimated the number of enemy soldiers on the island. To the 77th's dismay, this became evident as the invasion progressed.

★★★

April 16, 1945, dawned clear and sunny, with a chill in the air and quiet seas. Landing conditions were perfect. The usual announcement came over the loudspeakers to man battle stations and prepare for the assault. We clambered over the side, down the cargo netting, and into waiting LCVPs. We then pulled away and were transferred into LVTs (Alligators). Our landing wave, which would be the first to assault Green Beach, began circling in the rendezvous area.

As warships continued the heavy preparatory bombardment of the beaches, our circle of LVTs inadvertently drifted in too close under the big guns of the *Idaho*. When the battleship fired a volley from a set of batteries, the shock wave rocked our LVT and deafened us. The heat was so intense that it singed our hair and eyebrows, and even raised blisters on some men's faces. We rapidly pulled away from there.

Two battalions of the 306th were scheduled to land on Green Beach, advance diagonally across the island, capture one of the airfields, and then proceed to secure the other airstrips and arrive at the foot of Iegusugu Mountain. Meanwhile, the 305th would hit the southeast beaches, capture the town of Ie, and attack the southern portion of Iegusugu Mountain. Two days after our assault, two battalions of the 307th were scheduled to land east of the 305th's beachhead and join the battle against the Japanese.

We were old hands at this by now, having made landings on Guam, Leyte, and in the Kerama Retto. I went in with the 1st Battalion, which was abreast and west of the 2nd Battalion. We met only light resistance while taking the beachhead, but, of course, meeting "light resistance" still isn't very satisfying to the units participating in the action.

After we left the beachhead and approached the airfields, we encountered land mines. Some of them were huge 500 pound bombs buried tail down in the ground. The Japs had placed small anti-tank mines on the noses of the bombs

Supported by a battleship, American troops in LVT s (Alligators) assault a beach during the Ryukyu campaign. *U.S. Army*

just a few inches below the surface, and then covered them over with dirt and rocks. When armored vehicles drove over the mines, the resulting explosions blew huge holes in them and could completely overturn a tank.

Later in the day, our regiment's 3rd Battalion landed behind us and was kept in reserve. We advanced rapidly toward Iegusugu Mountain at the far end of the

The Japanese on Ie Shima used aerial bombs as mines. Later, the men in this squad were all killed when a mine exploded as they were attempting to disarm it. *U.S. Army*

Amphibious tank destroyed by a land mine near the beach on Ie Shima. *U.S. Army*

On April 18, 1945, (l. to r.) Fred Chippiga, Ray Singer, and Wayne MacGregor proceed along a Japanese tank trap toward the 305th regimental CP. *U.S. Army*

island, only being held up by pillboxes and caves on a small ridge north of the first airfield that we took.

On the second day, April 17, we were ordered to hold our positions. This would allow time for the 305th to drive further northeast and make contact with our right flank.

Early on April 18, our attack jumped off and our front line moved forward around the northern base of the mountain, with my battalion being on the easternmost side of the attack. That morning, our CO (commanding officer) sent me back with a communication to be delivered to the 305th on our right flank. Taking Fred Chippiga and Ray Singer with me, we dropped our packs and set out in a southwest direction across one of the airstrips.

On Ie Shima, the enemy had dug several huge tank traps paralleling and crossing the airfields in order to slow down or immobilize our armored vehicles, making them more convenient targets for Jap artillery and anti-tank guns. Because the anti-tank traps were at least four or five feet deep and afforded men on foot with some protection from artillery and small arms fire, we proceeded down them whenever we could.

When arriving at the 305th's CP (command post), we asked to see the CO. He was pointed out to us and I delivered the message. At the time, a small crowd of 10 or 15 men was crowded around the CO and I couldn't imagine why they didn't spread out, since occasional artillery rounds still were falling in the area. They were talking to a small, weathered, middle aged man, who someone excitedly said was Ernie Pyle, the famous newspaper correspondent.

Having read some of Pyle's war communiques from Africa and Europe in newspapers and magazines, I was anxious to get his autograph. Japanese monetary notes (Yen) had been given to us before we invaded the Kerama Retto, so I took one of the bills out and approached Pyle. He said hello, shook my hand, and was very friendly. When I asked him to sign the Yen note, he readily did so.

I placed the note back in my pocket and later put it in a letter to my mother. She received the letter, but the Yen note was missing. Of course, all of our mail was censored. Apparently, a censor, realizing the significance of a Japanese Yen note signed by Ernie Pyle, had stolen it.

Chippiga, Singer, and I, after delivering the message and receiving a reply for our CO, returned eastward across the airstrip toward our company.

When we arrived, Sergeant Crawford asked us if we'd heard that Ernie Pyle had been killed.

We told Crawford we'd met and talked to him just this morning!

Crawford said they'd heard over a tank radio that Pyle was killed a short time ago, shot through the head by a machine gun bullet.

Pyle was riding in a jeep with Colonel Joseph B. Coolidge, the 305th's CO to whom we'd delivered the dispatch. They were bound for an observation post in an area thought to be secure, when suddenly, machine gun fire struck the

77th Infantry Division
cemetery on Ie Shima.
Andrew Medal

Ernie Pyle's gravesite.
Andrew Medal

vehicle. Pyle and Coolidge jumped out of the jeep and into a ditch. When Coolidge and Pyle raised their heads up to look around, they again drew machine gun fire. The burst missed Coolidge, but struck Pyle in the head, killing him instantly.

Though the area seemed fairly secure, this incident is just another illustration of the character of the Pacific war—there really were no safe areas. Every soldier was in almost continuous danger—from the beachhead supply units and artillery emplacements in the back areas on up to the infantrymen in the front lines.

Pyle's body wasn't recovered for several hours because of continued shooting in the locality. When darkness fell, troops finally were able to reach the site and bring his body back. Pyle subsequently was buried in the 77th Division cemetery on Ie Shima. His gravesite initially was marked with a simple wooden cross similar to that of hundreds of other 77th Division soldiers interred beside him.[1]

Later, after Okinawa was secured, the 77th erected a concrete memorial over the spot where he'd been shot and killed. The inscription on the monument stated, "At this spot, the 77th Infantry Division lost a buddy, Ernie Pyle, 18th April 1945."

★★★

Iegusugu Yama, "The Pinnacle," under artillery barrage. *U.S. Army*

Casualties on Ie Shima already had exceeded what General Bruce and his divisional intelligence staff had estimated beforehand. And, the Pinnacle yet remained in Japanese hands. It loomed up ahead of us—an enormous, forbidding-looking fortress.

Meanwhile, the 305th and 307th were stalemated in their assault on Ie town and taking heavy casualties. Consequently, it was decided that the 306th would launch the primary attack against the mountain. On April 20, the assault began with a 10-minute artillery barrage that we hoped would drive the Japanese from their pillboxes, blockhouses, and caves. When we began our advance, it was apparent the barrage had little, if any, effect upon the enemy deep within the mountain. Immediately, the Japs came out, assumed defensive positions, and opened up a tremendous concentration of fire against us.

Our 1st Battalion platoons advanced primarily by crawling and creeping, keeping our heads down, and firing at the Japs whenever a target of opportunity appeared. By nightfall, the 306th had taken heavy casualties, but had secured a firm hold on the mountain's north face.

General Bruce radioed the overall commander of the Ryuku campaign, Lieutenant General Simon B. Buckner Jr., saying: "Base of Pinnacle completely surrounded despite bitterest fight I have ever witnessed against a veritable fortress."

A War Department observer, in a report commenting on the attack, confirmed Bruce's claim:

> It was the most remarkable thing I have ever seen. The attack looked like a Fort Benning demonstration. I saw troops go through enemy mortar concentrations and machine gun fire that should have pinned them down, but

Attack in progress against the Pinnacle. *U.S. Army*

instead they poured across that field and took the mountain against really tough opposition without even slowing down.

The Pinnacle was honeycombed with tunnels, pillboxes, blockhouses, machine gun emplacements, and trenches. Its numerous natural caves had been dug and expanded further into consolidated defensive positions, some three levels deep and providing numerous access points for defenders to assume firing positions against attackers. In many of the caves that contained artillery pieces, sliding steel doors protected the guns, and railroad tracks had been laid down, allowing artillery to be taken outside, discharged, and then pulled back in for protection.

On April 21, our regimental S-2, Captain Stephen K. Smith, called for volunteers to go with him to the top of Iegusugu Mountain. He wanted to unfurl "Old Glory," letting our men know that the island was being conquered. I happened to be out on patrol at the time and missed the opportunity to go.

One always has thoughts about what he might've or could've done. I know, however, that I would've volunteered in a second to help take our flag up the mountain. Then again if I'd volunteered, perhaps I wouldn't have been around later to write this memoir. In any event, two members of my squad, Junior Cotter and Joe Geiger, both with mountain climbing training, and three other men from our company, volunteered and set out for the summit.

Passing through our regimental lines, they started up the backside of the peak, picking the steepest slope where enemy defenses were less concentrated. As

The Pinnacle from a different perspective. *U.S. Army*

the patrol struggled up the steep incline and scaled a 50-foot cliff, they encountered increasing sniper fire from Japs entrenched all around them. They kept going all the way to the top, unfurling and displaying the "Stars and Stripes." They didn't have a flagpole, so Cotter and others held the banner up for everyone to see. However, enemy fire became so intense that they finally had to drop to the ground. It was unsafe to display the flag any longer. They returned to our company position under continuous machine gun, rifle, and mortar fire. Later, all were awarded the Silver Star for valor.[2]

On this same day, machine gunner Private Martin O. May of the 307th was in a position supporting his regiment's attack. He broke up a Japanese assault with accurate, intense bursts from his .30 caliber machine gun. Facing a second attack of swarming Japs, he threw grenade after grenade into their midst, protecting the withdrawal of his company from an untenable advance position. Despite being severely wounded and with a machine gun rendered useless by enemy mortar fire, he refused to withdraw. He maintained his position, throwing more grenades into the mass of attacking troops, until he was wounded a second time, and fatally.

Later, more than 20 Japs were found lying dead in front of his position. For "his determination and indomitable spirit in the face of overwhelming odds," Private May was posthumously awarded the Congressional Medal of Honor, one of five given to men of the 77th Infantry Division during the Ryukyu campaign. His valiant action was largely responsible for maintaining the American lines at

Climbing up the Pinnacle; the man at right is armed with a flamethrower. *U.S. Army*

This is the view that the Japs had of our troops during our assault (photo taken after the capture). *U.S. Army*

the base of the mountain, from which we shortly continued our successful assault and captured the peak.[3]

During the next several days, our attacks consisted mostly of mopping up operations against isolated caves and dugouts. However, on the evening of April 22 and the early morning of April 23, the Japanese launched a banzai attack against us. They charged into our lines, shooting and throwing grenades, and some even carried spears. They were wiped out, but not before some penetrated our perimeter.

When the mopping up of the Japanese stragglers who'd survived the bitter fighting finally was over, we were loaded onto an LST and left the island on April 26. The casualties in this operation were 4,796 Japanese killed and only 149 captured. Our losses were approximately 200 killed and 1,000 wounded. The fight for Ie Shima was a quick, terrible, convulsive effort by the 77th. Although the battle lasted less than 10 days, up to this time it was the bitterest fighting that we'd experienced—worse than Guam and Leyte.

⭐

NOTES

1.   Andy Medal, by coincidence a resident of my hometown of Grangeville, Idaho, likewise served on Ie Shima, and after the battle took a picture of Ernie Pyle's grave marker. He eventually gave a copy of it to me. It's the photo of the simple white cross included in this chapter.

2.   In recent decades, there has been much controversy over the right to desecrate or even burn and destroy the American flag as an exercise of free speech—a right guaranteed by our Constitution. For my generation and the generations before us, it should be remembered that the "Grand Old Flag" was a special symbol of our country and the precious concept of "Liberty and justice for all." The esteem and respect that we showed it is illustrated by the actions of men like Cotter, Geiger, and the rest of the patrol. By flying the flag, even briefly at that crucial time in the fighting, it lifted the spirits of our troops. It gave them confidence and served to indicate that bunker by bunker, and trench by trench, we were taking the island and winning the fight.

3.   For assaulting and capturing the Pinnacle, the 1st Battalion of the 306th, to which I was attached, received a Presidential Unit Citation. This was the highest award that could be conferred on a military unit. The Department of War's criteria for such a commendation stated: "[T]hat the unit had distinguished itself in battle by extraordinary heroism, exhibiting such gallantry, determination and esprit de corps in overcoming unusually difficult and hazardous conditions, as to set it apart and above other units participating in the same engagement... [I]t must have distinguished itself by conspicuous battle action of a character that would merit the award, to an individual, of the Distinguished Service Cross [our nation's second highest medal for valor]." (Circular 333, Section IV, Dec. 22, 1943)

8 OKINAWA (RYUKYU ISLANDS)

*T*HE TRIP ABOARD THE LST from Ie Shima to the Hagushi beaches, Okinawa, was short. By the next day, we were ashore and waiting for orders to again enter combat against the Japanese.

The Okinawa invasion was conducted by the Tenth Army, comprised of two Corps. The XXIV Corps included four Army infantry divisions—the 7th, 27th, 77th, and 96th. The III Marine Amphibious Corps consisted of the 1st, 2nd, and 6th Marine divisions.

These were veteran outfits, hammered into tough, elite fighting units by past noteworthy campaigns—the 7th at Attu, the Marshalls, and Leyte; the 27th in the Marshalls and Saipan; the 77th on Guam and Leyte; the 96th at Leyte; the 1st Marines at Guadalcanal, New Britain, and Peleliu; the 2nd Marines at Tarawa and Saipan; and the newly organized 6th Marines was made up of many men who'd served in the Marshalls and Marianas.

The invasion occurred on Easter Sunday, April 1, 1945, which was designated as L-day, or in military terminology "Love"-day. The overall operation had the code name Iceberg. Though it's mostly overlooked today, this was one of the great invasions in history, larger in a number of aspects than even the Normandy landing. The distances involved in the Okinawa assault were on a vast scale—ships came from all corners of the Pacific. And, it

William Rouse of the 96th Division died April 1, 1945, during the Okinawa landing. LCT (Landing Craft Tank) dropped the ramp too soon and Rouse drowned when his tank drove off a reef and sank; the other crewmen escaped (photo taken in the Philippines). *Sylvan R. Thompson collection* was the most powerful fleet ever assembled—more than 1,500 ships and over a half million men. The total number of soldiers in troopships or who would be in action on L-day totalled 184,000, which was comparable to the number of American, Canadian, and British troops in the armada that attacked the broader D-day beaches in France on June 6, 1944, landing 150,000 men.[1]

Naval vessels were spread out in every direction, and on every horizon—the troopships alone numbered almost 450. Iceberg's overall commander was Rear Admiral Raymond A. Spruance, while Lieutenant General Simon Bolivar Buckner Jr. led all ground forces. Buckner was a former West Point commandant and the son of a Confederate Civil War hero. While deeply respected, his combat leadership experience was limited to the Army's retaking of Attu and Kiska in the Aleutian Islands during 1943.

The greatest naval artillery barrage of the war was directed at eight miles of the Hagushi beaches in southwest Okinawa. As April 1 dawned, the bombardment lifted with the order to "Land the landing force." The assault waves set out for the beachhead, which was located on the west coast north of Okinawa's principal city, Naha, population 66,000. A casualty rate of 80 to 85 percent was expected in the first day of action (this estimate would've been greater than the Marines' terrible losses during the first 24 hours on bloody Iwo Jima about six weeks earlier).

Two Army divisions, the 7th and 96th, landed in the southern part of the beachhead, while two Marine divisions, the 1st and 6th, came ashore in the north section. The 27th Division was held in reserve, and my division, the 77th, was still busy cleaning up opposition in the Kerama Retto and a smaller nearby group, the Keise Islands. The 2nd Marines would be held in reserve at sea, too, after making a demonstration feint against the southeast tip of Okinawa.

Contrary to every prediction, the troops on L-day went in standing up—there was very little resistance. No one could understand it. By nightfall, 60,000 men were ashore. Joyously, the infantrymen surveyed the friendly beach. It was unbelievable.

One 7th Infantry soldier famously quipped, "I've already lived longer than I thought I would."

The total U.S. casualties for the day were less than 150. Due to good weather and little resistance, our forces moved rapidly during the next two days. The Army divisions drove across the island to the east shore and then turned south, with the 7th Division on the east side of the island and the 96th division to the west. Meanwhile, the 1st and 6th Marines turned northward in a continuous sweeping operation, quickly overcoming mostly light Japanese resistance in the next three weeks and securing the central and northern parts of Okinawa.

The landing had occurred on April Fool's Day and during the next week everyone wondered, "Where was the Japanese Army?"

Rear Admiral Richmond Turner on April 8 radioed Rear Admiral Chester W. Nimitz, the chief naval commander in the Pacific, "I may be crazy but it looks like the Japs have quit the war, at least in this section."

Nimitz's reply was cryptic and prophetic, "Delete all after 'crazy.'"

Our forces would soon discover, indeed, that the enemy still was on Okinawa and in great numbers, with a well-conceived strategy for meeting the invasion. In the southern bulb of the island, over 100,000 Japanese soldiers lay concealed in vast fortifications and caves. The Japanese commander, Lieutenant General Mitsuru Ushijima, and his staff had planned a skillful defense relying upon preserving their forces, rather than exposing them in vulnerable beachhead positions or squandering them in wild banzai attacks. Like his adversarial counterpart, General Buckner, Ushijima had been commandant of his nation's military academy.

The Japanese expected their well-entrenched soldiers and massive artillery, along with swarms of kamikaze planes coming from southern Japan, to inflict such catastrophic and unacceptable losses in American men, ships, and planes that the U.S. commanders would have no choice but to withdraw from Okinawa. And, even if the Americans eventually did prevail on the island, it might sap the will of the United States to undertake an even more costly and horrendous invasion of the Japanese mainland.

On Okinawa, they intended to bleed the Americans white in a protracted slugfest.

The 763rd Tank Battalion attached to the 96th Division moving up on April 1. Note rice paddies and Okinawan lyre-shaped tomb at left. *Sylvan R. Thompson collection*

★★★

As the two Army divisions moved south, they came up against the first serious line of Jap resistance. In a matter of just a few days, the GIs were stopped cold when facing the heaviest Jap artillery barrages of the Pacific war up to that time. Kakazu Ridge was the first of three great defensive lines that the Japanese had prepared on Okinawa. The second and most formidable was the Maeda Escarpment and Shuri defenses, and the final one was based on the hills Yuzu-dake and Yaeju-dake near the southernmost tip of the island.

From April 14 to the 19th, our troops absorbed excruciating losses and were stalemated by the tremendous enemy mortar and artillery fire. Meanwhile, the 27th Division joined the line on the right flank of the 96th. On April 19, General Buckner ordered a great assault against the Jap positions by all three Army divisions—from east to west, the 7th, 96th, and 27th. The jump-off for the attack was supported by an incredible barrage from six battleships, six cruisers, and nine destroyers, as well as almost 700 Marine and Navy planes providing close infantry support. In addition, nearly 30 American artillery battalions on nearby small islands and Okinawa proper hurled additional tons of shells all along the five-mile front. The huge barrage lasted for hours, but when the Army divisions attacked, the Japanese stopped them cold again.

Bombs and shells simply weren't very effective against the massive underground fortifications skillfully prepared by the Japanese. Unless there was a direct hit on a blockhouse, cave, or

A 763rd Battalion tank knocked out on April 4 by Japanese 47 mm anti-tank gun. Inset, upper right, shows anti-tank gun shell holes. One crewman, Holmes Loften, died from burns; the other four men survived. *Sylvan R. Thompson collection*

protected artillery position, the Japs escaped harm and, after a barrage quieted down, they came to the surface prepared to meet advancing GIs and tanks. An example of the dreadfully effective resistance that was put up by the enemy occurred on April 19 when U.S. units assaulted Kakazu Ridge. The stalled American infantry called for support, and a battalion of Sherman tanks was sent up. Of the 30 tanks attacking enemy positions, 22 were destroyed that day by Jap artillery fire and infantrymen carrying explosive charges.

Japanese small-unit tactics at Kakazu Ridge (and elsewhere) focused on separating American tanks from any supporting infantry, and then individually eliminating the armored vehicles. The Japs thought American armored units would attempt to attack through a saddle on the east slope of Kakazu Ridge. Here, they prepared an array of weapons—machine guns, small artillery, and mortars. They planned to wipe out or drive off the infantrymen, isolate the tanks, and then systematically destroy them with 47 mm anti-tank guns. In the rugged terrain of southern Okinawa, tanks advancing without supporting infantry almost certainly faced destruction.

Jap suicide attackers carrying satchel charges or anti-tank mines would scramble under tanks to detonate the explosives, demolishing the undercarriages and often themselves. Satchel explosives, which weren't shaped charges and thus were less effective than other anti-tank ordnance, frequently only disabled a tank by blowing off a tread or causing other damage. However, a disabled tank was an easy target for the Japs' deadly 47 mm anti-tank guns.

The enemy had other well-devised tactics for defending against armor. Jap infantry would creep up close to a tank and throw smoke grenades at it, thereby blinding the tankers' view of the surrounding area. Then they'd spray machine gun and rifle fire at the tank and throw fragmentation grenades, forcing the men inside to close the gun ports and hatches. Jap soldiers then ran up and put satchel charges or anti-tank mines under the treads. When these detonations disabled the vehicle, Jap soldiers climbed on top, pried open a port, and dropped grenades or satchel charges inside.

It became imperative for every U.S. tank, when attacking, to be closely supported by infantry. The enemy tactics worked so well at Kakazu Ridge, however, that the Japs for a time could boast, "Not an infantryman got through." When the ridge eventually was taken, almost 60 of our tanks had been destroyed.

★★★

The big April 19 attack was a failure. Nowhere did we successfully breach the Jap defenses. The irregular terrain and geographical confinement of the combat zone didn't allow for the vast sweeping tank maneuvers that were so successful in Europe. In France, Germany, and the Low Countries, armored columns made quick advances to strike key objectives, while often bypassing pockets of the enemy, which easily could be mopped up later or forced to surrender.

A 96th Infantry Division heavy weapons squad carrying machine gun tripods, barrels, and ammunition up Kakazu Ridge. *U.S. Army*

However, as the commanding general of the 96th Division on Okinawa said: "You can't bypass a Jap because a Jap doesn't know when he is bypassed."

Resistance was strong, casualties were sickening, and the lack of progress was painfully evident. It was obvious that our line would have to be reinforced or a different plan of attack initiated. General Bruce, the 77th's commanding general, had proposed while we still were on Leyte that a landing be made on the south end of Okinawa, away from the main landing beaches and behind the massive Shuri fortifications. After our conquest of Ie Shima, Bruce again broached this plan to General Buckner and cited the 77th's spectacular success when landing behind Japanese lines at Ormoc in the Philippines. The Marines likewise suggested such a landing, although using the 2nd Marines instead of the 77th.

Evidently after much soul searching, Buckner decided to continue the grinding, bloody, straight-ahead advance. He cited various reasons for his decision: he wouldn't be able to provide adequate logistics to units involved in a second front; the proposed southern beachhead was confined by coral reefs, and by steep cliffs, from which the enemy could contain or divert an invasion force; and, the Japanese retained reserve units for the exact purpose of confronting any such landing.

It was known that the Japanese 24th Division and 44th Independent Mixed Brigade were situated in the southern tip of the island, uncommitted and waiting for a time to be used to best advantage. Tenth Army staff officers from both the III Marine and XXIV corps also advised against a new landing.

In the latter part of April, Admiral Nimitz and members of his staff flew to Okinawa, conferred with General Buckner, and agreed with his decision. Accordingly, Buckner sent word to bring up the 1st Marines to relieve the 27th Infantry, which had been severely mauled in two weeks of intense action. Meanwhile, the 77th also was ordered forward to replace the battered 96th in the middle.

The front line, as then established, would include from east to west the 7th and 77th divisions, and the 1st Marines, and the bloody yard by yard advance would continued as before.

☆

NOTE

1. Ian Gow, *Okinawa, 1945: Gateway to Japan* (New York: Doubleday, 1985), 77; James H. Hallas, *Killing Ground on Okinawa* (Westport, CT: Praeger, 1996), 2–3; and Robert Leckie, *Okinawa: The Last Battle of World War II* (New York: Viking, 1995), 49, 61.

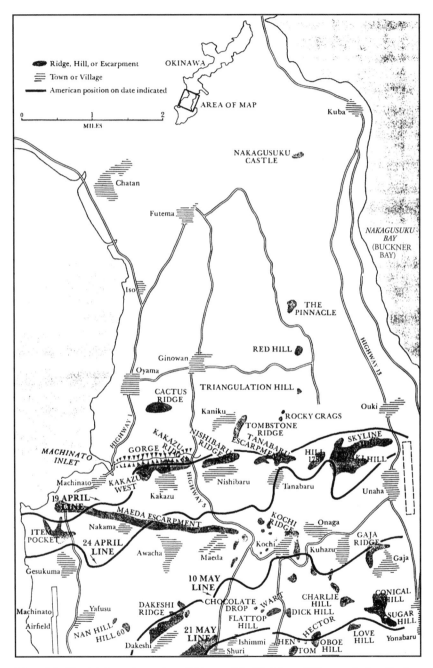

Map of the Shuri defenses in southern Okinawa. Modified from *Okinawa, the Last Battle.*

9 THE MAEDA ESCARPMENT

ON APRIL 29, 1945, my company boarded trucks as the 77th prepared to leave the Hagushi beaches bivouac for the front line. We were packed in as tightly as possible, and the convoy proceeded south on bumpy, dusty Highway No. 5, which extended down the interior part of Okinawa. The huge logistical effort required to sustain the mass of men on the island became clearly evident. We passed numerous tent camps for rear echelon troops, and huge piles of ammunition and supplies mostly covered with camouflage netting.

Then we passed our artillery positions, many of which were in action at the time. Proceeding further south, we began hearing the terrible rumble of artillery explosions in front of us.

Coming to a saddle on a ridge, the trucks pulled off to the side for a rest stop. This was Kakazu Ridge, seized only a few days earlier by the 96th Division, which suffered appalling losses. In just the first day (April 9) when attempting to take this ground, the 383rd Infantry Regiment suffered almost 350 casualties. The Japanese fought the 96th to a standstill, and then on April 12 launched a counterattack, which failed also after they suffered horrendous losses. Like two great Sumo wrestlers, the two sides fought savagely until both were exhausted, battered, and bled of many of their best troops.

For almost two weeks, despite the continuous and horrific combat, there was little change in the lines before the 96th finally succeeded in taking Kakazu Ridge. It'd been at this time that the American high command, realizing the decimated and exhausted state of the frontline divisions, ordered up the 77th and the 1st Marine Division to renew the offensive.

From the ridge where the convoy was parked, we could see the road winding down into a valley and skirting along a hideous, towering escarpment. This was our objective—the Japanese main line of resistance. The sight of it equalled our worst nightmares. This awesome and formidable defensive line was called the Urasoe Mura, or Maeda Escarpment after a small village located just south of the cliff-like projections that we were facing.

Our artillery was pounding the ridge, spreading volleys along it east and west. Between where we stood on Kakazu Ridge and the Maeda Escarpment—a distance of about 750 yards—the landscape was dotted with twisted, broken trees, their bare trunks shattered during the battle. Monstrous, water-filled bomb and shell craters extended endlessly and a thick pall of smoke obscured the sun, casting gloom over the valley.

My first thought was, "This is what hell must look like."

Smoke and dust rose up from the continuous shelling on the escarpment, and the valley was littered with the ugly detritus of war—broken vehicles, trucks, and tanks, shell casings and empty ammunition containers, helmets, empty tin cans and garbage, and dead Japs. In a nearby clearing, there were perhaps 20 or 30 American bodies stacked in a line on top of each other, like cordwood. This immediately reminded me of photographs I'd seen of the Western Front in France during World War I.

Without doubt, this was the most terrible and frightening landscape I'd ever observed. I also realized that in only a few minutes we'd be moving into the front lines. Our orders were to assault the escarpment and take it from the Japs. From our experience, however, we knew that Japs didn't retreat. You had to kill them where they stood, and kill nearly every one them, as few, if any, would surrender. And, they fought with a fury and fanaticism that amazed and shocked us.

In addition to the continuous battlefield noise, we noticed an almost overpowering smell rising from the decaying Japanese corpses lying among the shell holes and along the road. Several thousand must have died during the stalemate at Kakazu Ridge. Also, the massive numbers of Japs and Americans living in foxholes and fortifications had been urinating and defecating in their own positions—they hadn't any choice but to do so. They seldom moved more than a few hundred yards in a week's time. Foul and stank air was part of the battlefield fabric, and the repulsive smell met the nostrils long before you reached the front lines.[1]

As I stared down into the valley, all types of imaginary horrors rose up before my eyes; then I heard our sergeant yelling "Mount up."

The trucks crawled and bumped down the road and across the valley. The vehicles stopped at the foot of a huge, forbidding cliff. Sergeants again began shouting at us to dismount and dig in.

Then the dying began.

Even as we jumped out of the vehicles and started moving out, Jap artillery began inflicting casualties and men were crying out in pain and yelling "Medic, medic."

★★★

To the left, the escarpment's ridgeline dipped into a saddle and rose up to Hill 150, then another saddle further east dropped and rose up to Hill 152. Highway 5 bent east around the escarpment toward the Japanese fortress of Shuri located farther south. Slightly to the right of us stood a giant castle-like projection called "Needle Rock."

At Shuri, the Japanese commander, General Ushijima, had established a huge underground command post. It'd taken thousands of laborers many months to construct what were perhaps the most extensive and formidable fortifications in the Pacific. Dug deeply into the coral and limestone, it was virtually impervious to bombs, naval cannon fire, and artillery barrages. The vast tunnel network included a powerful ventilation system that provided fresh air, and running water was piped in for dining and hospital facilities. A web of tunnels connected the numerous strong points, dugouts, and fortified caves opening out on the forward and reverse slopes of the ridges.

At Shuri and in other carefully prepared defensive positions all across southern Okinawa, some dug as much as 100 feet down, the Japanese were sheltered from the full impact of our bombardments. Except for fortifications that we took from the enemy and could use, our men mostly occupied shallow foxholes, hastily scraped out of the island's hard coral ground, which didn't offer anywhere near the kind of protection that the enemy had.

The Tenth Army's battle line extended across one of the narrowest parts of Okinawa. After relieving the 96th Division, we'd have the 7th Division on our left flank and the 1st Marine Division, who were replacing the 27th, to the right. This three-division front was contained in only a five-mile distance, extending east to west from Nakagusuku Bay to the East China Sea. Also assigned in the area were supporting artillery and service units.

Altogether 90,000 to 100,000 Americans eventually would be crowded into the front during the Okinawa campaign, and, it could be assumed, we faced a similar number of Japs, all of whom were occupying dug-in positions. (If our troops had stood shoulder to shoulder over that five mile distance, they would've had to stand in ranks at least seven deep.)

As badly as the 96th Division was decimated, the 27th Division on the right flank was even worse off. On April 20, it'd suffered 506 casualties, the greatest loss for an Army division on any single day during the Okinawa campaign. After a couple of weeks in the line, for all practical purposes, it'd ceased to exist as an effective fighting force. (On Saipan, the 27th also had suffered severely in taking "Death Valley" and in repulsing a final desperate banzai attack—both of which were major achievements.) Its positions were taken over by the 1st Marine Division at about the same time as we came up to the front. The 27th was attached to the Island Command for garrison duty and participation in smaller actions elsewhere in the Ryukyu campaign.

★★★

When we unloaded from the trucks, we probably moved about 100 to 150 yards up the escarpment to our new positions. It was only another 50 to 75 yards to the top. The Japanese, of course, knew that replacements were taking over the 96th's lines. Wanting to welcome us and make us pay as dearly as possible for entering the battle, they'd intensified their artillery and mortar barrage.

The 77th advanced into the 96th's lines as they withdrew. Most of us moved right into their foxholes or occupied abandoned Japanese positions. The 96th's soldiers were completely exhausted. They'd desperately tried to advance through the saddle between hills 150 and 152 with supporting flame-throwing tanks. Jap soldiers were incinerated in their underground positions, or were flushed out by the hundreds and killed by infantry small arms or machine guns mounted on the marauding tanks. After much fierce fighting, however, the Japanese still held on near the ridgeline and forced the 96th back to the positions we now occupied.

The 381st Infantry Regiment suffered 60 percent casualties, almost 600 of them just in the four days before we took over their positions. Some platoons were down to five or six men. They were so debilitated and demoralized that they left some of their dead behind as they withdrew.

Okinawan tomb. *Melvin C. Lindeman collection*

Our headquarters personnel occupied a concrete Okinawan tomb. Like hundreds of other tombs on the island, it was shaped like a lyre, symbolically representing a woman's womb. A small, tunnel-like entrance led into a main room where the ashes and bones of deceased ancestors were preserved. The tombs could hold 10 to 20 soldiers and were excellent defensive positions, used by both the Japs and us.

Arriving up front, Lou Ryman and I picked a cave where we felt quite safe from the Jap artillery. It started to rain, however, and water dripped on us inside the dugout. Outside, we continued to hear cries from the wounded.

Sergeant Sall then called us over, and ordered us to help the communication section lay telephone lines to the top of the escarpment. Lou and I picked up a reel of phone wire and began unrolling it toward the ridgeline, flinching almost every step of the way as artillery blasts exploded in front, alongside, and behind us. Soon, we approached a sheer cliff where a number of telephone lines were tied to a battered tree

Two infantrymen laying down communication wire. *U.S. Army*

snag. We put the reel down and waited for the communication team to set up the system.

We heard the cry, "Medic, medic." Then, someone yelled at us, "Get over here and help carry this guy down the hill."

Lou and I scrambled over and each of us grabbed an arm and leg of a man who'd been injured in the back. Tripping and stumbling, we carried him down-hill. In a short time we reached the battalion aid station and left him there.

Then, we were told, "Get back up to the top of the hill, they need help."

So, we turned around and started struggling back up toward the base of the cliff. The Jap shelling mostly came from large 105 and 150 mm guns. The noise in our lines was incredible—thunderous, shattering explosions were interspersed with the hideous, soul-wrenching screams of our wounded.

We were positioned just below the top of the escarpment. On the opposite side, that is the southern slope, the enemy occupied their principal pillboxes, caves, tunnels, and blockhouses, which were out of direct sight of our artillery. Another advantage of the Japs' downslope positions was that they could see our attacking infantry and tanks silhouetted against the skyline when we came over the ridge top.

Our immediate objective was the reduction of the enemy positions directly in front of us. For the next three days, it was the most horrifying experience imaginable. We continually attacked and the Japs counterattacked. We shot at the enemy and in turn received fire from them. We threw hand grenades. We dropped satchel charges into caves, dugouts, and pillboxes.

★★★

As they had at Shuri and elsewhere, the Japanese used great ingenuity and ex-pended much labor in preparing their defensive positions on the Maeda Escarp-ment. Tunnels several floors in depth opened into rooms used for hospitals, mess halls, sleeping quarters, and supply storage. These tunnels, too, were intercon-nected with surface pillboxes, blockhouses, and cave openings. Once, one of our men threw several phosphorous grenades into a cave and observed smoke com-ing out at 16 other connected openings on the ridge. Often, tunnel and cave openings that housed artillery pieces had metal doors built into them for protec-tion against counterfire, as we'd already seen on Ie Shima.

Our intense artillery barrages, aerial bombardments, and naval gunfire failed to eliminate the vast enemy positions. Ultimately, the reduction of these fortifi-cations depended on small unit tactics. Our fire teams would pour rifle and au-tomatic weapons fire at a cave opening or blockhouse portal, forcing the Japs to move back deep inside. Then a soldier with a flamethrower sprayed napalm into the opening. Following this, a demolition man ignited a charge and held it for a few seconds before throwing it inside so the enemy wouldn't have time to hurl it back out. In this manner, hundreds, if not thousands, of caves and fortifications

Firing at a Japanese position during "blowtorch and corkscrew" operations. This lightly armored tank destroyer also is fixed with .30 and .50 caliber machine guns. *U.S. Army*

were sealed shut during the campaign, often killing those inside by concussion or suffocation.

Coordination between infantry and tanks, especially those with new flame-throwing equipment, was particularly effective. Typically, rifle squads with satchel charges, BARs, or other automatic weapons assisted the tanks. As a tank enveloped a Jap position with a plume of napalm or fired its cannon point blank into an opening, the enemy retreated back underground. Our infantry then moved down from behind the Jap position, in what the enemy called "straddle attacks." The Japs, having retreated into the deeper recesses of their defensive positions, then were killed, trapped, or cut off by the satchel charges or other explosives thrown in by the infantry. The Japanese were terribly afraid of these tactics, and reportedly believed there wasn't any defensive position, no matter how strong, that couldn't be taken by these means.

These were designated "blowtorch and corkscrew" procedures. Napalm or liquid flame served as the blowtorch, and phosphorous grenades, satchel charges, or other explosives were the corkscrew. Tank-infantry teams were the most effective means of overcoming the Maeda and Shuri defenses. It was done with co-operation, courage, and sacrifice in innumerable small unit actions. Each assault on an enemy position had the potential of becoming a desperate excursion in close quarter combat, resulting in casualties. At any time, Jap soldiers could fire point blank at us or pour out from underground positions.

"Blowtorch and corkscrew" tactics against a Japanese cave. *U.S. Army*

Hour by hour, yard by yard, cave by cave, and pillbox by pillbox, we moved forward taking ground. In the end, it was the individual Marine or Army dogface—with a satchel charge, rifle, or grenade in hand—that made the difference.

★★★

Night was the worst time of all. Japs could be heard moving around near our foxholes. They'd toss grenades and often charged our positions, sometimes resulting in hand-to-hand fights. We'd launch flares, or called in huge illumination flares shot up from our warships located just offshore. When flares suddenly illuminated our area, we often saw Japs coming at us. We'd fire as fast as we could, usually stopping them just outside of our foxholes. On this shattered, ravaged, nighttime battlefield, we'd kneel in our foxholes, rising only when the enemy showed themselves. Over and over again, we'd shoot and club at them, driving them back, until other attackers appeared and again we vented our rage on them.

We lived like beasts in holes that were persistently filled with rainwater. Our soaked clothing, covered with mud, piss, and shit, eventually rotted on our bodies and the soles of our wet boots separated from the upper parts, leaving toes and flesh exposed, with the stockings long since deteriorated.

We blamed the Japanese for our misery, and hatred of them filled our hearts. We somehow failed to realize, that just 50 or 100 yards away, they too were experiencing the same wretchedness. Not all did, though. Some were deep beneath the surface, safe from the incessant shelling. They occupied dry quarters, perhaps three, four, or even five stories underneath the battlefield where, for a time, they were practically impervious to attack.

On our right, the 307th fought savagely for five days, trying to gain control of Needle Rock. Nine times they took it and nine times they were driven back by Jap bayonet and grenade counterattacks. A cliff too steep to climb without aid was a barrier on the approach to Needle Rock. Consequently, the 307th had brought up four 50-foot ladders and Navy cargo nets obtained on the beaches.

In the initial attack, the ladders were set up, reaching to the top of the cliff. Then, volunteers climbed the ladders, pulling up the cargo nets and securing them at the top. These men lay flat against the cliff to avoid enemy machine gun and mortar fire. Then, the platoons began climbing up the cargo netting.

The first nine men going over the top were from Company A. Every one of them was killed or wounded. After several attempts, men finally were able to get on top and throw satchel charges into the pillboxes and blockhouses that were massacring our boys. The casualties didn't deter Company A. By dusk, two platoons were established on top of the escarpment, laying down counterfire at Japanese positions. That night, however, they were all driven back by enemy counterattacks.

Over the years, I've often thought about the sacrifice of the first nine

307th troopers climbing the escarpment.
U.S. Army

men who climbed the cargo nets and charged the Jap positions on the slope beyond. I don't know their names, but I can imagine the sergeant saying something like, "Kowalski, get up that ladder. Stop that firing."

Then, Kowalski's gone. They don't hear from him.

"Johnson, you're next, up the ladder."

Nothing's heard from Johnson.

Then, "Hansen," "Majeski," and so on.

One after another, each climbed the netting and disappeared over the top—all were casualties. None complained or dissented—they had no thought but to do their duty by getting to the top and fight the best they could, even if it meant sacrificing their lives so that the rest of the platoon could follow behind them. My God, what courage! What selflessness! Where did we get such soldiers? Our country truly was fortunate at that time to have men who'd do things like that.

The 307th asked the divisional engineers to fill a water truck with a thousand gallons of gasoline and drive it up as close as possible to the top of the escarpment. When the truck arrived, several hundred feet of hose was attached to the distributor valve. The hose then was dragged over the ridge top and they pumped gasoline into Jap caves and underground fortifications. After the gas was distributed and the tank emptied, satchel charges and phosphorous grenades were thrown into the enemy positions, blasting them into fiery ruins.

Slowly, as our lines gained more ground, flamethrowing tanks were brought up through the saddle between hills 150 to 152. They finally worked over the Jap positions, allowing us to gain some control of the ridge top.

★★★

Gradually, we took over the escarpment. On our right flank, Private Desmond Doss, a medic attached to Company B of the 307th, performed an outstanding act of courage. Doss was a Seventh Day Adventist and a conscientious objector. He wouldn't fire a gun, but was one of the bravest men in the division. Time after time, as the 307th struggled to take the top of the escarpment and was involved in constant attacks and counterattacks, Doss remained with the wounded men, administering to their needs.

When everyone else withdrew to avoid Jap grenades, machine guns, and mortar fire, he'd stay up front, tying the wounded into a rope litter that he'd prepared to let them down the side of the cliff. It's estimated that in one day he personally cared for 75 wounded men in this manner. For this, he was awarded the Congressional Medal of Honor.

Also, it's noteworthy that eight company commanders in the 1st Battalion of the 307th were wounded in little more than a day. The 1st Battalion went up to the escarpment with about 800 men and seven days later came back with only 324.

Each night, Japs carrying demolition charges and land mines tried to infiltrate along our entire regimental front. The attempts usually were made in squad or platoon strength. I personally wasn't involved in any hand to hand fighting, but some of our men did grapple with the enemy in the night.

You'd hear yelling, scuffling, and maybe a shot, then someone shouting, "I got the son-of-a-bitch!"

The next morning, a dead Jap would be lying outside of a foxhole.

The forward slopes of the escarpment had been cleared of the enemy in fierce fighting, but Jap machine gun and mortar fire on the reverse slopes was almost as bad. As we attempted to move forward, the Japs operated from caves and pillboxes behind us that we'd missed in our attacks. Only by sending tank-infantry teams back in the face of intense enemy automatic weapons and mortar fire were we finally able to eliminate these isolated enemy positions.

In the center of the 77th's line, just below the escarpment where I was located with the 306th, Jap artillery fire was incessant. We'd become experts at identifying approaching shells by their peculiar sounds. The heavy stuff from 105 and 150 mm cannons came in with a roar, sounding something like a train barreling down railroad tracks right at you. When hearing this, a man out in the open often had time to dive into a foxhole before the round hit and exploded.

A particularly terrifying aspect of heavy artillery fire, however, occurred when Jap gunners fired regularly spaced rounds at us. The first round might hit 200 yards away, the next at 150 yards, the third at 100 yards, and the fourth at 50

Enemy blockhouse on the Maeda Escarpment. An American M1 Carbine rifle lies at right.
U.S. Army

yards—now you were cowering in your foxhole, trying to get as low as possible and wondering if the next round would fall right on top of you.

One of the most frightening weapons was the monstrous 320 mm spigot mortar. Its 675 pound round made a shrill screaming sound as it ascended. It easily could be seen, too, looking like an oil barrel falling through the sky. It caused a fearful eruption when it struck.

Short range artillery—such as 37, 47 and 75 mm cannons—fired flat trajectory rounds that came with a scream and a whistle, and were on you almost immediately. In fact, we often heard the whistle and scream after the shell actually had gone by and exploded. If you heard the whistling scream, it usually meant you were all right because the round had detonated elsewhere.

The terror of waiting for incoming artillery shells to strike was sheer agony. Close-by blasts shocked your entire consciousness and made your ears hurt. It sent you into a quivering state as you hugged the dirt in your foxhole and prayed, prayed, and prayed that the next round wouldn't get you. This situation was even worse after a direct hit on a nearby foxhole killed the occupants, splattering blood and pieces of flesh, intestines, and bones on men in other foxholes. I believe any man who's been in a heavy artillery barrage will say it's the most terrible thing endured during war.

On Okinawa, we faced the Japanese 32nd Army, which had more concentrated artillery pieces and mortars than any other Japanese combat organization that we fought against in the Pacific. Not only did the enemy have a large number of cannons on Okinawa, but they used them more effectively than in other campaigns. For the only time in the Pacific war, Japanese artillery was under a unified command. Much of this artillery was of heavy caliber. Counting numerous naval coastal guns, they had more than 300 artillery pieces of 75 mm or larger. They also used large mortars, including 88 mm types, and twenty-four of the huge 320 mm spigot mortars.

Unfortunately for us, Okinawa also had been a training ground for their artillerists. The guns in their most formidable defensive positions, such as the Maeda Escarpment, Sugar Loaf, and the Chocolate Drop, had long been zeroed in for maximum effect against attackers.

★★★

It wasn't just the frightful, ear-splitting shelling, however, that terrified us. It was everything about being in battle—the rain, mud, filth, flies, smell, blood, and death. It was the dysentery that caused you to accidentally shit your pants. It was seeing your buddy killed, his body smashed or torn to pieces. It was being hungry, thirsty, lonely, and deeply afraid of what was out there in the dark. It was the trembling when a lieutenant told you to move out and knowing you were going to get shot at.

On several occasions when under fire, I lay shaking on the ground, trying to squeeze my cold body into every crack and crevice in the earth, making myself as small as possible. I thought, "Why me? God, what have I done to cause you to want me to die? Why, oh God, why me?"

On the Maeda Escarpment, I saw men come down from the cliffs crying and swearing that they wouldn't go back, it was more than they could face. In 10 minutes, however, they were scrambling up over the rocks and slopes, moving forward again into the maelstrom of fire.

☆

NOTE

1. If you've driven by a large cattle feedlot, you have an idea as to what the odor was like.

10 JAPANESE COUNTERATTACK

*F*OR THREE TERRORIZING DAYS, we would endure the worst continuous Japanese shelling of the war as we lay in foxholes on the Maeda Escarpment. We swore that artillery was the invention of the devil. When subjected to it hour after hour and lying in a foxhole holding back screams, sometimes I wanted to yell, "Stop, stop, stop!" at the top of my lungs.

On May 3, we were told to expect the Japs to launch a massive all out counterassault the next morning. That evening and during the early morning hours of May 4, the 77th Division, as well as the 7th Division on our left flank, was subjected to the heaviest enemy artillery barrage of the entire Pacific conflict. Colonel Stephen Hamilton, regimental commander of the 307th, had served with the 77th Division in France during World War I and fought in the great Meuse-Argonne offensive.

He later said of the shelling we received: "Except for that terrible barrage on the Champagne front in 1918, in which the Germans tried to wipe out the French forces, last night was the worst shelling I have ever experienced."

In the Japanese preparation for the assault, over 4,000 shells landed in our regimental area in little more than 24 hours. The Japs' 24th Division, a fresh but battle hardened organization, would lead the attack on the 77th. Until only recently, General Ushijima had been holding the 24th in reserve, deep behind the battle lines. These veterans of duty in Manchuria, bolstered by new recruits on Okinawa, had been resting and preparing for the time when their combat experience and 14,000 men were most needed. That time was now!

Lieutenant General Isamu Cho, second in command on Okinawa, had persuaded Ushijima that the occasion was right for a counterattack. This was done over the protests of a more realistic staff officer, Colonel Hiromichi Yahara. Despite some misgivings, Ushijima, too, decided that the time had arrived.

The 306th was given estimates that the attacking Jap units in our front would consist of at least a battalion of three complete companies, and possibly a second battalion, together with supporting armor from the Jap's 27th Tank

Regiment. The enemy's overall plan was to throw the main strength of the attack against the 77th Division in the center of the line. After breaking through our defenses, the Japanese then intended on turning west behind the American lines, thus cutting off and isolating the 1st Marine Division on our right flank. We were informed that the enemy would start the assault by sending up red flares.

★★★

Just before dawn on May 4, two red flares shot up in front of our lines. We laid grenades and ammunition clips on our foxhole parapets and fixed bayonets. I stared into the darkness trying to pick out any sign of movement.

When dug in at night, we'd learned to shoot only when Japs were fully in our gun sights because muzzle flashes gave away our location, which might result in an ambush or assault on our foxholes. In fact, when Japs came at us in the dark we usually threw grenades at them.

This morning, however, the enemy began coming across the broken ground toward us as dawn broke. Foggy conditions, though, made it difficult to see at any distance in front of our lines. We stared into the glare of the rising sun, squinting and trying to pick out whatever might be out there in the mist.

...Casualties in Okinawa Drive

By George McWilliams...May 6 (Sunday).—(I.N.S.)—Fleet Adm. Chester W. Nimitz announced today that the invasion of Okinawa thus far has cost [to May 3]... 2,337 soldiers and marines killed, 11,432 wounded and 514 missing in action. Navy casualties as of May 2 were 5,551 killed, wounded or missing...

Japanese ground casualties through May 4 were listed as 33,462 killed and 700 captured, meaning that nearly 15 Japs have died for every American killed in the bitter struggle raging on the island, 325 miles south of Japan.

Three thousands of the Japs were slain Friday when the enemy launched a general tank-supported counterattack in the southern sector of the flaming battle line...

The Jap drive was aimed principally at positions held by the Seventh and 77th Infantry Divisions ...

Next morning Lt. Gen. Simon Bolivar Buckner . . .took advantage of the enemy's disorganized state by ordering an advance on the right flank which brought leathernecks of the First Marine Division to Hill No. 187, east of the Asa River mouth and only a mile and half north of Naha.

The hard fighting devildogs also opened an attack against another hill north of Shuri where strong Jap emplacements and fortified cave positions have been holding up the American advance in a large sector.

Suddenly, there was motion—wraith-like Jap figures were coming toward us. Six, seven, eight, nine, or more khaki-clad, squat soldiers were advancing methodically toward us through the fog, all in a skirmish line and moving at a slow trot. They broke out of the mist about 100 yards away with rifles held in front at the ready. They jogged slowly toward us.

"Hold your fire," someone shouted. "Let them get close enough so that we won't miss."

As they trotted across the open ground, we could see bayonets on their rifles and the gleam of their eyes. One wore glasses. When they were about 20 or 30 yards away, Sergeant Ames yelled, "Let 'em have it!"

We opened fire. I zeroed in on the one wearing glasses. Within seconds half had fallen. Several of the others still were standing, but you could see bullets hitting them. Then they all were down. It was like shooting ducks in a gallery. Those 10 or 12 men, however, showed incredible bravery. They must've known they didn't have much chance of reaching our lines. Yet they kept coming at a trot with their rifles held in front, trying to close with us. When examining the bodies, we found several had been carrying American C rations.

★★★

In regard to the overall Japanese offensive, the enemy fought fiercely while ignoring huge casualties. In pressing forward against the 77th, they made their deepest penetrations. In the area bordering Highway 5 between Kochi and Maeda, where the 306th was dug in, individual grenade battles and machine gun and small weapons exchanges continued all morning.

Military historian Major Roy E. Appleman later stated in the official history of the XXIV Corps: "Penetration was made in that area to the regimental command post of the 306th Infantry, where, in heavy fighting, about ninety of the enemy were killed."[1] Here, we shattered this prong of the Japanese assault and stopped their forward progress.

As Japanese units attacked over the rolling hills east of Maeda, the 77th's artillery was brought to bear and destroyed many of them. The nine enemy tanks supporting the attack were all knocked out by artillery or bazooka fire from the infantry. The Japanese, as daylight brightened, were caught out in the open and simply slaughtered, adding to our division's toll of enemy dead. (The 77th later estimated, mostly from body count, that from April 29 when we moved into the line and until May 6 when the Jap assault had

OKINAWA JAPS IN BIG ATTACK

[AP] Tenth Army attacked heavily along most of the Okinawa front…against continued stiff resistance from cave and pillbox-entrenched Nipponese…

The 77th Division's attack in darkness was the most spectacular push. The doughboys were met by intense small arms fire. After daylight, the Japanese counterattacked, trying to drive the Yanks back out of Taira. But the assault was repulsed and Bruce's infantry pushed on south from the village toward Shuri…

stalled, our division killed approximately 3,500 Japanese. Pointedly, no prisoners are reported taken—zero.)

When the enemy attacked over the hilly area in front of Maeda and along Highway 5, their artillery dropped smoke shells into the low ground, concealing their infantry from our view. This enabled them to get into our lines, causing a great number of casualties. Unable to see them, we were ordered out of our foxholes and directed to attack them with small arms and bayonets, until they finally withdrew to the south.

Either out of desperation or shear audacity, the Japs had come at us right through their own artillery and mortar barrages, disregarding their own safety. Some of our companies had put out wire barriers, but the Japanese simply dropped their packs, crawled over and through the entanglements, and came at our men in bayonet charges.

As they appeared out of the smoke, our machine guns opened up and decimated their lines. Their attempted penetration was stopped, but heavy fighting continued for most of the day. The Japanese again fired smoke into their forward positions, but this time to help their men withdraw. In my area, we followed them into the smoke and killed most of them. They left approximately 250 dead, plus two tanks that'd been knocked out.

By May 8, the massive attack was over and they'd retreated back into the strong defensive positions that they'd occupied before the assault. It was obvious that the counteroffensive had completely failed.

★★★

The 1st Battalion of the 306th began advancing south along a ridge that ran parallel to Highway 5. About this time we heard that the war in Europe had ended and Hitler was dead. Celebratory volleys of artillery fire and shooting erupted all along the American lines.

Sometimes we picked up on the news when talking to men in tank destroyers in the late afternoon or evening. On their tank radios, they received the Armed Forces Network, Tokyo Rose programs from Japan, and other broadcasts. It was interesting to listen in. However, the tanks usually pulled back behind our lines at night.

For the infantryman, tanks actually were a mixed blessing. Their firepower was much needed to overcome caves and bunkers; however, each tank usually required a squad of foot soldiers for protection against Jap infantry. We didn't like guarding tanks in action because they drew the enemy's attention. Also, if Jap artillery and anti-tank fire became too intense, tanks simply pulled back behind our lines, often leaving the infantry up front exposed to hostile fire.

On about May 8 or 9, Sergeant Ames called our squad together and said we were going out to an observation post (OP) that'd been established a day or two earlier. He told us to get our gear ready, but didn't explain what the purpose of the patrol was or even exactly where we were going. Ames always believed more in action than conversation.

We started out in a southeast direction along the ridgeline past hills 150 and 152. Then we turned south above where Highway 5 bent around the ridge and continued toward Shuri. We approached a rocky outcropping with a saddle between two points, probably a distance of 20 to 30 yards. Ames had been told that we needed to be careful when crossing this area. We might receive machine gun fire.

When Ames said something, we listened. Though a man of few words, he was courageous, intelligent, and an excellent leader. We prepared to cross one at a time. Ames pointed at me first and motioned for me to go. I lowered my head and burst out of the rocks into the open with my rifle in my right hand, my body bent over and my legs pumping like a fullback breaking through the line of scrimmage into the secondary. Machine gun slugs ripped and snapped by me, but I made it without being hit. Ames then sent each man individually running through the open gap, until all were safely across, and then he too sprinted to where we were waiting.

We now were below the ridgeline where the machine gunner couldn't see us. We followed along in a southerly direction until coming to a large rock where the observation post had been established. We crawled forward into a depression underneath the overhanging rock, where some men squatted and peered through binoculars to the southeast at the Japanese lines.

From the observation post, Highway 5 could be seen meandering on the valley floor in a southerly direction towards Shuri. We could see the hills above Highway 5 to the left and directly to the south stood the Chocolate Drop. A little further east we observed Ishimmi Ridge, and then an open plain stretching about 2,500 yards to the town of Shuri.

One of the men at the OP was a naval artillery liaison officer. I still remember him calling in target coordinates to a battleship, and hearing a Navy gunner replying on the radio, "Battery one, salvo, on the way."

Then the liaison officer shouted "Splash" as the shells hit Shuri Castle. He gave adjustments for the next salvo, "Elevation up 100 yards, right 100 yards," until the shells fell exactly on target.

We remained at the outpost for only about 15 or 20 minutes. Across the valley to the south, fire and smoke rose up from where our artillery was hitting the Jap lines. We also watched three F4U Corsairs attack with rockets. As one of the Corsairs dived toward a target, it exploded and disappeared in small pieces from sight. We concluded that the fighter plane, when coming in low for the rocket attack, had slipped under our artillery barrage and one of our shells had hit it.

Sergeant Ames, after an informational exchange with the men in the OP, said we were heading back to our company area and to follow him. When reaching the exposed area in the rock outcropping, Ames again planned to send us across one at a time. He went first and made it. I followed, and although shot at, I wasn't hit.

Ernie Schaer from Lake Oswego, Oregon, a new replacement who'd joined our platoon on Ie Shima, was next. Midway across, he suddenly dropped as if hit by an axe. Ames, Joe Geiger, and Junior Cotter, disregarding the enemy machine gunner, all ran out, grabbed Ernie, and pulled him across. Though exposed to continuous bursts, they made it safely. We could tell that a heavy Nambu 7.7 machine gun was firing at us because it literally tore apart and smashed to pieces a rock ledge next to where Ernie was hauled to safety.

Both Geiger and Cotter were breathing hard after performing this rescue.

"God, that was close," I told Junior.

A bullet had hit Ernie squarely through the shoulder and lower neck, but missed the artery, spine, and trachea when cleanly passing through him. It was a miracle, but still, he was hurt badly, going into shock, and bleeding profusely. As we began applying medical aid, he turned ashen gray, broke into a heavy sweat, and seemed to have difficulty breathing. I pulled him further down the trail a few feet to a grassy, level spot.

"Oh, Jesus," he said. "Help me, goddamn it, Mac, it hurts."

Kneeling beside him, I took his hand and started talking to him: "Calm down, Ernie, we're going to get you out of here."

I continued, "You're not going to die, hell, you're going home, you're going to make it fine, you lucky bastard."

I didn't feel all that confident about his chances because his eyes were beginning to roll back in his head and he looked real bad, but I wasn't going to let him know it.

We put pressure on the entry and exit holes to stem the bleeding and applied gauze bandages as carefully as we could. We tried, however, not to cut off the air that he was sucking in and out of his neck. We also broke open a morphine syrette and gave him a shot, followed by a second one a few minutes later. We took turns carrying him back toward our company area, where we managed to have someone come out with a stretcher and carry him the rest of the way to an aid station. Ernie was taken back to the beach, and eventually evacuated to the States and given a medical discharge.[2]

NOTES

1. Roy E. Appleman, *The XXIV Corps in the Conquest of Okinawa* (Washington, DC: Historical Division, War Department Special Staff [WDSS], 1946), 316–17.
2. After the war, when Ernie returned to Lake Oswego, Oregon, I used to hear from him occasionally.

11 THE CHOCOLATE DROP

*A*FTER TAKING THE MAEDA ESCARPMENT and fighting south down the ridgelines parallel to Highway 5, the 306th faced a diminutive, unusual-looking hill quaintly called the Chocolate Drop. No trees and little, if any, vegetation grew on it. It was just a little brown protrusion looking like a chocolate drop resting on a slightly tilted saucer. It didn't seem possible when observing it, but the Chocolate Drop was one of the most formidable Jap fortresses on Okinawa.

It was a densely honeycombed citadel and ideally situated to counter ground assaults. There were no trees or shrubs for hundreds of yards around to offer cover for advancing troops. The ground in the lower part of the saucer and to the northwest was marshy and unsuited for tanks. And, to make things even worse, one of the largest mine fields on Okinawa surrounded it.

Seemingly impregnable, the Chocolate Drop was anchored to two other heavily fortified terrain features—Wart Hill in the middle, and Flat Top to our left, a long ridge running southeast. Consequently, from west to east, the Chocolate Drop, Wart Hill, and Flat Top all were mutually supportive. And as always,

Chocolate Drop Hill under attack by tanks and the 306th Infantry Regiment. *U.S. Army*

Southern Okinawa.

the Japanese defensive posture would be the same—heavily dug in soldiers, wielding tremendous firepower and willing to fight to the death, were occupying powerful, well-integrated strongholds.

Colonel Hiromichi Yahara, the highest-ranking enemy staff officer to survive the Okinawa battle, later stated that Chocolate Drop Hill was of critical importance in the Japs' island defenses. It was key to protecting an entire chain of fortresses in front of Shuri. If it fell, then other redoubts near Shuri would topple one by one like dominoes. Accordingly, it was defended with a fierceness equalling any of the enemy's most determined and desperate actions in the Pacific war.[1]

Seizing the Chocolate Drop was the 306th's objective. The 2nd and 3rd battalions began the attack on May 11, while our 1st Battalion was held in reserve.

306th Infantry troops firing at Japanese positions. The man at near right holds a BAR that has been stripped of its front bipod and top carrying handle to reduce weight, a common practice in World War II. *U.S. Army*

The withering fire coming from the Chocolate Drop and Wart Hill stopped them short.

Then, for three continuous days, all three battalions of the 306th joined in, pounding and assaulting the Chocolate Drop, Wart Hill, and Flat Top, but we didn't succeed in taking any of them. When attacking any specific point, intersecting enemy mortar, machine gun, and small arms fire coming from reverse slope positions shattered us. Jap firepower simply was devastating the regiment and we were suffering unthinkable losses.

Any former 77th infantryman will forever remember the Chocolate Drop with horror. In attack after attack, grenades, mines, artillery shells, mortar rounds, and bullets tore and ripped our ranks apart, reducing companies to platoons, platoons to squads, and squads to only a handful of men. In the 2nd Battalion, Company E was reduced to 24 men, Company F to 13, and Company G to 42, for a total of 79 riflemen. When at full strength before coming overseas, of course, each of these companies would've had 200 to 210 men. The 3rd battalion likewise suffered severely.

With the ranks so severely thinned, it became necessary for regimental headquarters to order a regrouping of the 2nd and 3rd battalions into one battalion. When constituting this reorganization, however, it became evident that there weren't even enough men left to fill a single battalion. Consequently, they were formed into a company instead.

Supported by nine tanks, yet another attempt was made to take Flat Top, but all of the tanks were hit and knocked out. As a consequence, forward progress came to a halt. Having lost nearly 600 dead and wounded infantrymen in four days, the 306th was relieved on the morning of May 15 by the 307th. The remaining men were sent back behind the lines for a much deserved rest.

★★★

To many Army and Marine veterans of Okinawa, implicit in their memories even today are those terrible ridges and hills with incompatible names that echo down from decades ago—Chocolate Drop, Love Hill, Strawberry Hill, Sugar Loaf—names totally incongruous with the actuality of those terrible places.

Early in the battle, while the 1st Battalion was still in reserve, Gene Funk, Junior Cotter, myself, and three other men from our company had been sent to the 2nd Battalion to act as litter bearers because of the extraordinary number of casualties. When acting in this capacity, I earned my second Bronze Star with a V for valor. Funk and Cotter also were cited for heroism during the attack on the Chocolate Drop and received similar awards. The citation read in part:

> For heroic achievement in connection with military operations against the enemy at Okinawa R.I. on 15 May 1945. Because of unusually heavy casualties, a litter squad of six men was sent to the 2nd Battalion. MacGregor was assigned to this squad. He cheerfully and willingly helped to evacuate wounded in the face of heavy enemy mortar and sporadic machine gun and sniper fire. At the height of the action, word was received that a soldier had been severely wounded in the vicinity of "Chocolate Drop Hill." Although fully aware of the danger involved in reaching the wounded man, MacGregor volunteered to evacuate him… In spite of great personal danger, MacGregor made way to the wounded man and transported him to the rear through continuous heavy enemy fire. MacGregor's courage and determination under enemy fire reflected great credit upon himself and the military service.

I mention this not for any kind of self-aggrandizement, but to delineate what kinds of actions merited awards. Luck often decided who received medals. Many acts of heroism never were observed and consequently weren't given any recognition. Furthermore, only commissioned officers could make recommendations for medals. An enlisted man might see and report an award-worthy act, but it was up to an officer to determine whether or not to submit an application for granting a citation.

FOE RESISTS U.S. ADVANCES BEFORE NAHA

By Edward Thomas, United Press War Correspondent. Aboard Admiral Turner's flagship off Okinawa—(UP)—Japanese mortar, sniper and artillery fire stalled the American advance in heavy fighting on southern Okinawa today.

Marines battling in the northern approaches of Naha, the capital city, and soldiers punching at the defenses of Shuri were brought virtually to a standstill by strong enemy resistance.

The Japanese used a variety of weapons—including the anti-tank "Molotov cocktail"—against the two marine and two army divisions attacking along the five-mile Naha-Shuri-Yonabaru defense line.

The Sixth marine division dug in on the northern rim of Naha, a rubbled community with a pre-invasion population of 65,000.

Ahead of the leathernecks lay wide mud flats of the Asato river valley. A crossing would take the marines practically under the muzzles of Japanese guns.

The Sixth repulsed an attempted counter-landing by Japanese north of the estuary. Marines destroyed six to 10 enemy boats on a reef, killing approximately 40 Japanese.

In the center of the American line, the 77th army division reported slight local gains up to 200 yards in stiff combat which failed to dent the main defenses of the town of Shuri, lying midway between the coastal towns of Naha and Yonabaru.

To receive a medal, a man normally had to do something that went above and beyond what was expected of him in performing his normal, anticipated duties as a fighting soldier. For example, a rifleman wiping out a fortified position and killing several enemy soldiers in the process might not receive a citation. It was an action expected of him as a soldier. By way of a specific example, when Sergeant Crawford shot and killed the three Jap machine gunners on the run on Guam, he didn't receive a medal. However, say if he'd been out of ammunition, sprinted and caught them, and then captured or killed them with his bare hands and a bayonet, he might've earned a citation. In my case, running out in front of the lines and carrying back a wounded man under fire wasn't something expected of us. In today's language, it wasn't in our "job description." It was an action "above and beyond the call of duty."

Every combat veteran knows, however, that medals often reveal little about a soldier's conduct in battle. Most heroic acts weren't seen or reported, and too many decorations went to officers in regimental or divisional duties behind the front lines—a situation with fellow officers wittingly or unwittingly conspiring to "You write me up, and I'll write you up." Medals were sparingly given in the infantry except Purple Hearts for combat casualties, and we got plenty of those.

Destroyed armored vehicles at the foot of Sugar Loaf Hill, taken by the 6th Marine Division on May 18, 1945. *U.S. Army*

So, medals often didn't mean that much to us. However, when memories of the Chocolate Drop and Sugar Loaf later rang in our consciousness, just knowing that we survived these places was reward enough.

★★★

When the 307th replaced us on May 15, they advanced in column—from east to west, the 3rd, 2nd, and 1st battalions. As the battalions moved forward, I encountered an officer with the 307th's Company K on the far left, and he requested that I stay with them as a rifleman since they were short of men. Meanwhile, Funk, Cotter, and the other three men from my company serving as litter bearers had returned to our outfit.

Consequently, I advanced with the men of Company K as they moved up on the left. By noon we were nearing the Chocolate Drop. We pushed ahead under heavy fire about 300 yards and took the bottom slopes of Flat Top. We then dug in a short distance below the ridgeline. All attempts to advance over the ridge top were met by a wall of enemy rifle and machine gun bullets. Grenades were hurled back and forth over the crest of the hill as we fought for control of the top.

The Japs were sheltered in caves, tunnels, and trenches on the reverse slope. In close combat, a hand grenade was the most effective weapon against these types of positions. Grenades are relatively heavy, however, and we could carry only so many in our grenade pouches, pockets, and backpacks. Some soldiers carried additional grenades by looping the handles over their ammunition belts or by taping them on. This wasn't a good idea. When passing through brush or crawling on the ground, a pin might be pulled out, and if the priming handle were somehow released, the grenade would explode. Also, it took too much time in critical situations to cut a taped grenade loose from a web belt or shoulder harness.

Consequently, boxes of grenades were lugged up by hand to our front positions just below the ridgeline. There were 40 fragmentation grenades in a box. We took the grenades right out of the box and threw one after another over the top at the Japs on the other side. They were doing the same to us. It was a ruthless killing match. My arm actually got tired from throwing so many grenades. Fortunately, the hill wasn't composed of hard coral, thus we were able to scrape out shallow foxholes in the soil for protection. Though the hillside was too steep to really adequately dig in, to some extent the incline protected us; many of the Jap grenades thrown or rolled down at us bounced on past our foxholes before exploding.

Some men were kept busy just hauling up the heavy grenade boxes from the company CP. At this juncture, one of the amphibious tractors had worked its way forward, stopping several hundred yards back behind a rise to keep out of sight of the Japs. Any kind of vehicle out in the open would draw enemy fire. We knew the Alligator had come to evacuate the wounded, but a man was sent to ask the crew to go back and bring up a load of grenade boxes.

Each time we advanced to the ridge top and tried to get over, rifle and machine gun fire drove us back. Although it'd rained during the night, the day turned hot, and we were sweating and worn out from fighting, carrying grenade boxes, and tossing grenades. Japs could be heard talking to each other on the other side of the hill and then we'd receive mortar fire. Someone yelled that the lieutenant was down. He died a short time later. Only one officer remained in the company at that time. After nightfall on May 15, we fought off several Jap counterattacks.

★★★

The next day, Company K and other elements of the 307th's 3rd Battalion continued to assault Flat Top and the Chocolate Drop. The actual killing ground wasn't so much on these hills, as it was down below and between them. Tanks were lost to mines in the flat. Here, the ground was wet and marshy, the footing poor, and it slowed everyone down. With no cover when crossing this open area, we were targets for Jap snipers, machine gunners, and mortar crews. The enemy, of course, had planned it that way—the Chocolate Drop, Wart, and Flat Top complex was a nightmare for attacking infantry.

When reaching the steep hillside and trying to get to the Jap caves and blow them shut, the enemy again rolled grenades down on us. Then, they hit us with knee mortars and intense machine gun fire. We finally reached the north side of the crest of Hill 140 (Flat Top), but again weren't able to go over the top. Every attempt to do so met heavy, devastating resistance.

Consequently, men began working their way around the bottom of the steep ridge-like eminence, while other units assaulted the Chocolate Drop to try and stop the deadly fire coming from it and Wart Hill. When the shooting from these positions was reduced—even though we didn't succeed in taking them at that time—our troops worked their way around the Chocolate Drop, sealing off caves with flamethrowers and satchel charges. Finally, we took the north slopes of Chocolate Drop. Our dead below it reminded one observer of a skirmish line lying down to rest.

The scene was frightening. Gun muzzles by the hundreds barked and tatted, men scrambled and cowered seeking cover, shells shrieked and exploded, tanks gushed flames into enemy portals, blasts missiled deadly rock and coral fragments, bullets and steel splinters whizzed and snapped in the air, stricken armored hulks belched fiery smoke, and wounded and dying soldiers screamed and the cry "Medic, Medic" echoed everywhere. It was a terrible, exhausting fight for the 77th Division, but was matched in ferocity by the 6th Marine Division's taking of Sugar Loaf off to the west, and by the struggle for Conical Hill by the 7th and the 96th, which had rejoined the line on our immediate left.

We couldn't have taken either Flat Top or the Chocolate Drop without the support of tanks, but I believe we lost 14 or 15 during this time. It was here that one of the most tragic casualties of the war occurred. Sergeant Fred Hensel went into the mine fields to investigate the area where a number of tanks had been knocked out or damaged, He stepped on a land mine and became a "basket case," surviving but losing all four appendages, both arms and both legs—a living testimony to the horror of war.

★★★

During this period, Japanese radio broadcasted a typical Tokyo Rose message in English heard by many of our troops on Okinawa[2]:

> Sugar Loaf Hill—Chocolate Drop—Strawberry Hill. Gee, those places sound wonderful! You can just see the candy houses with the white picket fences around them and the candy canes hanging from the trees, their red and white stripes glistening in the sun, but the only thing red about those places is the blood of Americans. Yes, sir, those are the names of hills in southern Okinawa where the fighting's so close that you get down to bayonets and sometimes your bare fists. Artillery and naval gunfire are all right when the enemy is far off but they don't do you any good when he's right in the same foxhole with you. I guess it's natural to idealize the worst places with pretty names to make them seem less awful. Why Sugar Loaf has changed hands so often it looks like Dante's inferno. Yes, sir, Sugar Loaf Hill—Chocolate Drop—Strawberry Hill. They sound good, don't they? Only those who've been there know what they're really like.

Flat Top Hill under attack by the 306th. *U.S. Army*

On May 17, after resuming the attack around the northeast side of Flat Top, we managed to clean out and seal up several large caves on the south face. We continued fighting our way to the top, but again failed to hold and were driven back down. The assault wouldn't have even reached the base of Flat Top without the help of tanks, and three more were lost that day to anti-tank fire. The only remaining officer in Company K was killed while trying to lead us up to the crest of the ridge. Every officer in the company had been wounded or killed—none were left.

The casualty rate among junior officers in the Pacific war was high. Jap snipers made it a practice of trying to kill them first. When our troops moved forward, the enemy often let the men in front advance so they could get a shot at an officer or radioman behind them. Platoon and company commanders—the second lieutenants, first lieutenants, and captains—had a shorter combat life expectancy than almost any other people in our ranks. Replacement second lieutenants sometimes became casualties so quickly that the men they were sent to lead hardly learned their names.

By this time, Company K had only about 20 or 25 men left—it was less than a platoon in size. Continuing our way around the bottom of Flat Top, we tried to reach the caves located further along on the reverse slope. Again we were deluged by mortar and machine gun fire from Chocolate Drop, as we tried to pass over the crest of Flat Top and come down on the Japs on the other side. Again, the enemy threw grenade after grenade at us from their unseen positions on the reverse slopes. Finally, we realized we simply couldn't take the hilltop. Gradually, we were driven off. We crawled, slipped, and fell on our way back down.

Then we got panicky! Had we left anyone on the hill? Did everyone get back down? We accounted for the missing one by one—a man had the back of his head blown off by a rifle shot, another was hit by grenade fragments and couldn't have been alive when we left, and so on until we knew what'd happened to each missing soldier. Only then were we satisfied to settle down and dig in once more. By this time, Company K's casualty rate probably was approaching 100 percent; most of the veterans were gone and the company depended on replacements.

One of the company's surviving men staggered over to me and sat down on the edge of my foxhole. He put his head in his hands and leaned forward looking at me. Tears ran down his cheeks.

"Why," he asked. "Why? What if we'd taken that goddamn hill, there's another one on the other side, isn't there? When is it going to end?"

I couldn't answer. I didn't know an answer.

During the night of May 17, under cover of darkness, the wounded were evacuated, while reinforcements, water, rations, and ammo were brought up. Among the replacements was a new officer who brought several men with him. I noticed that most carried carbines, so I figured they were new replacements that hadn't been in combat yet, and probably were rear echelon troops scraped together to help fill our depleted ranks.

Most combat infantrymen didn't favor carbines. For one thing, they usually were assigned to officers, and the Japs assumed that anyone carrying one was a platoon or company leader and thus a priority target. Men with any experience in the front line usually replaced carbines and Reisling submachine guns (commonly called "squirt guns" or "grease guns") with M1 rifles or the Thompson submachine gun. The latter, in fact, was a much sought after weapon. I preferred the M1 Garand rifle. It would operate under the most miserable of conditions in mud, water, whatever, and could nail Japs at 150, 200, even 250 yards, which neither the carbine or the submachine guns could do.

Contrary to the way we'd operated in previous campaigns, replacements on Okinawa sometimes were sent up to our front line units while we were locked in combat. Occasionally, these new men came up in the dark, were introduced to some members of the

Big Okinawa Fight Nears Decisive Stage

May 18 (Friday).—(AP)—The battle for Okinawa was reaching a decisive stage today as troops of the Tenth U.S. Army battled in the capital city, Naha, and closed in from three sides on Shuri, keystone of the Japanese "Little Siegfried Line."

Elements of the Sixth Marine Division penetrated to the heart of debris-cluttered Naha yesterday after throwing a small bridgehead across the Asato River estuary on the west coast...

A surprise attack by the 77th Infantry Division drove through rough ground to the outskirts of Ishimmi Town, within 2,000 yards of the heart of walled and moated Shuri in the center of the line.

squad or platoon, and then told to take cover in a foxhole, whose former occupants, often as not, only recently had been killed or wounded. For an 18- or 19-year-old replacement not long out of high school, few experiences could match this for sheer terror. They'd crouch there sleepless under the strange, flickering half-light of flares sent up by the Navy, flinch from whistling and whining small arms fire, cower under shattering artillery and mortar explosions, and shudder when hearing infiltrating Japs moving in the blackness. The new man might be killed before dawn and none around him would know him by sight or by name.

The new lieutenant crawled and scrambled from one foxhole to another, introducing himself and asking for our name, rank, and a little background information about our experiences. When telling him I was a member of the Intelligence and Reconnaissance Platoon from the 306th Infantry Regiment, he asked why in hell was I with Company K of the 307th? I told him my story.

"Well, we're short handed," the lieutenant said, "but I can't keep you here. Get back down to your own outfit."

★★★

The next morning, I started down the trail toward the last known position of my company and eventually found them. When relieved on May 15, the badly depleted 306th went behind the lines to a rest camp with pyramid tents and sleeping cots. For more than two weeks, they'd been sleeping in nothing but foxholes,

Behind the lines at the rest camp: (l. to r.) Gene Funk, Lou Ryman, Wayne MacGregor, and Irish Doherty.

so now most of the men simply wanted to lay on the cots and rest, and write letters home to relatives and sweethearts.

Special facilities had been set up, however, to provide diversion and help relieve the stress that'd been building up in the men for weeks. A library tent contained a number of volumes, mostly soft cover, for those interested in reading. Volleyball nets were put up for men wanting sports action, and movies were shown in a large tent. Most importantly, there were shower facilities and the dining areas served fresh cooked meals, rather than C, K, or 10 in 1 rations.

The worst thing about being in a rest camp, though, was knowing it wouldn't last. Usually after about three to five days, we'd have to return to the front lines. As our departure neared, everyone began stressing out. However, I didn't hear anyone griping to the effect that they wouldn't go back. I never heard of anyone in my company who refused to fight.

None of us wanted to enter combat again, but we realized that the only way we'd ever return to America was by defeating Japan.

NOTES

1. Hiromichi Yahara, *The Battle for Okinawa* (New York: John Wiley and Sons, 1995), 67–70.
2. Japanese government radio didn't identify any of its female announcers as "Tokyo Rose" when broadcasting across a vast reach of the Pacific. Basically, it was a name that American GIs came up with. In actuality, a number of English-speaking Japanese women were utilized to deliver propaganda programs. One of them was Iva Ikuko Toguri, a young Japanese-American graduate of UCLA who was visiting an ill aunt in Japan when the war broke out. Not able to speak Japanese effectively and trapped in a country she found alien to her, she nevertheless was eventually recruited to serve as a radio announcer. For a time her call sign was "Orphan Annie, your favorite enemy" when giving 15 minute talks aimed at undermining American morale. Tried after the war for treason, she served ten years in prison.

12 STALEMATE IN THE RAIN

B Y THE TIME I REJOINED MY OUTFIT, they'd already had two days of rest. After another couple of days in camp, the 306th was ordered back to the front, where our battered and very severely reduced battalion would be held in reserve. As usual, the first thing we did when reaching our new positions was dig in.

The next day, May 21, the skies opened up and began dumping sheets of rain for days, soaking everyone and everything, and turning the roads and fields into muddy bogs. Since Okinawa isn't in the tropics like Guam or the Philippines, the rain was cold. After the deluge started, we were wet and miserable practically all of the time, hardly ever warming up or drying out.

Muddy conditions shut down logistical support to the front lines beginning May 21, 1945.
U.S. Army

Disintegration of Foe Seen

May 21 (Monday).—(AP) ...Some disintegration of Japanese resistance on Okinawa was seen today by Maj. Gen. John R. Hodge as three Yank divisions moved to encircle Shuri, a key enemy stronghold on the island, from which the knockout blow can be delivered against Japan.

General Hodge, commander of the 24th Army Corps, told newsmen at Okinawa there was "some indication that the Japanese are disintegrating as an overall fighting unit." He noted a sharp decrease in enemy artillery shelling.

Only 30,000 Japanese troops are believed left...

Tank-led marines of the First Division drove through intense small arms and mortar fire to ridges on the northwestern outskirts of moated Shuri and found that ancient capital of the Ryukyu chain, like the near-by Okinawa capital city of Naha, reduced to rubble and debris.

The leathernecks fought 800 yards through elaborate defenses to gain the commanding heights. Hand-to-hand fighting occurred on the slopes.

Maj. Gen. Andrew D. Bruce's veteran 77th Division infantrymen, repulsing three counterattacks, captured a strongpoint 900 yards northeast of Shuri yesterday as the 10th Army's slow envelopment of that Okinawa fortress city continued against fierce resistance...

During the daytime as we moved about, it wasn't bad, but in late afternoon when crawling into a foxhole and laying there under the continuous rain, we were soaked, muddy, and freezing. We took our steel helmets off the liners and bailed out water when our foxholes began filling up. Our ponchos were poor protection in thwarting the rain, either if worn or when used as a covering over a foxhole. Our feet, wet all the time and frequently immersed in water up to the ankles, began developing what World War I soldiers called "trench foot."

The smell of death was everywhere. Our dead, of course, were removed and buried by the Graves Registration people. On May 21, in fact, my squad was sent out to guard them as they went up near our front lines to recover American dead (see chapter 13). No one, however, had bothered to do anything with the rotting Japanese bodies lying all around us. When our lines had moved forward in other campaigns, engineers bulldozed large trenches, pushed the enemy bodies in, sprayed the mass burial with DDT or sodium arsenate, and then filled the trenches in with earth. In our current situation, however, this couldn't be done until the combat zone moved forward. However, our lines were static—there hadn't been an advance for days.

Lou and I couldn't stand the smell of a couple of bodies laying fairly close to our foxhole, so we dragged them 20 or 30 feet further away and threw them down a hill. It was an awful thing—hundreds of maggots squirmed underneath each of the dead Japanese. As we picked the bodies up and moved them, the spots where they'd lain were crawling with masses of white, grubby maggots. It turns the stomach just to think about it.

Fleas and lice were another problem. The island was infested and seemed especially so in the enemy positions that we moved into as we advanced. The situation became so bad that on several occasions Army transport planes, C47s, with spray equipment flew low over the front lines spraying everyone with vermin-killing DDT—the dead, our troops, and even the enemy.

★★★

During this time, Sergeant Ames came over to our foxhole and said, "MacGregor, the CO would like to talk to you and he wants you to come back right now."

I walked over to the company CP. When reporting to our CO, he said Army headquarters had sent a special request. He and certain other company commanders were directed to nominate one individual in their companies who had the intelligence, battle experience, educational background, and character to be considered as a possible candidate for an appointment to West Point. Those nominated initially would be given oral interviews back at XXIV Corps headquarters.

He said he was nominating me from our company and had arranged transportation. I'd be taken back that afternoon.

Just getting away from the constant Jap shelling, mud, and the smell of death was reason enough to go. I could hardly contain my enthusiasm when I went back and told Lou what'd happened. After we ate our C rations for lunch, I walked back down to the road where several tank destroyers and some jeeps were

77th Division troops wearily trudging toward the front lines past tanks stalled in the mud. *U.S. Army*

parked. I then was taken back to Corps where, after introducing myself, I was sent into a tent where a major proceeded to interview me.

After the interview was concluded, he said, "MacGregor, I notice you're wearing glasses. How much of a problem is it?"

I had to be truthful. I told the major I couldn't see across the tent without my glasses. My vision was 20/200 in both eyes, and I always tried to carry an extra pair of glasses when in combat.

He leaned back in his canvas chair, spread the palms of his hands on the table, and looking at me, said, "Son, I'm sorry. I'd like to be able to tell you that you had a chance for an appointment from the Corps, but I can't. You simply wouldn't be an acceptable candidate with your eyesight."

He thanked me for coming and stood up. I saluted, and he shook my hand. Then, as I turned to leave, he said, "One more thing, with that kind of eyesight, how in the hell did you ever get to be a scout in a recon platoon in the infantry?"

"Well," I said, "when I was a senior in high school, two buddies and I had permission from our mothers to go down and take enlistment physicals. We went to the Army Air Force recruiting station and volunteered. Both of my buddies were accepted, but, when I took the physical, I couldn't read past the initial letter on the eye chart. So, I never made it. But then, on my eighteenth birthday, I went to qualify for enlistment in the Army and spent an hour or so waiting in a room where an eye chart was located. I memorized it. This time, when being tested, I didn't have any difficulty. Until today, nobody ever asked me about my eyesight, and it's not something I ever want to bring up."

He smiled, and I heard him chuckling as I left the tent.

When getting back to the company area, I walked up to the foxholes and headed to where Lou and I were dug in. Lou could tell that things hadn't gone well.

When I told him what'd happened, all he said was, "Shit, those idiots back at Corps always have had their heads up their ass."

★★★

The rains continued and our positions became even wetter than before. One day, as I sat on the edge of my foxhole, Junior Cotter walked up. I noticed he carried a large sheath knife in one hand and a thin wire with a number of teeth on it in the other.

"Junior, where in the hell did you get those teeth?"

He looked at me and said, "Well, I've been cutting them out of the mouths of dead Japs and making a necklace. You know, this has gotten to be pretty popular. There are two or three guys that have these necklaces."

My jaw dropped, and I blurted, "For god sakes, Junior, you know better'n that. If there are some stupid sons of bitches who'd do a thing like that, that doesn't mean you have to. Get rid of those goddamn things."

Making coffee over a fire during a break in the rain: (l. to r.) a company communications man, Governor Bryant, and Irish Doherty, June 1945. *U.S. Army*

He looked at me, "Yeah, Mac, but some of them are gold."

"I don't give a goddamn, you got no business knocking teeth out of dead Japs, and you sure as hell shouldn't have any necklace made out of 'em."

His head bent down, his shoulders slumped, and he looked dejected. "You really don't think I ought'a keep these?"

"Hell no, Junior, that's not anything for a man to do, and you're a hell of a lot more of a man than to do something like that. Throw them away."

With that, Junior stood up and walked away. He never told me if he discarded the teeth, but I never saw him carry them around after that. I assume my talk had helped some and he'd gotten rid of them.

Collecting teeth was bad enough, but I remember a few days later seeing a guy from the weapons platoon who'd made a necklace out of finger bones. I thought to myself, how sick can you get. Today, it's hard to believe that those things happened. At the time, however, we'd become so accustomed and inured to the depravity, death, and destruction all around us that, to some people at least, knocking out teeth or cutting off fingers simply didn't seem that bad.

★★★

The torrential rains that started on May 21 continued, turning the battlefield into a sea of mud and bringing all ground action to a halt for a time. The 1st and 6th Marines were on our right flank, and the 96th Division had replaced the 7th

Division on our left. We were in the middle facing Shuri, the strongest defenses on the entire island.

In the deluge, tanks bogged down, trenches filled up with water, and even amphibious tractors couldn't negotiate in many areas. Providing supply and logistical support to our front line troops became extremely difficult. Trucks, jeeps, tanks, amphibious tractors, DUKWs (amphibious wheeled vehicles), or any other type of vehicle simply couldn't operate in the forward areas. Consequently, our troops resorted to carrying in supplies and equipment on foot, and the wounded were taken out the same way.

Ammunition, medical supplies, food, everything, had to be hand carried the last 1,000 or 1,500 yards up to the front. Men in the front-line foxholes were sent back to bring up their own supplies. Every step taken in the mud when sinking down six inches or a foot was an agonizing effort. As mud balled up thickly on your boots, your feet felt like they were encased in concrete. Just walking took a great effort and we proceeded at a snail's pace. Mud also clung to clothes; in fact, to everything. While this was going on, of course, the Japs continued to shell us. They intermittently targeted not only our front lines, but also battalion and regimental areas, and even supporting units such as the artillery.

Our living conditions must've closely resembled what the Allies and the Germans experienced on the Western Front during World War I. Holes and trenches dug into hillsides collapsed or caved in because of the saturated ground. We shivered in the cold rain and our food was limited to C rations, or 10 in 1 rations. The constant pounding by Jap artillery made it almost impossible to get any

Waiting for the sun to reappear: (l. to r.) Ray Singer, Lucky Last, Sergeant Howard Crawford, and Lieutenant Barnes Compton. *U.S. Army*

consistent sleep. After lying for days in flooded positions and wearing soaked, rotting clothing, our skin wrinkled and whitened, and patches of it fell off. When scraping an arm or hand, skin came away like wet cardboard. The morale of some men began to crack.

There simply wasn't any movement in our front lines, and very little activity from the Japanese, except for artillery and occasional mortar fire. Our shells, of course, continued to whine incessantly overhead, bombarding the Jap positions. With activity slowed, however, we could leave our foxholes and make small fires to warm coffee or heat C rations. Misery and stress showed on every face. Our eyes had begun to have a blank stare and everyone was wan and pale. There was an unhealthy aura about us. This continued for almost two weeks.

We just hoped that the Japs were as bad off as we were.

★★★

By the end of May, almost 65,000 Japanese reportedly were "counted" dead, and an additional 10,000 "possibly" had been killed in the Okinawa campaign. Except for about 5,000 or so enemy soldiers that our division killed in the Keramas and on Ie Shima, plus a thousand or two eliminated by the Marines in central and northern Okinawa and on some other small nearby islands, the vast majority of these appalling enemy fatalities occurred in the southern Okinawa defensive zones. According to divisional reports, about 12,000 were killed by the Marines and 41,000 by the Army divisions.

A big difference when comparing these figures to a similar count of enemy losses in North Africa and Europe is revealed by a statement from the III Amphibious Corps—only 128 Japanese soldiers had surrendered to the Marines up to this time, and the Army divisions had taken just 90 prisoners. My division, the 77th, reported capturing only nine during this period; three of these Japs, in fact, had surrendered to my squad.

In the European Theater, by contrast, casualty reports for a similar number of Axis dead also usually noted the capture of a large number of their soldiers.

Though hard fighters, Germans would surrender when they knew they were beaten or cut-off on the battlefield. The infrequent Jap prisoners, however, often were taken only because they were unconscious or so badly wounded that they couldn't retreat, fight to the death, or kill themselves. The Japs simply were tremendous adversaries.

Wounded Japanese prisoners. *U.S. Army*

By early June, even though the battle was far from over, we'd already suffered substantially more casualties than in any other campaign in the Pacific. There also were large numbers of neuro-psychiatric cases, or combat fatigue. A mental breakdown could strike even the strongest soldier after a period of time when men lived in the mud and cold, were constantly exposed to enemy fire and the terror of Jap counterattacks, especially at night, and were struggling along on insufficient food and sleep. Some shook and cried, wet their pants, and their eyes glazed over. They seemed to be in a state of shock. Often they couldn't even move out of their foxholes. Everyone was scared, however—some just more so than others.

The number of combat fatigue cases seemed to generally depend on how long an individual was in combat and how much enemy action he'd been exposed to. It's not known why some men broke down completely, while others didn't. Everyone seemed to agree, however, that if anyone was exposed to combat long enough, eventually they'd develop some degree of psychological collapse.

Altogether, there were more than 25,000 cases of "non-battle casualties" on Okinawa, most of which were classified as combat fatigue. This was more cases than anywhere else in the Pacific. It's believed that this was due to the long period of time that our soldiers were engaged in intense combat on Okinawa—a total of almost three months—plus being subjected to the heaviest enemy artillery fire and the most persistent enemy defensive resistance of any Pacific campaign.

For our division, most of the combat fatigue cases occurred during the Maeda Escarpment and Chocolate Drop fighting. When a soldier's mental state reached a nadir—when he totally broke down and couldn't operate effectively any longer—he usually was sent to a rear rest area where medical personnel looked after these cases. Some could be treated, and, partially recovered, they returned to their outfits after two, three, or four days.

Others, however, were in such a severe state of emotional and nervous collapse that they simply couldn't return to combat. In a number of instances, their psychics were forever damaged—some men never recovered from the terror they'd experienced.

☆

13 ISHIMMI RIDGE

O N MAY 21, SERGEANT SALL instructed Sergeant Crawford to take two squads and escort a group of Graves Registration personnel up to Ishimmi Ridge to recover bodies. My squad was one of those ordered to go.

Four days earlier, on May 17, Company E and attached units from companies H and C, all of the 307th Infantry, had assaulted Ishimmi Ridge. At the start of that action, our forward positions had been situated about 1,250 yards from the ridge. Company E and the attached men made an unusual night attack against the Japanese. Surprising the defenders, our men took the ridge and dug in.

The Japanese, upon realizing the incursion within their lines, utilized every resource at their disposal in attempting to drive back or overwhelm our men. The enemy felt that the assault had formed a crucial wedge in their positions, threatening the entire Shuri defensive line. They launched a mortar and artillery barrage, and sent infantry forward in bayonet and grenade attacks. The fighting was intense, with men even grappling hand to hand. Our soldiers fiercely resisted, but the position simply was too exposed, and too far out in front of our main lines to hold out without support.

Decimated by Japanese attacks, the 307th men finally were reinforced and relieved by infantry after several days. Despite the desperate circumstances, the wounded were evacuated as Company E and its attached men withdrew, but they couldn't carry the fatalities back with them. The dead lay where they'd fallen.

By then, our main front line had advanced to incorporate the area where the intense fighting had occurred. It was at this time that the two squads from my platoon were ordered to escort and protect the Graves Registration teams.

From our position on the ridges west of Highway 5, we proceeded through the rain in a southerly direction towards Shuri. Crossing to the east side of Highway 5, we entered an unbelievably torn-up and crater-pocked landscape, without a living bush or tree standing anywhere. There hardly was a foot of ground

ISHIMMI
RIDGE

SHURI
CASTLE

ISHIMMI

Ishimmi-Shuri Castle battle area. Our two squads walked directly through the area in the foreground while on our way to Ishimmi Ridge. *U.S. Army*

that hadn't been ripped up. The shell holes were filled with water and the entire area was muddy from the saturating rain.

We could see Ishimmi Ridge from a distance, identifiable because of several shell-shattered tree snags sticking up on it. The ridge stood about 30 or 40 feet above the valley that we were walking across. Upon climbing the short distance to the narrow ridge top, we saw a scene of utter destruction. The bodies of our soldiers were lying in and around their positions. Some were lying inside or half-out of foxholes, while others were sprawled on top of the ground in the perimeter—all in the poses in which they'd been killed. We'd long been hardened to the sight of Japanese bodies, but seeing so many of our own dead was another matter. It sickened and saddened us.

There were more than 100 American dead lying as they'd fallen. The ridge, too, had been churned up by artillery and mortar explosions. Most of the craters were filled with water and some had two or three rotting bodies lying inside. Interspersed with our dead were numerous Japanese corpses, many of them intertwined in death with their American adversaries—killed together in the savage hand-to-hand fighting.

I walked over to the northeast side of the ridge, where I saw an American lying half in and half out of one of the foxholes. Water covered the bottom of the foxhole and part of the soldier's body. He was a young blonde man whose face had been partially blown away. His body had started to turn green and was so bloated with putrefaction that his dungarees were stretched as tight as a blown up balloon. The corpse also was covered with flies and maggots.

I thought I'd drag him out, so that the Graves Registration men could more easily put him into a body bag. I reached down and grabbed a leg protruding over the top of the foxhole, but as I pulled, the entire leg came out at the hip in my hands—I stumbled backwards holding the leg in my arms. Trying to keep from falling, I stretched my right leg out solidly behind me and stepped right onto a Japanese corpse. My momentum drove my foot into the stomach, rupturing the intestines. Up to my ankle in blood and decaying flesh, I instinctively raised my foot and backed away, pulling along a string of guts caught on the toe of my boot. Horrified, I violently shook my foot while backing up, unable to conceive of what I was seeing. Continuing to move away, my foot remained tangled in the intestines, pulling them out of the body cavity, like a large, ugly gray rope.

I finally broke free. The smell was unbelievable. Having pulled the leg and guts away from the two bodies, the gas inside of them was released. This stench, along with the smell of other bodies in the area, was unbelievably nauseating, making it almost impossible to keep from vomiting.

The Graves Registration teams had brought up folded stretchers. After unfolding the stretchers, they'd roll the corpses onto them. Some of the dead had bandages on them, which meant, of course, that they'd been injured and their wounds had been tended to, and they'd continued to fight until killed. One could imagine the terror that they must've experienced. Pounded by artillery and mortar barrages, and entirely surrounded by the enemy, they'd waited and prayed for help to get through, but it didn't come in time to save them. However, their undaunted courage sustained them to the end and was another example of the heroism commonly displayed by American soldiers on Okinawa.

Most of the Graves Registration men wore long rubber gloves reaching well above the wrists. They'd unfold a stretcher, put a body bag or poncho on the stretcher, set it next to a corpse, and then two or three of them would reach under the body and move it. Frequently, a corpse began to fall apart. The heads, especially, often fell off and rolled downhill, with a Graves Registration man in pursuit. Other times, a limb detached from the torso and was only held in place by the fatigue shirt or trousers. Flies swarmed over the corpses and maggots squirmed underneath them. Some of the men had been dead for four days and were in an advanced state of deterioration. Many of them lay in their foxholes face down in three or four inches of water, riddled with bullets or metal fragments.

In the warm geographical environments of the Pacific campaigns, the dead, both American and Japanese, almost immediately upon being killed were blown by flies. In a short time, maggots hatched and began devouring the remains. Within a day or two, the bodies began decomposing, followed by putrefaction, and then disintegration. As the bodies swelled, the juices inside oozed out, creating a foul, repugnant odor. The dead turned green, then black, and soon were more than a third their normal size. They'd burst, then fall apart, often becoming unrecognizable—a gross, foul caricature of a human being.

While the teams worked at retrieving and bagging the bodies, we began receiving some shellfire. Everyone was getting nervous, particularly when a sniper began firing at some of the Graves Registration men. They tried to hurry up, but this caused even more of the bodies to fall apart. It was an extremely difficult task. If someone grabbed a corpse by the boot, the leg was so decomposed that the boot usually came off with rotting flesh inside, leaving the leg bone sticking out through the bottom of a pant leg. Becoming frustrated, some of the Graves Registration men took their entrenching tools off their packs and began shoveling pieces of corpses into body bags or onto ponchos. Eventually, the teams had all of the bodies or body parts that they could move at that time and they asked us to escort them back to our lines.

For weeks, my life since moving up to the Maeda Escarpment had been a hideous nightmare. Bad as it'd been, however, it paled beside this cesspool of death on Ishimmi Ridge. If people everywhere could see what the residue of battle consists of—the bodies of their soldiers, their children, lying torn asunder, flesh decaying and falling off the bones, and insects, birds, and other animals feeding on the decomposing corpses—perhaps it would cause a revulsion, a loathing, an abhorrence of such a magnitude that wars would become obsolete—an unthinkable way to settle differences between nations.

However, this will never happen because relatively few people actually see and experience the terrible consequences of war. Only those doing the fighting really understand the results, and the torment that is left when the shooting ends. The effect it had on me was lasting. I asked God to get me home alive, without any permanent, disabling wounds. I swore an oath that if that happened, I'd be an advocate of peace for as long as I lived.

"Get me home, God," I'd say, "and I'll never fight anyone again, ever."

★★★

Shortly after Company E was rescued and relieved on Ishimmi Ridge, Lieutenant Robert F. Meiser, a platoon leader in that unit, wrote an explicit account of that action in a duty report. It begins with mention of the brief period when the company was held in reserve and received many green replacements, followed by the dramatic details of the desperate fighting, May 17–20.

> For six days prior to May 17, 1945, the 307th Infantry was in [77th] division reserve. On May 15th, E Company was moved to a reserve area on the reverse slope of the Urasoe-Mura [Maeda] escarpment with Highway 5 adjacent on the left. In this area the company reorganized in preparation for future commitments.
>
> This short period of action had been the first time in battle for about 70 percent of the E company men. [These replacements] had had little opportunity to become acquainted with each other, their non-coms, and to recognize their officers.
>
> At [1830], on May 16th, Company E's commanding officer, Lt. Theodore S. Bell, called his platoon leaders to accompany him to the battalion Observation Post. There, high atop a rocky pinnacle, Company E was given the order to make a surprise night attack on distant Ishimmi Ridge.
>
> The plan was to advance, single file, 450 yards beyond the escarpment to the Line of Departure. From there our objective was 800 yards to Ishimmi Ridge, which was the very core of the Shuri defense line. The order of march would be the 2nd, weapons, 3rd, and 1st platoons. In addition, a section of heavy machine guns from Company H were to be attached, plus a reinforced rifle platoon from Company C.
>
> The men were told details of the attack. They were instructed to lock and load their weapons, fix bayonets, and use them if enemy were encountered in the advance. Canteens were filled, extra ammunition issued, and all made ready.
>
> At 0215, May 17th, the company was awakened and in pitch darkness prepared to move out. The company moved slowly due to the ruggedness of the terrain and the inability to see any distance. Water-filled shell holes had to be avoided and several ditches detoured. Flares were going up regularly but everyone hit the ground in that instant before each shell burst.
>
> By 0350 the squads began forming in line, each in a close skirmish formation. We were now down in the valley, and still about 800 yards from our goal. Our guide was three or four limbless trees on the two highest points of Ishimmi Ridge and those were only faintly visible in the clearest of flare light.
>
> Promptly at 0415 the company left the Line of Departure. Fear of being discovered by the enemy was our greatest worry, as we could have easily been ambushed in this land which was physically occupied and thoroughly controlled by Japs.

Flares caused numerous delays but we were never caught moving, which might have proved our undoing. On the way up, no attack was made on us, but the sound of battle was all around. Rifle and machine-gun fire was heard continually and the whine of heavy artillery shells was incessant.

Dawn began to break as we came upon our objective. About 50 yards from it, the 3rd platoon echeloned to the left of the 2nd and nearly on line, forming the left front and flank. The 2nd continued straight forward to occupy the center and foremost position, while the platoon from Company C held the right front and flank. Our rear was protected by a well formed semicircle of the 1st platoon.

We now found that the 125 yard part of the objective we were able to occupy was a very prominent, table top ridge. It was quite flat and made up of rock and coral where digging was very difficult, and in some places impossible.

The top center of Ishimmi Ridge was very narrow, being only about seven or eight yards wide, and then fanning out to either flank in a leaf-like pattern. Directly to the rear of the narrow section of the ridge was a pocket, 20 yards in diameter, in which the company Command Post was located, and this, ultimately, was the location of the company's final stand. To our right rear, 250 yards distant, were two grassy mounds of earth, each about 30 feet high and affording perfect observation into our positions. Likewise, to the center rear was a finger ridge extension which afforded the enemy an excellent OP as well as machine gun positions.

At 0505 we were on our objective, and as daylight was coming we hastened to dig in. The enemy on the ridge was completely surprised and was not aware of our presence for nearly 20 minutes. While initially caught napping, they soon made up for lost time and all hell broke loose at 0530. Mortar shells, heavy and light, began falling on our area in such fury and volume that one would believe the place had been zeroed in for just such an eventuality. Machine gun and rifle fire began pouring in from all directions and within a short time even enemy artillery began shelling us.

As daylight came, we finally realized that we were in a spot and that the enemy controlled the position from every direction, including the rear. The [3rd] Platoon on the left was receiving murderous fire, especially from both flanks and the high Shuri Ridge across the valley to our front. Foxholes were only partly completed and to raise one's head meant death on that fire-swept plateau. Mortar shells very often dropped directly in the foxhole, usually taking at least one man's life or badly wounding several. The same action was taking place [with the Company C platoon] on the right flank as that area was almost identical to the one on the left.

In the rear, the 1st Platoon was faring no better and was taking a terrific pounding from all types of fire. However, they maintained continuous and effective fire on the enemy, especially to the right and left rear, greatly reducing his advantages there. Our light mortars were in this area and though only partially dug in, the mortar crews fired as long as the mortars were serviceable. By 1000 the first day, enemy action had knocked out all but one of the mortars and killed or wounded nearly all the crewmen.

The 2nd Platoon had gone over the center of the ridge and dropped into a long Jap communication trench which was about six feet deep. Small dugouts in this trench contained about 10 or 12 sleeping enemy who were quickly disposed of by bayonet or rifle fire. However, tunnels from inside the ridge led into either end of the trench and the enemy soon attempted to force their way upward. At first, surprise was so complete that a Japanese officer and his aide, laughing and talking, came toward us in the trench, walked completely past one of our men and were killed without realizing what hit them.

By making use of the tunnels the Nips were soon able to set up knee mortars about 100 yards to either flank and fire systematically from one end of the trench to the other. Each position had two mortars which were firing simultaneously, doing great damage to the earthworks of our line as well as producing heavy casualties in our ranks. Riflemen were blown to bits by these mortars and many were struck in the head by machine gun fire. The blood from the wounded was everywhere; on the weapons, on the living, and splattered all around. The dead lay where they fell, in pools of their own blood. Though the platoon medic was wounded early in the morning, he took care of the injured as fast as possible, but was unable to keep up and soon his supplies were exhausted.

By 0700 both of our light machine guns had been knocked out, one being completely buried. The few remaining crewmen became riflemen and stayed right there throughout the day. During the morning a few Japanese had managed to crawl up from the deep ravine to a line just slightly beneath our position and began hurling grenades upwards at us. Grenades were tossed back and soon the infiltrators were killed or driven backward, but we had suffered too. The battle continued furiously all morning and by noon the 2nd Platoon had suffered heavily, about 50 percent being killed or wounded. The number of Japs killed had mounted steadily, but they were still able to reinforce almost at will and attempted numerous frontal and flanking counterattacks.

Meanwhile the 3rd Platoon [on the left] had had a steady grenade battle and had repulsed three fixed bayonet attacks by the enemy coming from their left flank. However, the men of this platoon had very little cover and were being whittled down man by man until more than half of them were out of action, including their platoon leader. Dead men were pushed hurriedly from the all too small holes in order to make more room for the living. In some cases the firing was so heavy as to even prevent this, and the living and bloody, mangled dead were as one in their foxholes. By 1800 the first day there were only a handful of men left alive in this platoon and they were clinging tenaciously to the few remaining positions of their own right flank.

The section of heavy machine guns was located on the hill itself, one each in the 2nd and 3rd platoon areas. These weapons were recognized by the enemy immediately and the Japs proceeded to "polish them off." They did a good job, blowing one gun to shreds as it was being placed on its tripod. The other was smashed beyond use after it had fired one-half of a box of ammunition. The crewmen were nearly all killed and those remaining alive seized rifles of dead comrades.

During the first day the 1st Platoon in the rear had continuous trouble from both flanks and the rear. Deadly fire was delivered on this platoon from the two earthen mounds all day and it was only late in the afternoon that our artillery was able to blast the two knobs and flush the enemy out. The platoon had suffered heavily in killed and wounded, but maintained their perimeter defense, although their ranks had been thinned considerably.

In spite of the terrific pounding we were taking, battle discipline was excellent. It seemed as if the men realized the danger of faltering and each and every man stuck to his allotted position, fighting back savagely while there remained a breath of life in his body. Wounded men insisted on being propped up, given a rifle and another chance to even the score with the enemy. Individual acts of heroism and sacrifice were witnessed continually and many probably went unseen.

In the CP area trouble started early, too. Four enemy were killed in a grenade battle on reaching the site. There were several large crevices in the left edge of this pocket and the Japs were sleeping there when we arrived. They soon started the fireworks and with great difficulty were finally exterminated.

The artillery observer had two radios along but one was set afire the first day and the other blown to pieces early the second day.

The first day had been unusually hot, with a burning sun and no breeze at all, so by nightfall our water was gone. No rations were to be had, but provisions and help were expected that night. At 1800 Lieutenant Bell ordered the 2nd and 3rd platoons to consolidate and withdraw to a perimeter around the CP. It would have been impossible to have tried to hold our original positions even in daylight and suicidal for the night. Wounded were to be moved to the area around the CP and there await evacuation that night.

The withdrawal of the 2nd Platoon began at once with the removal of the wounded. There were six badly mangled men in that position and all had to be carried out. They were placed on ponchos and pulled sled-fashion by the 10 remaining men of the 2nd Platoon. The last four men of the 3rd Platoon acted as protection against two snipers and one machine gun which had zeroed in on a shallow place in our only route of withdrawal. When we were ready to move a man through the exposed area, the four guards would fire steadily and thus enable us to move wounded out one by one. Even in this way one of the wounded was killed by a burst of machine gun fire and a litter carrier was badly wounded. Some time was taken to destroy equipment we could not use or would not need. Nothing usable was left for the enemy. This movement was finally completed at about 2030 and our defense set for the night.

Our rescue force did not reach us that night as the Japs had placed an ambush and cut them to ribbons. No one slept a wink all night as the bombardment continued constantly. The Jap artillery remained active, mortar fire maintained its tempo, and four "buzz bombs" were dropped on us. Grenades were tossed most of the night and infiltrating enemy were either killed or driven off. The brilliant light of the flares enabled us to spot many of the enemy before they were completely upon us.

Throughout the first day American M18 self-propelled guns supported us with everything they had and laced fire on pinpoint targets. Many times they had to fire so close to our position that we were showered with rock from the strike, and the noise of the burst was ear-splitting. Their direct fire into bayonet fixed Japanese squads saved us from numerous fanatical charges into our weakened positions. Our long range supporting heavy machine guns aided immensely in breaking up Jap charges and their continuous harassing fire gave the enemy no end of trouble. The mortar support given us, especially in the valley to our front, inflicted countless casualties on the enemy and certainly broke up numerous charges so that we could pick off the stragglers.

The second day's fighting continued more furiously than the first, the enemy redoubling his efforts to dislodge us. The previous day everyone had been confident of success and far too busy to think otherwise. Because of the strategic importance of this one piece of ground we were ordered to stay "at all costs." Though tired, hungry, and thirsty, the men remained determined until the end, prepared for a last ditch death stand. Grenades had long since been exhausted, but every spare clip of ammunition was salvaged and the few spare, workable rifles placed in handy positions. Bayonets were taken from scabbards. The few less seriously wounded made preparations along with the others and all were ready to sell out to the enemy, but only if he were willing to pay a high price in blood.

Throughout the second day the wounded were in fearful condition, their moans and cries for help being continuous. Medical supplies were exhausted and wounds had to go untreated. In the burning heat, the stench of the dead was suffocating and flies collected in great numbers. The enemy pressure increased steadily, particularly in the employment of knee mortars. At one time eight of their weapons, firing in pairs, were pounding us.

Our own and supporting fires continually tried to knock out these enemy mortar positions, but they were well protected and undoubtedly retreated into caves under bombardment. That afternoon another attempt was made to reinforce us, but by 1600 only five men and the commanding officer of Company C were able to safely cross the bullet swept plain to our rear. These men immediately found foxholes, but their commander was shot through the head while running to our CP, and fell on the parapet of that foxhole.

Late in the afternoon we were notified that a litter-bearing team of about 80 men would attempt to reach us that night.

The enemy attack was extremely fierce throughout the day and early evening, but slackened a little after dark. At about 2200 on May 18th, the first of the litter men began to arrive. As soon as they came in they were taken to a disabled man, who was placed on a litter and whisked away as soon as possible. There were a few walking wounded and these were sent along with the litter teams. The Japs soon realized what we were doing and opened up with rifle and machine gun fire. By moving swiftly and ducking flares, all the wounded were evacuated safely from our position in two and a half hours. Eighteen men had been carried out and several others had been able to walk with a little assistance.

Canteens were thrown from foxhole to foxhole and into the CP, where they were filled and tossed back.

Dawn of the third day found us hanging on only by our finger nails, but there we were and more determined than ever to stay. The battle opened with all its fury again and the enemy threw everything on us for the third consecutive day.

Attacks were steady throughout the day and were repulsed only with the greatest difficulty. Our supporting weapons had our flanks well under cover and kept enemy activity under strict observation. Whenever enemy movement was noted they immediately opened fire. Enemy mortar fire did continue at a fast and accurate rate, and even though our numbers were few, more were either killed or wounded.

Finally, rifle fire began to increase, a sure sign of some kind of movement, and at 2200 the relief began to come in. [These were men from Company L, 306th Infantry.]

The relief CP immediately was established in our old position and then the job of placing the men began. It was very dark and only by knowing where each hole was at, were we able to set up the defense as ours had been. A few of our remaining men had been wounded during the last day and they were now taken out by litter teams. Snipers pecked away at us continually, but by 0300 on May 20th, all the relief had been positioned and the last six of our group ready to leave. The new commanding officer was told what to expect and where it would come from, and having given this information we prepared to move out.

As we started to leave, a bursting shell to our right rear wounded two of the new men and we decided to evacuate them as we went back. One man was badly torn up and was carried back in a poncho, while the other could walk if able to lean on someone else.

Then the last of our party left Ishimmi Ridge. A white tape had been placed on the route for part of the distance, so we had little trouble in getting back to our Line of Departure.

Late the next morning the men were counted, and in the final check up there were 28 men, one NCO, and two officers left of the 129 who had gone up three days before. Of the heavy weapons groups of 17, only 4 returned. The Company C unit's strength of 58 was whittled down to 13 men. Therefore, total casualties, from the original personnel of 204 men, were 156 killed and wounded. By far the greatest percentage of these had been killed. However, this night attack, though costly, was highly successful and their lives were not given in vain. Ishimmi Ridge was the very heart of the Jap defenses before Shuri.[1]

★★★

As the meat grinding Okinawa campaign continued day by day, there were fewer and fewer of the original personnel remaining in the line companies. Due to attrition from incessant mortar and artillery attacks and machine gun and small arms fire, many of the older veterans simply were disappearing. By older, I mean in "battle experience," not in "age." The killed, wounded, or battle fatigued veterans were replaced by mostly green recruits—often 18- and 19-year-olds who hadn't received adequate preparation for what was expected of them, nor did they have an understanding of the horrors that they'd be facing. Of course, I was only 19 years old myself and originally the youngest man in my platoon, but I'd fought through several campaigns, and been wounded and decorated, thus I was considered an "old veteran" in our platoon.

Staff Sergeant Alfred C. Junkin, a platoon sergeant who went into the Ishimmi salient with Company E and was wounded there, wrote to his battalion commander regarding the inexperience of the replacements in combat for the first time:

> Our 30 replacements [in my platoon] showed great courage, but were too new to the job. One of them saw two Nips who got a sergeant 30 feet away, but his finger froze on the trigger. Another saw Japs standing on the horizon and shouted wildly for an older man to shoot them while his own rifle lay in his hands. Another saw enemy a few yards from his hole, aimed and fired an empty rifle. In the excitement, he had emptied his magazine and had forgotten to reload.
>
> Sir, I mean no disrespect by the above comments. The record speaks for itself… I am proud to belong to the 77th and especially Company C. But I deplore the necessity of taking green recruits, who hardly know how to load a rifle, into combat. My platoon of 42 men was smashed down to the last two men in the grenade and demolition battles on Pinnacle Rock on May 4th and 5th. With 30 replacements and old men borrowed from other platoons, it happened a second time on May 17th and 18th [on Ishimmi Ridge]. I know that you have the interests of the men of our battalion at heart. And I believe you will agree that these teenage youngsters fight with great courage, but are just too green and inexperienced to do the job.[2]

Junkin was awarded the Distinguished Service Cross, our nation's second highest military award, for his heroic conduct. Several others in the Ishimmi Ridge action earned Bronze or Silver stars.

★★★

The problem described by Sergeant Junkin was one faced not only by units in the 77th, but by all of the divisions fighting in southern Okinawa. Casualties were so numerous that the replacement depots barely kept up in providing new men for the front line units. Our horrific losses had far exceeded pre-invasion estimates. A large number of the replacements were 18- and 19-year-old kids just out of basic training. They were needed desperately right away and there simply wasn't sufficient time to get them properly trained for front line conditions on Okinawa. Sending them ill-prepared into combat at that stage was unfortunate. Thus, to survive they needed considerable good luck and the personal ability to learn and adapt quickly while serving in the front lines—some did and others didn't.

The 77th Division had set up a replacement training program, but the new men were being sent to line units so fast, particularly in the first three weeks of May, that it didn't function adequately. The new replacements themselves told us that this brief training consisted of little more than marching in step and doing calisthenics, while they also served in kitchen duty.

When entering combat, the new men, too, sometimes disregarded the most rudimentary principles taught in basic training, including the admonition against "bunching up." Being close together seemed to give them a sense of security when, of course, the exact opposite was true. "Bunched-up" troops are significantly more vulnerable to concentrated enemy fire, resulting in a likelihood of greater casualties. For infantrymen in action, chances for individual survival normally are best when everyone is spread out.

A number of replacements didn't even have time to get acquainted with the men in their new squads and platoons—some recruits literally came up one day, and were dead, or wounded and evacuated, the next day. The veterans might not have known a replacement's name, either. Some veterans, in fact, avoided friendships with them. They didn't want the additional heartache of seeing another friend killed or maimed, which was likely with a new recruit. Many veterans kept to their old buddies.

Most green replacements, of course, had barely begun to develop the ingrained instincts necessary for combat survival, but they also didn't have an understanding of the special tactics required for assaulting fortified positions on Okinawa. An effective front line infantryman not only needed to be physically fit and combat-wise, but he also had to understand our "corkscrew and blowtorch" and "straddle attack" operations against blockhouses, caves, tunnels, and trenches. This required small unit training and special preparation to maintain the tank-infantry teamwork required to take a strongly fortified position with a minimum potential for casualties. Obviously, it was difficult or impossible to provide this training to replacements, who were immediately needed to fill the ranks of our severely depleted squads and platoons.

Every combat veteran knows, of course, that no amount of training can really prepare a soldier for combat. Those men that manage to get through the first few days of action have a better chance for survival in the longer run. A certain element of luck is involved, too—not only for replacements, but also for any veteran on the front line for weeks at a time. However, more effective training should've been made available to the green replacements and rear echelon troops that were recruited for front line duty on Okinawa. This would've prevented some of the terrible inadequacies, as well as additional tragic casualties.

However, even as inadequate as their preparation was, how was it that a significant number of replacements did fight so well? For example, Lieutenant Meiser noted that 70 percent of the men participating in Company E's attack on Ishimmi Ridge were new replacements. Yet, they conducted a skillful assault on a distant objective in the black of night, wrested out an entrenched enemy with bayonets and rifle fire, established an effective defensive perimeter, and withstood everything that the Japs could throw at them, including waves of enemy infantry with fixed bayonets. Then, when heavy losses made it necessary to withdraw from their initial perimeter after a full day of fighting, they destroyed any equipment that might be useful to the enemy and consolidated their defensive position around the company CP in an intrepid and disciplined manner. Here they resisted another two days of intense Japanese attacks.

Such actions could be expected of a company of veterans, but it is especially noteworthy for a group of green replacements. Despite the hesitancy and inexperience noted in some cases by Sergeant Junkin, these men had proven to be determined, effective soldiers under what appears to have been exceptional leadership provided by their officers and non-coms.

For many years, military doctrine had proclaimed that if a combat unit—say a company or battalion—had suffered 30 percent or more casualties, then its fighting spirit and ability to conduct an assault were severely restricted. If the casualty rate exceeded 50 percent, then a unit's combat efficiency was shattered. This certainly wasn't true on Okinawa, however. Many platoons and companies (and even battalions and regiments), both Marine and Army, took 50 percent or more casualties, or even exceeded 100 percent, and still remained effective. These units remained in action, obviously, because their ranks were filled by replacement troops who'd managed to quickly learn enough combat skills to have a chance of remaining alive and becoming effective fighters.

As hard as it was for a green recruit to fill a vacancy in a squad of veterans, it was even tougher for a new officer. Though a buck Private or Private First Class was scared to death and hardly knew a damn thing yet about the reality of combat, at least he didn't have to lead anyone. All he had to do was listen and follow orders. If he did, he might survive longer than just the few days and nights that was the average. (During World War II, half of all individual replacements sent to rifle companies at a time when these units were actively engaged in combat were killed or wounded after only three days.)

A green officer coming up to lead a platoon or a company, on the other hand, was a real enigma.

★★★

Most replacement officers—particularly the first and second lieutenants—were young, new to combat, and inexperienced in leading troops. They had yet to learn, of course, how we lived and survived in the front lines. For example, they wouldn't know whether artillery was incoming or outgoing, if it was large or small caliber, or if they should duck or remain standing. When one of our own outgoing artillery shells passed overhead, it amused us "old veterans" to watch a panicky replacement officer quickly fall to the ground. This occurred, too, with incoming enemy shells that we knew wouldn't strike anywhere near us. We'd remain standing nearby unperturbed, while a new officer, who'd "hit the dirt," meekly rose up from a prone position to his feet.

Humor aside, these situations made us acutely aware that most replacement officers didn't yet have the knowledge and experience required for responsible leadership in combat. The crucible of enemy fire and the use of his wits had provided the combat infantryman with the experience and knowledge needed for

ASSOCIATED PRESS [June 21.] Conquest of Okinawa Island officially ended today while flame-throwing tanks still were burning Japanese out of suicide pockets...

Americans killed since United States total casualties of 35,116 were last announced a month ago included two generals—Lieut. Gen. Simon Bolivar Buckner, Jr., Tenth Army commander, and Brig. Gen. Claudius M. Easley of the 96th Division.

Gen. Joseph W. Stilwell, veteran of China and Burma, will take over command of the Tenth Army...

United States Tenth Army forces finishing up the Okinawa campaign under command of Lieut. Gen. Roy S. Geiger of the Marine Corps, had closed the Japanese into such tight pockets by last night that all artillery support was called off. They relied on demolition charges, automatic weapons and flame-throwing tanks, of which the Japanese are deathly afraid. "They run," said on tank officer, "and sizzle."

...Enemy garrisons in two small pockets are being mopped up."

...The Japanese, developing suicidal air tactics to a violent pitch, crashed upon and sank with their kamikaze (divine wind) pilots...18 United States Fleet units during the campaign, and damaged at least 49 others. The damaged ships included battleships and carriers, although none was listed as sunk.

In Washington, the Navy said recently that total losses in the Ryukyus operation included 25 ships sunk and 54 damaged.

The cost of the futile Japanese aerial defense of Okinawa was 4,000 planes...

survival. The replacement officer, however, had yet to prove that he could keep himself alive or command in such a way that men wouldn't be needlessly killed. Usually, he was judged against an officer whose place he was filling—someone who'd been wounded or killed, and who, in many instances, had been respected and admired. Sometimes, there even was a hint of resentment among the men in this regard when a new officer filled the former position of a favorite officer.

If a new officer had the intelligence and foresight to initially listen to the NCOs and follow their suggestions, he might make it through the first few days and eventually become an effective combat leader. But, ordinarily, if a new officer refused to confer with the sergeants, if he'd disregard advice, if he had a superior attitude and insisted on giving all orders regardless of the consequences, then that officer often just ended up getting killed. This, of course, was a tragedy, but it was even more so if his inept actions caused the deaths of men serving under him. A new officer needed to be under fire for awhile and show that he could take it, and he needed to successfully lead some missions or patrols, indicating that he'd learned how to be an effective leader—then, his men would develop confidence in his leadership.

After a soldier had been in combat for awhile, he learned that an officer could get you into a lot of trouble by being too bold and taking chances in situations where a more prudent and effective leader wouldn't. An officer not only needed to be a good tactical leader, but had to understand and have compassion for his men, and feel that they were important. He needed to understand their physical and emotional characteristics and limitations, and how to best utilize their individual abilities. They expected him to know when to go forward, and when to hunker down, waiting for things to develop—to determine whether or not we should move out, and in what manner and direction. We didn't expect them to be heroic, but we wanted them to have the courage to face enemy fire. We were willing to follow them, but we also expected them not to unnecessarily expose us to danger.

Despite these reservations about new officers, I hardly ever saw any enlisted man flatly refuse to follow an officer's order regardless of the circumstances. We all were scared and didn't want to take unnecessary risks, but during my entire time in the Pacific I never saw or heard of an act of cowardice in my platoon. In fact, refusing to obey an order from a respected officer was almost unheard of in any of the units that I knew. Fortunately, the majority of officers that I served under were excellent, especially the West Point graduates. This wasn't necessarily the case with some of the "90-day-wonders," however, who were just out of the officers' training schools. A number of them simply weren't prepared for the leadership role into which they were thrust.

The new officers were assigned to lead tough, experienced, and battle hardened men who weren't about to follow a foolish, dangerous order to the letter. Most of the new officers, even the ineffective ones, knew they'd better not bark out some ridiculous, witless command to 10 or 20 dirty, tired, and exhausted men who were well armed, had been killing Japs for days, and who remained in largely autonomous, isolated positions in the front lines. To persistently do so might even result in an unpopular officer's death due to "friendly fire" from his own men, and I'm sure this happened on rare occasion. I personally never saw anyone who was ordered to move forward by their assigned officers flatly refuse to do so.

We understood that a platoon had to have cohesion to be effective—someone had to lead and the rest had to follow. Despite having reservations at times, it never really occurred to me to disobey an order, even when I didn't have a great deal of confidence in the officer giving the command. I might openly question an order, but if it was repeated to me, I did it. This obedience had been drilled into us during basic training. Because of our camaraderie and not wanting to let our buddies down, and due to our training and discipline, men simply wouldn't disobey a lawful order. To do so might cause the death of a buddy.

One final thing, no matter how dangerous or desperate our situation, most of us believed it'd be the other guy who'd get killed. When young, most of us are convinced that nothing dire is going to happen—you feel you're invincible and going to live forever. I thought I might get wounded, perhaps, but being killed was something I shoved into the deep recesses of my mind.

It wasn't until after the Okinawa campaign, when we were preparing to invade Japan, that it suddenly hit me—I'd already lived longer than I had any right to! For the first time, I began brooding about the future. What was going to happen next?

Up until that time, however, Lou and I had told each other that we were going to make it, and this kept us going through all those months of combat.

★★★

By June 1, it was obvious that the Shuri line had been broken. The 1st Marine Division had fought its way up Wana Draw to take battered Shuri Castle. This, as well as intense pressure from the other American divisions, had proved disastrous for the Japanese. General Ushijima ordered the defenders in the Shuri line to conduct a secret, and largely successful, withdrawal six miles to the south, an action that was aided by heavy rain that slowed the American response.

My regiment, the 306th, as well as the 307th, was pulled back and put into divisional reserve. We didn't know it yet, but the worst of the fighting was over for us.

The 305th, however, was attached to the 381st Infantry Regiment of the 96th Division. The incessant rainfall finally ended on June 5. For the next couple of weeks, they continued the advance south against the remaining Japanese units, who with their backs to the sea were making a last stand by anchoring on two adjacent hills, Yuzu-dake and Yaeju-dake, at the tip of the island. The latter was called the "Big Apple" by the 96th Division infantry assaulting it—a nearly impassable morass of soft clay seriously impaired tanks there. The final enemy defenses, now hampered by poor communications, greatly reduced manpower, and a severe shortage of supporting artillery, began collapsing, but the Jap positions still were dangerous, formidable objectives for our troops.

The savage fighting on Okinawa had no respect for rank. General Simon Bolivar Buckner was killed by Jap artillery fire while up front at an observation post on June 18, just as the final Japanese resistance was disintegrating. Buckner was the highest-ranking American officer killed by enemy fire during World War II. (General McNair, who I mentioned earlier, was of higher rank, but McNair was killed by friendly fire—a U.S. bombing attack in Normandy.) Shortly thereafter, Brigadier General Claudius Easley, the assistant 96th Division commander, also was killed, by machine gun fire.

On June 22, General Ushijima and his second in command, Lieutenant General Isamu Cho, committed suicide as American troops closed in on the top level of their

Plaque at left reads: "Lieutenant General Simon Bolivar Buckner Jr. killed on this spot, 18 June 1945, battle of Okinawa." *Melvin C. Lindeman collection*

headquarters cave facing out on the ocean. Having failed in their assigned task of defeating the Americans, they took their lives in the Samurai tradition by *seppuku*—Ushijima by ritual disembowelment, and both Ushijima and Cho by sword blows to the neck administered by fellow officers. Seven staff members also immediately pulled out pistols and shot themselves. For thousands of other Japanese soldiers and Okinawa civilians, too, suicide was preferable to surrender. Many Okinawans jumped off the island's cliffs.

Colonel Hiromichi Yahara, who'd argued unsuccessfully against the massive Japanese counterattack of May 4, had asked to join his commander in ending his own life. General Ushijima, however, specifically ordered Yahara to stay alive to tell the "truth" about the Battle of Okinawa.[3] Dressed as a peasant workman, Yahara tried to escape, but eventually was captured by our troops.

★★★

On Okinawa, of course, the Army and Marines fought side by side. On a number of occasions, units of the two services coordinated their attacks and worked very effectively together. I found the cooperation exemplary between the two branches both on Guam and Okinawa, and I gained deep respect for the combat efficiency and aggressive character of the Marines that flanked us. I believe the admiration often was mutual—as a consequence of our division's accomplishments and our successful beachhead landings, the Marines themselves often called us the 77th "Marines."

While I admired the combat skills of the Marine divisions, I never regarded our Army divisions as anything less than their equals. I personally felt, as did everyone that I served with in the 77th, that our soldiers were every bit as capable as the Marines. It's unfortunate, but it appears to me that the Marines have benefited from a certain publicity, particularly after the war, making it appear that they were the major service conducting the ground fighting in the Pacific, rather than being equal partners with the Army.

Throughout most of the Okinawa campaign, the 1st Marine and 6th Marine divisions flanked the 77th on the right. Every day, we faced the same dangers and hardships, the same resolute enemy entrenched in the same kinds of fortified positions. There weren't any differences in the Jap shells that killed and wounded Marines or Army infantry. We all bled the same way. The rain that fell on them, fell on us, and the mud that engulfed them, did the same to us.

During the Okinawa campaign, I knew the Marines showed efficiency and élan, but in my opinion the 77th and other Army divisions exhibited these same qualities, and in equal measure. The Marine and Army divisions moved with the same dispatch and decisiveness. Our flanks always moved up together. Consequently, it's somewhat bothersome that over the years some portion of the American public, at least, has come to believe that the Marines were the primary American force that defeated the Japanese in the Pacific.[4]

This appears to have been fostered by some Marine publicists who'd like to magnify the accomplishments of their units, while denigrating the role of the Army. My purpose here is not to diminish or criticize the achievements of the Marine units on Okinawa, but, at the same time, let's not eliminate credit where it should be given. While I was researching the background historical literature for this memoir, I too often came across comments that elevated the accomplishments of the Marines while downplaying and even criticizing the role of the U.S. Army infantry units.

These opinions sometimes came from individual Marines who'd fought in the Pacific and recorded their experiences, and sometimes they came from other authors writing about the Pacific campaigns. Even recently, some books and television documentaries still give the impression that Okinawa, like Iwo Jima, was solely a Marine operation. In fact, the Army and Marines cooperated, and extensively, in many of the major Pacific campaigns—in the Solomons, the Marshalls, the Marianas, Okinawa, and elsewhere.

To set the record straight, on Okinawa up to May 31, 1945—around the time of the fiercest fighting against the Shuri defenses—the Army's 96th Division had been in the Shuri line for 50 days; the Army's 7th Division, 49; the

OKINAWA BATTLE COSTLIEST IN MEN

June 21.—(AP)—The conquest of Okinawa was the longest and costliest of all the campaigns in the Central and Western Pacific [i.e., exclusive of the New Guinea, Solomons, and Philippines campaigns]...

The 82 days it took to break all organized resistance dwarfs the 26 days of Iwo Jima. The latter, however, is less than eight square miles in area, and Okinawa is roughly 485 square miles.

The figures for Okinawa, which include Japanese casualties...and American casualties only to May 24, compared with those of six other campaigns follow:

	Japanese		American	
	Killed	Captured	Killed	Wounded
Okinawa	87,343	2,565	9,602	25,514
Iwo Jima	23,244	1,038	4,630	15,308
Saipan	27,586	2,161	3,426	13,099
Guam	17,442	520	1,437	5,648
Palau	13,354	435	1,302	6,115
Tarawa	5,000	150	913	2,037
Tinian	6,939	523	314	1,515

77th, 32, and the 1st Marine Division, 31. The 6th Marine Division had been on the front line for just a little more than three weeks.[5]

Most of the casualties, both for the Army and the Marines, were incurred in the enemy's southern defensive area, which was approximately five to six miles wide (east to west) and eight to twelve miles in length (north to south). It was within this very limited space that the most crucial and prolonged struggle on Okinawa was fought. By June 1, approximately 65,000 of the enemy were reported killed here in the Shuri area, whereas 3,200 of the enemy had been eliminated by the Marines in northern Okinawa and about 5,000 by the 77th Division on Ie Shima and in other small island assaults.

During the entire Okinawa campaign, the Army lost 4,663 dead and missing, and the Marines 2,898. The wounded totaled 18,099 for the Army, and 13,609 for the Marines. In addition, the Army suffered 15,613 non-battle casualties, the Marines 10,217; the great majority of these, of course, were neuro-psychiatric in nature (combat fatigue). These figures total 38,375 casualties for the Army and 26,724 for the Marines.

The Marines were on the right flank of the Army during the campaign against the enemy's formidable southern defenses. For either service, there wasn't any material difference in the terrain, the weather, or the intensity of the Japanese resistance. Consequently, I've been disturbed on several occasions when reading comments by different Marine authors who criticize Army infantry units who fought next to them so valiantly on Okinawa. Hopefully, there are only certain individuals that feel this way. Taking sides in this manner actually is detrimental to the reputations of both of these fine services.

I understand that there is a certain amount of unit pride and inter-service rivalry that may be involved here, but whether the Army or the Marines faced the fiercest enemy opposition and most difficult terrain features simply cannot be determined. However, consider this. Okinawa was the only campaign during the Pacific war in which Army and Marine divisions fought for about the same period of time, under the same conditions, and with somewhat equal numbers of men (on May 31—45,980 Marines, and 51,745 for the Army). There was little, if any, difference in the performance and execution of their battlefield conduct and responsibilities. My experience indicated that the 77th, the 96th, and the 7th were the equal of any other divisions, Marine or Army, that fought anywhere in the Pacific.

NOTES

1. *Official Narrative of the Operation of the 77th Division on Okinawa, Vol. II*, National Archives and Records Division, RG:319, Stack 270/19/8/5, Box 337, 67–82. The version presented here in *Through These Portals* has been slightly shortened and edited.
2. *Ours to Hold It High: The History of the 77th Infantry Division in World War II* (Washington, DC: Infantry Journal Press, 1946), 269–70.
3. Hiromichi Yahara, *The Battle for Okinawa* (New York: John Wiley and Sons, 1995).
4. My granddaughter once asked me to help with an essay that she was preparing for her seventh grade elementary class concerning the Pacific war. She expressed surprise when I told her that I'd fought with an Army infantry division on Okinawa. She said, "I didn't know the Army fought there, Grandpa. I thought the Marines took Okinawa."
5. Roy E. Appleman [et al.], *Okinawa, The Last Battle: United States Army in World War II* (Washington, DC: Center of Military History, 1948), 386.

14 End of the Nightmare

N June 21, 1945, Okinawa finally was declared secure, though small pockets of Jap soldiers continued to resist for several days. The 305th continued in the mopping up of the scattered, unorganized enemy resistance in the southern portion of the island. Thus, the 77th Division, which had been the first large ground unit to engage the enemy in the Ryukyu campaign (i.e., the Kerama Retto assault), also participated with the last major American units completing the conquest of Okinawa.

All together, our division killed more than 16,000 Japanese and took 58 prisoners. Our total casualties for the Ryukyu campaign, including the invasion of the Kerama Retto and Ie Shima, amounted to approximately 1,100 killed in action, 4,000 wounded, and 2,100 non-battle casualties (nearly all of which were neuro-psychiatric or battle fatigue cases).

After the battle—shattered Japanese fortifications on Okinawa. *Melvin C. Lindeman collection*

This is a total casualty list of about 7,200. At the end of May, however, the 77th Division had remaining in its three infantry regiments, not counting attached units, a reported strength of about 9,600 men, many of whom were replacements. A comparison of these figures would suggest a total casualty rate, during just this one campaign, of about 75 percent among the combat infantry regiments. That means that about 7 out of every 10 men assigned to those regiments—including both the veterans at the start of the campaign and the replacements who came later—eventually became casualties. A heavy price, indeed, for one division to pay during its participation in this terrible battle.

As with the XXIV Army Corps' infantry regiments, tank units also suffered heavily. Nearly 60 percent of all tanks were either destroyed or heavily damaged during the Ryukyu campaign.

★★★

Knocked out tank, April 1945. *Sylvan R. Thompson collection*

Above and to the right: Two views of a destroyed M4 Sherman tank—"remodeled," in tankers' parlance. *Sylvan R. Thompson collection*

Before leaving Okinawa, I made it a point to visit the 77th Division cemetery. It was well kept. The stark geometry of row upon row of graves initially gave an appealing appearance, until you realized that underneath each beautiful white cross and star of David lay men that you knew, that you'd eaten chow with, and who'd fought beside you. In addition to this cemetery on Okinawa, the 77th Division also had cemeteries on Ie Shima, in the Kerama Retto, on Leyte, and Guam.

All contained the bodies of young men who'd gone to fight for their country in a burst of patriotism the likes of which our country has seldom seen. After the Japanese attacked Pearl Harbor, it seemed as if nearly everyone I knew in high school wanted to join the military. Most did, sooner or later—the Army, Navy, or Marines, any of the services—just so long as it gave them the opportunity to fight for their country. Japan's treacherous attack caused feelings of hatred and revulsion for our enemies. At the same time, however, most of us had a good feeling about being in a position to defend and protect our families, sweethearts, and the land in which we were born.

I walked down the rows of graves and looked at the names of boys I knew— Bowerman, Bonjiovanni, Bush, MacDonald, Maslowski, Steinberg—so many different names, nationalities, and ethnic groups, but all were Americans and now joined by a common bond of death, in a military cemetery thousands of miles from home. They'd died fighting for a cause they believed in; they'd given their lives to honor and protect family and country.

Dedication of the 77th Infantry Division cemetery on Ie Shima. *U.S. Army*

Remembering now, how I had stood there in that cemetery, I'm reminded of a rhyme that I'd once read or heard, and which somehow stayed with me over the years. It runs through my mind:

> What did you learn in school today, dear little boy of mine?
> I learned that war is not so bad
> I learned about the great ones that we've had
> We fought in Germany and in France
> And someday I'm going to get my chance
> That's what I learned in school today
> That's what I learned in school.

It makes me think of when I was a boy and how we used to play war, aiming our fingers or toy guns at other boys, shouting "bang, bang" and "you're dead." Why was it that we let our children grow up glorifying war and making them think that it's a great adventure, when actually it's the most gross, painful, and horrifying experience that can happen to anyone? It's debasing and cruel; but, of course, we children had no idea actually of what we were doing, or even thought that we'd someday fight in a real war.

As I turned to leave the cemetery, I saw a box near an entry gate containing several copies of a speech by Brigadier General Edwin H. Randall, which was presented at the cemetery's dedication ceremony. I took one out and read it. The speech ended with the verse:

> Here dead we lie because we did not choose
> To live and shame the land from which we sprung.
> Life, to be sure, is nothing much to lose;
> But young men think it is, and we were young.

American Battle Monuments Commission Listing of 405,399 American World War II Fatalities

*233,181   buried in the United States.

*93,242   interred in overseas ABMC cemeteries.

*78,976   "Missing in Action" and "Buried at Sea" identified at ABMC memorials.

American Cemeteries

The 77th Division cemeteries were temporary, as were all of the hundreds of other burial grounds established on battlefields around the world by the American Graves Registration Service. After the war, families had the right to have the bodies of servicemen and women brought home for reburial in the United States, or the next of kin could choose to have them reinterred overseas in new, beautifully landscaped, military cemeteries maintained by the American Battle Monuments Commission (ABMC). Occasionally, relatives directed that isolated graves be left undisturbed at the original sites.

Of the ABMC list of 405,399 Americans who died in all theaters of action during World War II, 233,181 are buried in the United States, often in National and State veteran graveyards, as well as in private cemeteries. Of the remainder, relatives chose to have 93,242 interred in the overseas American Battle Monuments Commission cemeteries. There also are 78,976 World War II "Missing" and "Buried at Sea" who are memorialized at ABMC sites.

In the Pacific, the ABMC maintains cemeteries and memorials at Manila (17,206 burials/36,282 missing), Honolulu (18,096 missing), and the West Coast (412 missing). Two-thirds (or 54,790) of all U.S. dead in World War II listed as "Missing in Action" and "Buried at Sea" were lost in the Pacific theater, which primarily was an ocean-based conflict.

The ABMC also maintains 13 European cemeteries for American World War II dead in France, England, Belgium, Italy, the Netherlands, and Luxembourg, plus one in Tunisia, North Africa, and a memorial on the East Coast. An additional 30,921 Americans who perished in 1917–18 during the Great War (these were the World War II generation's fathers, uncles, and older brothers) likewise are interred in some of these and other European ABMC cemeteries.

The Manila American Cemetery (17,206 burials/36,282 missing) is the largest administered by the ABMC anywhere for World War II fatalities. The two largest ABMC cemeteries for World War II dead in Europe are located in France at Lorraine (10,489 burials/444 missing) and Normandy (9,387 burials/1,557 missing).

The U.S. government provided one-time travel expenses to immediate family members wishing to visit the grave of a close relative—a son, daughter, spouse, father, etc.—buried in an overseas ABMC cemetery. Although the vast majority of fatalities in World War II were men, a significant number of women also lost their lives.

In addition to men and women in military service, the official listing of 405,399 burials includes civilian technicians, Red Cross workers, and entertainers that served our armed forces. Some other civilian and Merchant Mariner fatalities are not included in this listing. Philippine nationals who fought alongside their American comrades in arms in the Philippine campaigns are allowed burial in the Manila American Cemetery. All other ABMC cemeteries are exclusively reserved for American war dead. Remains of the "Missing" still are found from time to time on World War II battlefield sites.

For American Battle Monuments Commission listings and information, see the website: www.abmc.gov. For information about the numerous National and State veterans' cemeteries in the United States, contact: www.cem.va.gov.

December 8, 1941
Excerpts from Emperor Hirohito's
Declaration of War on America and Britain

We, by the grace of heaven, emperor of Japan seated on the throne of a line unbroken for ages eternal, enjoin upon ye, our loyal and brave subjects:

We hereby declare war on the United States of America and the British empire.

Men and officers of our army and navy shall do their utmost in prosecuting the war, our public servants of various departments shall perform faithfully and diligently their appointed tasks and all other subjects of ours shall pursue their respective duties; the entire nation with united will shall mobilize their total strength so that nothing will miscarry in attainment of our war aims.

To assure the stability of East Asia and to contribute to world peace is a farsighted policy which was formulated by our great illustrious imperial grandsire [Meiji, d. 1912] and our great imperial sire [Taisho, d. 1926] succeeding him and which we lay constantly to heart...

It has been truly unavoidable and far from our wishes that our empire has now been brought to cross swords with America and Britain. More than four years have passed since China, failing to comprehend the true intentions of our empire and recklessly courting trouble, disturbed the peace of East Asia... [and] relying upon American and British protection, still continues to be fratricidal opposition.

Eager for realization of their inordinate ambition to dominate the orient, both America and Britain are giving support to the [Nationalist Chinese] regime and have aggravated the disturbance in East Asia.

Moreover, these two powers, including other countries to follow suit, increased military preparations on all sides of our empire to challenge us.

They have obstructed by every means our peaceful commerce and finally resorted to direct severance of economic relations, menacing the existence of our empire.

Patiently have we waited and long have we endured in hope that our government might retrieve the situation in peace.

But our adversaries, showing not the least spirit of conciliation, have unduly delayed settlement; and, in the meantime, they have intensified economic and political pressure to compel thereby our empire to submission.

This trend of affairs would, if left unchecked, not only nullify our empire's efforts of many years for the sake of stabilization of East Asia but also endanger the very existence of our nation. The situation being such as it is, our empire, for its existence and self-defense, has no other recourse but to appeal to arms and to crush every obstacle in its path.

The hallowed spirits of our imperial ancestors [are] guarding us from any defeat...

15 CEBU (PHILIPPINE ISLANDS)

*E*ARLY IN JULY, we boarded LSTs and sailed for Cebu, a large island located just west of Leyte in the central Philippines. As usual upon our arrival in a "rest" area, we were put to work building our own camp. These were called rest camps, but we hardly ever had a chance to relax in any of them.

First, we had to clear brush and trees from the site and bring in sand. Then we erected framed tents for our quarters and also a kitchen and large dining area with tables and benches. The dining hall also served as a recreational area. In addition, a movie house with a projector was set up and coconut logs were laid down in rows for seating.

Once the camp was completed, however, there was scarce time for recreation. We immediately began training for our next campaign—the invasion of the large Island of Kyushu, located in southern Japan. Kyushu is one of four main islands that make up the Japanese homeland—the others being Shikoku, Honshu, and Hokkaido.

Then came news that an atomic bomb had been dropped on Japan on August 6. This one bomb—a tremendous weapon equalling the explosive power of 20,000 tons of TNT—had completely annihilated Hiroshima. Four days later, word arrived that a second bomb was dropped on Nagasaki with largely similar results.

We waited in anticipation for the Japanese surrender and shortly it was announced. Everyone temporarily felt filled with joy, but there wasn't any real celebration among the men in my platoon. We'd been fighting for so long that it was hard for us to believe that the war finally was over. Only until we arrived at our homes back in the States would we believe it. We feared, in a way, that the peace agreement somehow would fall apart and we'd end up back on APAs headed for Japan for one final, long, brutal campaign.

For several days, our divisional officers negotiated a surrender agreement with the enemy troops still holding out in the hills of Cebu. My regiment, the 306th, was ordered to proceed to where the Japanese were bivouacked, and

Remnants of the Japanese forces on Cebu surrender to our regiment. About 40 women stand in the mid-portion of the ranks. *U.S. Army*

disarm and convey them to Cebu City. This was accomplished without any difficulty or problems. We took about 5,500 Japanese prisoners. They appeared eager to surrender and caused no trouble whatsoever. In addition to the soldiers, we also took in a number of nurses and "comfort girls."

★★★

Since the end of the war, the dropping of the atomic bombs on Hiroshima and Nagasaki have raised a number of ethical and historical questions. Among others, was the use of the A-bomb really necessary at the time to force Japan's surrender? Why were large cities targeted? Could the bombs have been used effectively against other objectives, resulting in fewer casualties? Would we have dropped A-bombs on Caucasians (Germans) as well as Asians? And so on.

It sometimes seems to be forgotten that during the war not only the United States but also Germany and Japan were in a race to be the first to develop the atomic bomb. Our enemies made significant attempts in this endeavor; they knew it probably was feasible. However, the United States, with greater and more secure resources, better planning, and highly capable scientists, put the greatest effort into atomic research and achieved success.[1] If by chance, however, either of our main enemies had successfully developed an A-bomb first, I'm certain they would've used it against the other Allies and us. The proven brutish, heartless character of the fascist leaders in Japan and Germany leave little doubt about this.

An atomic bomb dropped on Japan, August 1945. *U.S. Army*

From the time that work first began on the atomic bomb, there appears to have been little question that it eventually would be used against the enemy's military, industrial, and commercial centers, and that civilian casualties undoubtedly would be incurred. The conflict in the Pacific was a total war—no quarter was asked and none given. Because of the conflict's savagery and the treachery at Pearl Harbor, objections to bombing Japan's cities (and thus the civilian populous) slowly eroded until, by the time of the atomic attacks, there was a general lack of resistance to their use in this manner.

Since early 1945, in fact, the frequent and extensive B29 fire bombings of Japanese cities already had been widely cheered in the United States. Hundreds of thousands of Japanese men, women, and children were dying in these nighttime fire raids, which continued even during early August when the atomic bombs were dropped. The March 10, 1945, raid on Tokyo had killed more people (130,000) than either of the later Hiroshima or Nagasaki atomic bomb attacks. (In Europe in early 1945, too, the Americans and especially the British had conducted similar massive fire bombing raids on Dresden and other German cities.)

It must be pointed out that in the summer of 1945, many in the top Japanese military and political leadership fully realized that their nation was "doomed." However, in true Bushido tradition, they intended to fight to the bitter end in suicidal resistance, enveloping Japan and its population in a catastrophic orgy of destruction. For these people, surrender to the Americans under any circumstances was entirely out of the question. Others in Japan held the hardly less fatalistic view that intense Japanese resistance to an ongoing invasion in the home islands "might" cause such unacceptable U.S. losses that the Americans would withdraw and negotiate an armistice. Fortunately, however, there was a small but growing minority of peace-minded Japanese leaders in and out of government who were surreptitiously encouraging surrender, preferably with the Emperor being allowed to retain his throne. In early August, with the dropping of the atomic bombs sandwiched around Russia's declaration of war on Japan (August 9), the Emperor would openly side with these elements, ending the war on August 15.

After the war, it was revealed that a target committee had been created to determine when and where atomic bombs should be dropped on Japan. It was suggested that the Imperial Palace in Tokyo or the ancient cultural center of

CEASE FIRE ORDER GIVEN...

Aug. 14. —(AP)—Japan has surrendered unconditionally, President Truman announced at 7 p.m., E.W.T. [Eastern War Time] ...

General of the Army Douglas A. MacArthur has been designated Supreme Allied Commander to receive the surrender.

Offensive operations have been ordered suspended everywhere.

V-J Day will be proclaimed only after the surrender has been formally accepted by MacArthur.

Mr. Truman read the formal message relayed from Emperor Hirohito through the Swiss government, in which the Japanese ruler pledged the surrender on the terms laid down by the Big Three Conference [Britain, Russia, and the U.S.] at Potsdam.

Kyoto be obliterated, but this was rejected because these were important cultural places. Such destruction, or any harm inflicted on Emperor Hirohito and his family, would have only further inflamed Japanese civilian resistance.

A few top-level decision-makers in Washington D.C. suggested that a bomb be dropped offshore or in a non-populous part of Japan as a pre-announced demonstration to the Japanese people. This idea was rejected—the Japanese might shoot down the plane carrying the bomb or consider the demonstration blast to be some kind of technically created sham, and thus they wouldn't appreciate the bomb's terrible destructive power. Also, there was a chance that the bomb might fail to explode—a real possibility with a new, barely tested technology.

The committee finally decided to target large cities and thereby try to terminate the war as soon as possible. This would produce the greatest psychological effect on the Japanese people and government. As a secondary objective, the example of the bomb's destructive power also would serve as a deterrent to our wartime ally, the Soviet Union, whose ultimate territorial aims in Asia and Europe were starting to be looked upon with suspicion by the United States.

The U.S. Secretary of War, Henry L. Stimson, and some others expressed shock and concern about the probable heavy civilian casualties. They felt that some people would feel that dropping atomic bombs on Japan was comparable to the atrocities committed by the Nazis in Europe. Eventually, however, Stimson's moral misgivings were somewhat overcome and he became an advocate for using these weapons, even though it might turn the Japanese so much against the United States that they'd never be an ally in any future disputes that might arise with the U.S.S.R. in Asia.

President Truman, in his diary, claimed that he had directed Secretary of War Stimson to use the atomic bombs only on "military objectives and soldiers and sailors."[2] Any intelligent person, of course, and certainly the President of the United States, would have known that there would be thousands of civilian deaths as a result of these atomic attacks.

★★★

Our leaders were hoping to avoid a U.S. invasion of Japan already scheduled to begin in the fall of 1945. It was expected that the assault's astounding losses would dwarf our casualties in Normandy and the European campaigns. In fact, veteran divisions in Europe were in the process of being transferred to the Pacific to participate in the latter stages of the attack. Also, 14,000 Allied planes and 100 aircraft carriers were expected to participate in the monstrous operation.

The first landing would occur on the southernmost island of Kyushu on November 1, 1945, designated as X-day. My division, the 77th, was chosen among others to participate in this attack. General MacArthur, the overall commander, had assigned 14 divisions for this phase of the operation:

Americal Division	33rd Infantry Division
1st Cavalry Division	40th Infantry Division
2nd Marine Division	41st Infantry Division
3rd Marine Division	43rd Infantry Division
5th Marine Division	77th Infantry Division
11th Airborne Division	81st Infantry Division
25th Infantry Division	98th Infantry Division

More than a quarter-million infantrymen and almost 90,000 Marines were assigned to the assault, code named "Olympic." The invasion would begin with the 25th, 33rd, and 41st infantry divisions landing on the southeast coast of Kyushu and driving west to connect up with the 2nd, 3rd, and 5th Marine divisions coming ashore and pushing inland near Kushikino on the west coast. Three days later, my division, the 77th, and the 81st and 98th divisions would assault the island's south coast and move north and west to cut off and bottle up the enemy forces on the tip of Kyushu. The 11th Airborne was scheduled to stand in reserve to provide support as needed.

Depending upon the success of the Olympic operation—estimated to take up to four months—an even larger invasion of the huge main island of Honshu would occur in the spring of 1946 in an operation called "Coronet." Consisting of perhaps five million men, it would be the largest amphibious assault ever attempted.

The Joint War Plans Committee issued a memo in the summer of 1945 estimating casualties for the Kyushu invasion. It was expected that "Olympic" initially would result in 132,500 casualties. However, if the assault on south Kyushu didn't bring the Japanese to their knees, then it would be necessary to invade the northern part of Kyushu, too, in which case casualties could be expected to approach a quarter-million. (Even vaster losses could be expected in Operation Coronet, of course, when the main island of Honshu and the capital city, Tokyo, were invaded.)

The American casualties on Okinawa were almost 13,000 killed, nearly 37,000 wounded, and roughly 26,000 neuro-psychiatric cases—a total Army, Navy, and Marine casualty toll of about 76,000. The Japanese garrison on Okinawa consisted only of approximately 115,000 men, of whom 110,000 were killed in the horrific struggle. These numbers pale in comparison to the absolutely astronomical casualties that could be expected in the invasion of the Japanese main islands, which were defended by more than 2,500,000 enemy soldiers from 57 divisions, 45 regiments, and other organizational elements. In addition, an estimated 32,000,000 civilian men and women were organized into huge militia units. This would be a human tragedy of indescribable proportions.

These invasion statistics shocked President Truman. He essentially had three alternatives for ending the war: (1) invade Japan with a resulting terrible number of American and Japanese dead and wounded; (2) order a naval blockade and a continuing massive aerial bombardment, which could result in millions of Japanese civilian casualties, mostly from starvation and deprivation; or (3), drop atomic bombs, which in all probability would quickly end the war.

Of course, for infantrymen awaiting orders to mount another amphibious assault, which would be bigger and bloodier than anything we'd ever seen before, questions of morality were hardly contemplated. We were hoping and praying that somehow the war would end. We weren't concerned about the high estimates of Japanese dead or even overly so with the overall figures for our own casualties. We primarily were concerned with whether we, individually and our buddies, were going to live or die.

The horrors of past campaigns were beginning to weigh on many of us who'd managed to survive. For the first time I began having doubts as to whether I'd make it through another battle. Any member of a veteran rifle company, especially, could look around and see perhaps only 20 or 30 original men left from the time when they shipped out to the Pacific. They knew the odds were stacked against them. All of us had, at one time or another, prayed for that "million dollar wound"—an injury serious enough for a man to be sent back to the States for medical treatment, but not one that caused the loss of a limb, eyesight, or which resulted in ugly disfigurement.

We had little sympathy for the Japanese, even the non-combatants. Having seen so much death, pain, and sorrow, all we wanted now was an end to the war. If it required the deaths of further hundreds of thousands of Japanese, so be it.

Most historians today agree that the atomic bombs brought the war to an abrupt conclusion. The best estimate of casualties at Hiroshima and Nagasaki are that between 150,000 and 200,000 Japanese victims perished. It's insightful to recall that the casualties in the Okinawa campaign considerably exceeded these numbers. On Okinawa, 150,000 civilians, 110,000 Japanese soldiers, and almost 13,000 Americans were killed—totaling 273,000.[3] And, this in just one campaign on a small 60-mile-long island.[4] The implications regarding what would've happened in a full-scale invasion of Japan are obvious. Is it any wonder now that practically any veteran who fought on Okinawa feels the United States was justified in dropping atomic bombs on Japan and bringing this savage war to a sudden end?

☆

NOTES

1. Some have speculated that if the course of the war in Europe had gone differently, a scenario could have developed in which we would have dropped atomic bombs on Germany, too. This likely would have played out if the June 1944 Allied landing in Normandy had failed and the Allies had retreated back to England's shores. Thus,

having thwarted the Allied threat in the West, Hitler would have transferred substantial numbers of his troops from France to the Eastern Front, thereby probably checking the Russian advance and extending the war well into the summer of 1945. Consequently, it is likely that the United States then would have resorted to using atomic bombs against Germany in the summer of 1945 as a whole series of these weapons became available. This would have been done to avoid heavy Allied losses in another attempted invasion of France or from continuing campaigns in Italy or elsewhere in Europe. Also, our animosity toward the Nazis practically equalled our disdain for the Japanese. As things actually turned out, of course, the war in Europe ended May 8, 1945, three months before atomic bombs were ready for use. For a good summary of this scenario had the D-day invasion failed, see Stephen E. Ambrose, *D-day, June 6, 1944: The Climactic Battle of World War II* (New York: Touchstone, 1994), 28–30.

2. Barton J. Bernstein, *Foreign Affairs* 74 (1) (January/February 1995): 147.

3. Ian Gow, *Okinawa, 1945: Gateway to Japan* (New York: Doubleday, 1985), 204; Williamson Murray and Allan R. Millett, *A War to Be Won: Fighting the Second World War, 1937–1945* (Cambridge, MA: Harvard University Press, 2000), 511; and George Feifer, *Tennozan: The Battle of Okinawa and the Atomic Bomb* (New York: Ticknor and Fields, 1992), xi, 557-58, 578.

4. It is informative to compare these appalling statistics to another incident of proportionate scale in the China-Japan conflict. In late 1937-early 1938 during their advance in China, haughty and conceited Japanese commanders were angered by what they perceived as the insolence of the inferior Chinese people to try and resist Imperial Japan's hegemony. Consequently, Japanese leaders condoned their troops barbaric actions in "The Rape of Nanking." In this debacle of unimaginable scale, 200,000 to 300,000 Chinese residents of Nanking, mainly civilians, were murdered (no one will ever know the exact figure). Chinese by the tens of thousands were machine-gunned, beheaded by Japanese officers with Samurai swords, or bayoneted while tied to stakes; women and girls were raped, killed, and mutilated; old people and children were victims too; thousands were buried alive. The institutionalized and indoctrinated cruelty within the ranks of the Japanese Imperial Army was simply unfathomable. Today, this event has largely been forgotten in the West. However, people in many Asian countries, particularly China, Korea, and the Philippines, still keenly remember this or similar incidents, much like citizens of Western nations recall the Jewish holocaust in Europe during those same times.

16 JAPAN

*I*N THE EARLY PART OF SEPTEMBER, the rumor mill began its work. Word was that we'd soon be heading for Japan and occupation duty. True enough, the 306th was ordered to proceed to Hokkaido, the large northern island. We'd been resupplied and outfitted and were fully combat loaded when we left Cebu for Japan. There was no zigzagging to avoid submarines and no blackouts aboard ship. Lectures about the Japanese, their customs, and family life were presented to us several times during the voyage.

On October 4, our convoy steamed into Hakodate harbor at the south end of Hokkaido. Most of us were apprehensive about the reception we'd receive from the Japanese. Although the enemy soldiers who surrendered on Cebu were submissive and caused no trouble, we didn't know what to expect when we reached the home islands. After our convoy halted offshore from Hakodate, once again we climbed over the side of the ship—this time for the last time—and scrambled down the

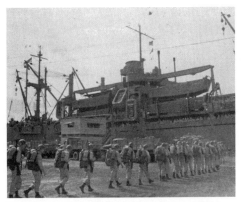

Newly re-outfitted 77th Division troops embarking on an APA for Hakodate on the northern island of Hokkaido, Japan. *U.S. Army*

cargo nets and into the landing craft. We then were taken to piers in the port area and went ashore.

We were transported to a university campus and assigned to what appeared to be dormitories. After living outdoors for so many months, these accommodations seemed luxurious to us. We were pleased to have access to indoor bathroom facilities that were modern, tiled, and had good fixtures. Initially, however, it was surprising to see that Japanese toilets consisted of what we called "tiled slit trenches," with water running through them, over which one had to squat when relieving oneself.

In every way the Japanese were obedient to our orders, requests, and requirements. At first, we saw few women or children. I'm sure it was because they'd been told that Americans would commit rapes and murders. After we'd been in Japan for a few weeks, the civilians could see that we weren't going to harm them. They soon became quite friendly and I was even invited to several Japanese homes for dinner.

While we were in Japan, veterans one by one were beginning to be sent home under a readjustment program based on the "point" system. Servicemen earned points in a variety of ways—one point was given for each month spent in the service, another point for every month served overseas, and an additional point for each month of combat duty. Each decoration and battle star was worth five points. Also, five points were granted for being married and five more for each child. Initially, a total of 85 or more points made a man eligible for discharge. Men with lesser points eventually began being sent home, too.

In many ways, parting was difficult for us. We felt like brothers. For a long time, we'd lived, eaten, and fought together and had seen buddies die. Now, as our men were sent home, breaking up the platoon, it was hard on all of us. We were happy for the men with the high points who left, but there always was an emptiness in our group after they'd gone. In October, Lou and I were informed that we had sufficient points to be discharged and we'd be going home.

★★★

During our time in the Pacific, the 77th Division had earned a reputation for superior combat efficiency. We'd spent more than 90 days at sea while in transport to different destinations. We fought on Guam, Leyte, the Kerama Retto, Ie Shima, and Okinawa. In addition, my unit, the 1st Battalion, had served during the Luzon invasion as a work battalion unloading supplies at the Subic Bay beachhead. We were involved in combat for more than 200 days, and an almost equal length of time was spent in areas where scattered enemy elements still were active and posed a danger.

Twenty U.S. Army infantry, cavalry, and airborne divisions were engaged in combat in the Pacific Theater during World War II.[1] The 77th suffered more casualties in action than 17 of those divisions. Only the 7th and the 96th had a greater number of killed or wounded in combat. All three of these divisions (i.e., the 77th, 7th and 96th) incurred the greatest percentage of losses on Okinawa. The 27th Division also is near the top of the list for overall casualties.

It seems popular now, among some people, to overly emphasize the fact that we prevailed against the Japanese because of a great advantage in material resources, equipment, and supplies, more numerous ships and planes, and

U.S. Army Infantry and Marine Corps Divisions Battlefield Casualties in the Pacific

Infantry Divisions

Division	Combat Deaths	Wounded in Action	Total Casualties
7th Infantry	2,334	7,258	9,592
96th Infantry	2,036	7,181	9,217
77th Infantry	1,850	5,935	7,785
32nd Infantry	1,985	5,627	7,617
24th Infantry	1,689	5,621	7,310
27th Infantry	1,853	4,980	6,833
43rd Infantry	1,406	4,887	6,293
37th Infantry	1,344	4,861	6,205
25th Infantry	1,497	4,190	5,687
41st Infantry	960	3,504	4,464
1st Cavalry	970	3,311	4,281
Americal	1,157	3,052	4,209
38th Infantry	784	2,814	3,598
40th Infantry	748	2,407	3,155
33rd Infantry	524	2,024	2,548
11th Airborne	614	1,926	2,540
6th Infantry	514	1,957	2,471
81st Infantry	515	1,942	2,457
31st Infantry	414	1,392	1,806
93rd Infantry	17	121	138
TOTAL	23,211	74,990	

Marine Corps Divisions

Division	Combat Deaths	Wounded in Action
1st Marine	3,470	14,438
4th Marine	3,345	12,045
2nd Marine	2,795	9,975
5th Marine	2,414	7,159
3rd Marine	2,371	8,045
6th Marine	1,630	7,700
TOTAL	16,025	59,362

The above statistics are derived from Shelby L. Stanton, *Order of Battle: U.S. Army World War II* (Novato, CA: Presidio Press, 1984), and the Marine Corps Historical Section, *Combat Casualties by Division*, Personnel Accounting Section, April 3, 1950. These numbers do not include neuro-psychiatric or non-combat casualties. Also, it must be pointed out that these figures present only "division" statistics. Other Army ground units, such as separate infantry regiments, suffered an additional 15,247 battle deaths. The Marines, whose divisions were larger than the Army's, also incurred another 6,454 combat fatalities not listed here.

Keep in mind, too, that the casualty data differs depending on the source. For example, the 77th's own records indicate that the division suffered 2,000 combat deaths and 6,282 wounded in action, for a total of 8,282 battle casualties. And, in "Order of Battle, Report of Casualties, Army Ground Forces, 10 January 1946," the 77th's casualties are listed as 3,037 killed, 10,531 wounded, and 133 missing; this total includes neuro-psychiatric and non-battle casualties.

The U.S. Army Air Force also suffered substantial casualties in the Pacific, but these figures appear not to be readily available.

technological superiority. It's true that the sheer weight of these advantages did eventually play a role in defeating the Japanese military, which fought with tenacity and courage, but that alone didn't ensure victory on the battlefield. Ground, sea, and sky still had to be taken from the Japanese and held. Ultimately, it wasn't the quantity of our servicemen, but rather their quality that made the difference. It was the individual American soldier, sailor, and marine, acting with great courage and sagacity, disregarding his personal safety and moving forward into peril, that bought victory in the Pacific. Overall, we had better leadership, too. Factories and industrial ascendancy, no matter how great, cannot alone win wars. People must do it.

When the Japanese attacked in 1941, they thought they could prevail in a protracted struggle with the United States and Great Britain. It was their strategy to conquer most of the western Pacific and East Asia, and by so doing, they'd obtain control of the vast natural resources in those areas (oil, rubber, rice, etc.) to sustain their armed forces in inflicting heavy casualties on our forces. They also seized and controlled much of the central Pacific, and sent vast numbers of men, ships, and planes into an "outer defensive perimeter."[2]

A Japanese fatality on Leyte. *Sylvan R. Thompson collection*

They felt that we didn't have the fortitude and determination to throw our resources and manpower against this defensive perimeter in a long, slow, and costly conflict. They planned on forcing us to negotiate an armistice, leaving the Japanese dominant in the western Pacific and with their greatly expanded empire intact. The Japanese military firmly believed that, in their Samurai tradition, they could force the American forces to back down. It was a serious miscalculation, and the Japanese people were to pay a terrible price for it.

At the start of the war, too, the Japanese had mostly good and sometimes even excellent equipment that in some instances was superior to ours. The Mitsubishi "Zero" fighter could out-perform anything that we could put up in the air against it early in the war, and their aircraft carrier force initially was easily the equal of the U.S. Navy's air arm. The I Type Model 400 submarine carried three fighter planes and could stay at sea for more than four months. The Model No. 93 torpedoes used by Japanese submarines, as well as the torpedoes launched from their destroyers and cruisers, were far more effective and reliable than ours early in the war. Not until 1943 did the U.S. Navy begin to effectively close the gap in this regard.

Though the American Navy normally had between half-again or twice as many battleships in service at any one time (about 15 to 20 of them), two Japanese battleships, the *Yamato* and sister ship *Mushashi*, were the most formidable warships ever built. Their tonnage was one-third larger than any capital ship in the American Navy, including the USS *Missouri* and three others of the Iowa class, which were America's most powerful battleships launched during the war years. The Japanese super battleships each had nine 18.1-inch guns, while the main guns on the largest American ships were 16 inch. The *Yamato* and *Musashi's* huge 70-foot-long guns potentially could fire a shell weighing more than 1½ tons for 30 miles, meaning it could attack American battleships before they could close range and return fire. As it turned out, the *Yamato* and *Musashi* were used sparingly by the Japanese, but these vessels were a constant threat to be reckoned with by our naval forces.

In regard to infantry weapons, their 7.7 Nambu machine gun was better than our bulkier, heavier, rapid fire weapons, and it fired twice as many rounds per minute. The 50-mm "knee" mortar clearly was superior (in fact, we simply didn't have anything comparable). It was light, making it highly mobile, and crews could carry more ammunition for it than we could for our 60 mm mortars. Ask anyone who was ever under attack by the knee mortars—they hated the damn things!

Also, the ranks of the Japanese Army were bolstered by tough, well-trained veterans with a long and proud martial history. They'd been fighting in China and Manchuria

Wayne MacGregor with captured Japanese "knee" mortar. *U.S. Army*

for years, and revelled in personal, hand-to-hand combat. Their officers were resolute, forceful, and experienced. They had a tradition of winning every war they'd been in, and they'd been taught that they were superior in every way to their American adversary.

Although outclassed in numbers and available equipment when the war began, our American forces always had the will to resist, even in hopeless situations, such as at Wake Island, or Bataan and Corregidor in the Philippines. As the war went on, the American people, with an indomitable will, skill, and resolve, mounted a massive, determined counterattack. We learned from our mistakes, developed better weapons, and improved our training methods. At their core,

American servicemen and women knew that what they were fighting for was right, and that the "new order" that Germany and Japan stood for was wrong. More than anything else, the faith, trust, belief, and strength of character of the American and Allied cause is what led us forward to victory.

At the end of the conflict in 1945, 16,300,000 Americans had served in the armed forces. Approximately 8 percent, or 1,300,000 men, served in either the Army or Marine infantry. More than 70 percent of all American casualties during World War II were suffered by the infantry units. And, of course, it'd been the infantrymen who lived in the worst filth, discomfort, and sub-human conditions of any our forces, and usually under the most continuous threat of a violent death.

★★★

Having received departure orders, Lou Ryman, myself, and seven additional men from our company, along with other 77th Division troops, were trucked to the Hakodate docks on November 7, 1945. A large ferry took us across Tsugaru Strait to the main Japanese island of Honshu. We then boarded a train and proceeded through the countryside toward the port of Yokohama, located adjacent to Tokyo about 350 miles to the south.

As our train entered the northern outskirts of the vast Tokyo metropolitan area, the devastation we observed was unbelievable. For mile after mile there was nothing but a ghastly, pulverized moonscape. There hardly were any standing buildings, just broken down walls and rubble. The surviving population had pieced together small board and cardboard huts covered over with corrugated tin roofs. Families—parents and small children—stood outside of the huts, stoically watching our train passing by.

Night after night during the spring and summer of 1945, hundreds of our huge B29 bombers had dropped incendiary bombs on Tokyo and other Japanese cities. The highly congested environs of the typical Japanese metropolis, consisting largely of wood, bamboo, and paper structures, had gone up in flames, killing hundreds of thousands of men, women, and children. Residential as well as industrial and commercial areas were annihilated, leaving miles and miles of city landscapes looking like desolate, charred deserts.[3]

In Yokohama, Lou and I managed to be quartered together in the same squad tent. We also received a weekend pass and visited Tokyo. The downtown area was terribly devastated with only shells of some buildings still standing. We made our way to Emperor Hirohito's palace. The Japanese considered him to be a descendant of the Sun Goddess and he was held in such reverence that most people in his presence wouldn't allow themselves to look at him directly. We wanted to see the residence of this Japanese "Deity," who we felt had almost been a personal enemy of ours over the past couple of years.

Lou Ryman and Wayne MacGregor at the Imperial palace, Tokyo.

The ancient, castle-like fortification was an architectural masterpiece occupying almost a square mile of ground in the middle of the teeming, overcrowded city. While walking around outside of the Emperor's palace, Lou and I had our picture taken.

During our air assaults, the B29s flying from the Marianas and planes launched from our aircraft carriers had orders to avoid bombing the palace and its beautiful grounds, which were culturally important sites. Its destruction, or personal injury to the Emperor, would've only increased the resentment and resistance of the Japanese population.

With the surrender, the Japanese had humiliatingly been dealt the first defeat in their nation's history, and their quest for a vast Asian Pacific empire, which many Japanese thought was an inevitable destiny, had been thwarted. A further shock to them came in the early part of the American occupation. Emperor Hirohito, by royal decree, informed his people that he wasn't a "god." For decades, this belief had helped predicate an impression among the Japanese people that they were greater than other races and as such were destined to govern the world. In other words, the underpinning of almost all that the Japanese had believed in and fought for during the Pacific war now was proclaimed to be false.

In personal appearance, Emperor Hirohito was a quite respectable but not imposing figure. He had a retiring, withdrawn personality, walked with a kind of stumbling gait, and wore thick-rimmed glasses. However, the Japanese had believed he was a direct-line descendant of the Emperor Jimmu Tenno, who had ruled Japan during the seventh century B.C. General MacArthur acted with firmness and authority toward Hirohito. But, recognizing the Japanese veneration for their Emperor, MacArthur also treated Hirohito with dignity and respect, which materially helped in promoting feelings of goodwill and cooperation between our two nations during the long occupation period in Japan (1945–51) and afterward.

☆

NOTES

1. The 98th Infantry Division was stationed in Hawaii.
2. Ultimately, the Japanese development of their "outer defensive perimeter" would have included Midway, and probably the eventual seizure of Hawaii as well, but the U.S. Navy's victory at the Battle of Midway in early June 1942 thwarted this goal.
3. "In six months, in 1945, Japan sustained damage from air attack [B29s and carrier aircraft] equivalent to that sustained by Germany in the last three years of the European War." John Keegan, ed., *Atlas of the Second World War* (London: HarperCollins, 1989 [reprint edition 1997]), 196.

17 HOME AT LAST

THE SHIP TAKING LOU AND I home from Yokohama to San Diego traveled on the great northern circle route. A violent typhoon in the North Pacific, however, extended the time of our passage by at least a week. The storm bent the propeller shaft, forcing the vessel to slow down. Almost three weeks would pass before we finally docked at San Diego.

Lou and I stood in the cold Pacific air at the bow railing and reminisced about what'd happened to us in the past couple of years. We'd gone into the Army as boys and were coming out as men. More than anything, we had a sense of fulfillment, of actually having helped, in some small way, to bring an end to the most terrible conflict in human history. Importantly, we realized that during the war we'd lost that feeling of selfishness that people so often have in their lifetimes. The thing that we were most concerned about when in combat was the guy next to us. There wasn't any way we would've let him down.

During the voyage, we also confided in each other regarding our future plans. Lou could hardly wait to return home and marry his girlfriend, Donna, as soon as possible. During my whole time in the Pacific, I never knew anyone as much in love with his sweetheart back home. Lou also intended to return to college. I'd always wanted to be a lawyer. My hopes and dreams were to go to college and earn a law degree, and develop a practice somewhere in Washington or Idaho.

When the ship arrived at San Diego, Lou and I said our farewells as he disembarked. I'd be staying aboard for the voyage to Tacoma and would receive my discharge from the service at Fort Lewis. The ship continued on to Los Angeles, where other men disembarked. Meanwhile, I'd made friends with a young man named Jim Battles, also a sergeant like myself. When inquiring as to whether we could go ashore and see Los Angeles, we were told that only commissioned officers would be given passes. All non-coms and enlisted men had to remain aboard ship.

As you can imagine, this unfair order didn't sit well with a lot of us. After brooding all afternoon, Jim and I finally decided to do something about it. The ship was still crowded with thousands of men. As the officers moved off the deck to go ashore, Jim and I fell in line and walked off the boat without being questioned. Looking back on it, I can't fully understand why we wanted to go into town. There really wasn't much for us to do there. Perhaps it was just rebellion, a way of showing that we were tired of all the "chicken shit" we'd endured in the military all these months. The war was over, and we'd fought and won, so why should any favors be given to commissioned officers? Their insignias of rank meant nothing now. We all were going home for one purpose—to be discharged and enjoy the freedoms and social equality we'd fought for.

On shore, we drank coffee and ate donuts at a USO, then left with other men that we met there. We went from one bar to another, drinking more than we should have. I'd never been much of a drinker anyway, and really hadn't touched much alcohol since high school. Sometime toward morning, about three or four o'clock, we took a cab back to the docks. After crawling out of the taxi, we went to the dock looking for our ship. It was nowhere to be seen!

Almost in a state of panic, and unable to believe that the ship could've left without us, we made our way to the Harbor Master's office. We succeeded in arousing someone there who opened the door for us. Bleary-eyed, he asked what we wanted.

When we told him our predicament, he looked as us blankly, replying, "Hell, that ship left at midnight. It's been gone for several hours."

The expressions on our faces dropped. It was as if someone had thrown a barrel of cold water on us. We couldn't imagine anything worse than being on our way back home for discharge, and then somehow "missing the boat."

Fortunately, Jim and I had learned enough in the past couple of years to realize we didn't want to sit around and wait for something to happen. Immediately, we started planning our own trip to Tacoma. After making our way downtown, eating a good breakfast, and buying a highway map of California, Oregon, and Washington, we took a cab out to the main highway and started hitchhiking north.

Tacoma lay over 1,000 miles away, but we made good time. Late the next day, we arrived in Tacoma and went out to the docks. After inquiring as to which piers were being used by troopships, we walked over there and patiently waited for the arrival of our transport. We noticed, however, that there weren't any bands, welcoming committees, families, or crowds gathered for the arrival of a troopship. There only were some booths, tables, and chairs set up by the Red Cross, whose personnel were huddled trying to keep warm, while serving coffee, soft drinks, and donuts. Usually the Red Cross charged for these items, which complaining GIs said should've been served free to servicemen. A drizzling rain fell, it was cold, and fog had moved in settling over the bay. Our ship wasn't coming in this day.

That night we slept at a YMCA, and early the next morning returned to the docks, and saw our vessel approaching on Puget Sound. During the past two days, of course, we'd been apprehensive about being "Absent Without Leave," or AWOL. Fears of court-martial and stockade time kept going through our minds. With deep anxiety, we stood with the crowd waiting for the ship to dock. We watched for men from the 77th to begin disembarking. The boat was crowded. We had to wait for what seemed like a long time, but possibly only 30 or 45 minutes, before our unit's troops began walking down the gangplank.

Finally, I saw Lieutenant Boylin, the officer in charge of our homebound contingent, leading our men off the ship and down to the dock. Jim and I stood no more than 20 or 30 feet from the gangplank. As Boylin stepped off the gangplank and walked towards us, Jim and I came to attention and saluted. Without breaking stride, Boylin looked directly at us and snapped, "Fall in," and we did.

I'd never been so relieved about anything in my life. Lieutenant Boylin never said a word to us about our unauthorized leave or missing the ship in Los Angeles. He didn't ask about what we'd done or how we were able to get to Tacoma. For this, I'm eternally grateful to him.

We were transported to a processing center at Fort Lewis, Washington, and assigned temporary quarters. We weren't allowed to leave the base, but I called Mother to let her know that I was in town; then called again to let her know when I'd be discharged and released. On the third day, December 19, 1945, Mother was waiting for me as I met her with my discharge papers in hand, home at last.

Sergeant Wayne C. MacGregor, Jr.
U.S. Army Separation Qualification Record
December 19, 1945

Intelligence Observer—Obtained information concerning strength, disposition and probable intentions of enemy forces etc; went on reconnaissance patrols of enemy territory; was lead scout in attacks against enemy; can read maps, use compass; is proficient in use of all Infantry weapons and tactics; advanced to position of squad leader, responsible for control, coordination, tactical employment, discipline and morale of his squad.

★★★

It seemed to me that little had changed during the 2½ years that I'd been away. For people at home, jobs had been plentiful, and now everyone was employed and involved with their own concerns. I thought America was trying to forget about the past and was focusing on the future.

Few people seemed to know of or even seemed to care about the savagery that had just ended six months earlier in the Ryukus. The struggle for Okinawa had occurred around the same period when other transcendent international events had transpired—the deaths of Roosevelt, Hitler, and Mussolini, Germany's capitulation, Russia's declaration of war on Japan, the dropping of the atomic bombs, Hirohito's surrender, and the official termination of hostilities on September 2, 1945. At another time, the fighting on Okinawa probably would've ranked among the most important news events of the year. For most of the American public, however, it'd already become a rather indistinctly re-membered campaign—one among many others that contributed to our victory in the greatest war ever fought.

Vast numbers of veterans, too—particularly the frontline troops, merchant mariners, combat airmen, nurses and medics, the battle fleet seamen, prisoners of war, and many others—were trying to put aside the fears and terrors of the past and settle down to making a future for themselves and their families. They'd experienced the worst of it on land, sea, and in the air, and generally avoided talking about what they'd been through. They mostly kept their memories, rec-ollections, and nightmares to themselves.

Even for the many others in the military who'd been assigned duties stateside, or in the massive overseas supply chains, or in rear echelon service—those who served with distinction, but not in situations of great peril, danger, or apprehen-sion—practically all of them knew someone who died in the war, and many la-mented their lost years away from homes and careers. They, too, mostly looked to the future, and largely ignored the recent past.

★★★

When I think of the 2½ years that I spent in the military, I find myself saying, "There's no way I'd do it again," and that's true. But at the same time, like a lot of veterans have said, I wouldn't have traded a million dollars for the experiences that I had out there in the Pacific. We were among the best and no one will ever take that feeling away from us

Everyone at times during his or her life is faced with strife, sorrow, and prob-lems that seem insurmountable. We all have our "hills" to climb, sooner or later. When I think about myself, I believe I was fortunate in facing my most difficult obstacles in life when I was a teenager, still young and resilient, in Spokane and the Pacific. This matured me and made me grow. My special "hill," however, had to be the Chocolate Drop. Nothing has ever equalled the awful difficulties that I faced there for a week in mid-May 1945. It was terrifying, but it brought out the best in me. It made me reach deep into the reservoir of my soul and pull up every ounce of courage, fortitude, and hope that I had inside of me.

I've been asked on occasion if I'd like to go back and visit the Pacific islands where we fought. I've no desire to do so. The memories of what occurred there

Nature Hiding Scars on Okinawa

By Tom Lambert. Okinawa, April 1 [1950]. (AP)—Five long years have softened and in some cases obliterated the traces of the bitter battle for this island, the last great campaign of the Pacific war.

The hills are verdant now, as they were before Japanese and American explosives churned them into an alternately dusty and muddy battleground on which thousands died.

A rustling tank, on its side in knee-deep water on Green beach, is one of the few signs left at the scene where the American marines and army swarmed ashore on Easter Sunday five years ago today.

A few landing vehicles on a reef and...a wrecked barge or pontoon here and there are other mementos. Okinawan fishermen pass them by without a glance.

At the present American defense base at Naha, the airstrip is lined with deadly-looking jet fighters with such incongruous names as "My Bundle of Fun" and "Miss Eunie Bee." The pilots, youngsters in football-type helmets, lack the strained look around the eyes that marked Okinawa's wartime pilots of conventional-engined jobs.

Up at Kadena airfield it is calm now. It was there five years ago that a planeload of Japanese landed and wrecked 32 United States planes before they were killed.

Offshore there are none of the American transports and warcraft that swarmed those seas while crews watched for the kamikaze suicide pilots of Japan. The enemy sank or damaged scores of ships and killed more than 4900 seamen, but in and around Okinawa the Japanese lost 7800 planes...

No tanks gouge up the Okinawa terrain now. The new improved highways carry modern automobiles, trucks and high-wheeled horse-drawn Okinawan carts.

A returning fighter would be hard put to recognize such one-time hot spots as Kakazu ridge, Shuri and Naha, Sugarloaf, Conical hill, the Chocolate Drop, Item Pocket and Hacksaw ridge.

The surrounding fields, once burned bare and stinking with death, now are green with rice and vegetables.

Around Chocolate Drop, a hard search discloses a few crumbling foxholes, the tread of a tank, a couple of riddled Japanese helmets, a handful of corroded machine gun cartridge cases.

Kids from the near-by orphanage yell there. That seems appropriate too, for those kids are war orphans.

Grass and a few flowers struggle on the face of Kakazu ridge, whose scabrous rocks once spat death.

Shuri castle is a rockpile testimonial to the power of the navy gunners and military artillerymen who slugged it to ruins, and to the youngsters who finally cleaned it out with rifle and grenade.

Around the base of Sugarloaf, remembered by the marines, there are a few old vehicles, notably two tanks with snouts pointed uphill—like runners who fell exhausted just short of the goal. Okinawan farmers cultivate right up to the treads, while youngsters play on the tanks.

Naha is pretty well built back, but the old concrete opera house is full of holes, one big enough for a tank to have made.

South, across the island near Suicide cliff, there is a bronze plaque on a coral rock to mark the spot where Lt. Gen. Simon Bolivar Buckner Jr. was killed by a shell just four days before his 10th army won the Okinawa victory...

Not far away is the place where Lt. Gen. Mitsuru Ushijima, Okinawa's defender, committed hara-kiri.

Off the west coast, at Ie Island, where weary little Ernie Pyle met death, farmers quietly till the soil. Not many Americans go there anymore.

The Okinawans themselves sport that G.I. look five years after the war.

There's an old woman with a dress made of an army blanket; here's a young woman in suntan slacks, and a little girl with an old khaki towel as her only garment.

The Okinawans have moved out of the cave tombs where so many took refuge during the fighting.

Those tombs are dark and quiet now, leading the visitor to melancholy reflections...

77th Division troopers on Leyte—who had passed "Through these portals." *U.S. Army*

are fading, but I'd rather recall them as I still picture them in my mind. I still see my comrades, young, vibrant, and full of life with the vision that young men have—that they can accomplish anything, win any contest, and whip any foe. And they did, but in doing so, many were lost, never to come home.

Today, the battlefields of Guam, Leyte, and Okinawa wouldn't appear as how I remember them. Most areas where our boys fell valiantly, attacking entrenched Japanese in caves, bunkers, and blockhouses, have been bulldozed, re-landscaped, and otherwise altered by agriculture, suburbs, and urban growth. Modern roads, new buildings, and high rises now stand where we fought and lived, where we were told to take "one more hill." No, I have no desire to return with other old men and have my precious memories disturbed by the progress of civilization and populations that have largely forgotten the pain and sacrifice of those years.

I might add that the time I spent in the Army helped me form character traits that I otherwise might not have acquired. I came home with a desire to help people. I believed that as an attorney, I might be able to fulfill that dream. Justice is by right an inheritance of every American, and I wanted someday to do whatever I could to insure that legacy.

Oliver Wendell Holmes, a Civil War veteran and U.S. Supreme Court judge, once said: "A man has not lived if he has failed to share the action and passion of his times."

I have lived and I have shared.

Epilogue

When you next attend a rodeo, sporting event, or parade, watch as the flag is presented by an honor guard or raised to the top of a flag pole. Notice the persons in the crowd who are the first to rise. Their hats removed and right hands placed over their hearts, they stand, trying to hold their ageing bodies rigid and at attention. There are fewer of them each year. They weren't professional soldiers. Many were little more than boys when their country called them, often still in or just out of school or college. Young men then, fit and strong, full of hopes and dreams, yet willing and eager to serve their country.

Time and age have thinned their ranks. They're senior citizens now. Some may have tears in their eyes. They're remembering comrades lying under stark white gravestones that stand in silent vigil in a foreign cemetery.

Remembering—the cemetery at Okinawa. *U.S. Army*

Their memories go back beyond the war, perhaps 65, 70, 75, or even more years. They remember when it was the right thing to remove your hat when a lady entered a room; to rise and offer your seat to a woman or child on a streetcar or bus; when people knew what the 4th of July really stood for; when politicians proclaimed their honesty and patriotism and you believed them; when a binding contract was consummated with a handshake or a nod of the head; when you'd leave your front door unlocked and weren't afraid to walk the streets at night; when there still were local wildlands that hadn't been fenced and didn't have roads; when people expected less and valued what they had more; when everybody knew the difference between right and wrong; when no one used foul language in the presence of a woman, particularly a wife or mother; when you really meant it when you said this was the best country in the world.

Not many of them are left, and too many have stories that never will be told. When you see these men, standing with pride as the flag passes, remember that you are watching the winding down of an era, the passing of a generation, the likes of which we may never see again.

Finis

Memorial Day came early this year. My wife Nancy and I drove to north Idaho and visited Moscow, decorating the graves of her parents, Rex and Carol. The cemetery plots had been honored by many—flowers and plants were placed on, or near, most of the monuments. Small American flags fluttered over the internment sites of veterans.

The weather was warm and sunny. The kind of day on which, when my daughters were small, I'd mow the lawn and they'd take turns riding behind me on the lawn tractor. Memorial Day, however, was a time of reflection in our family, and of remembrance and celebration. It was a day to rest; to refrain from preparing the yard for the coming summer—the pruning of trees and shrubs, rototilling, weeding, and planting rows of corn, lettuce, carrots, and hills of potatoes in the garden. But this year we didn't do the garden work, nor will we in the next, or probably ever again. The work is too hard. Nancy and I are getting too old.

From where we live on Camas Prairie near Grangeville, Idaho, I occasionally look northward out the picture window in the family room. I gaze out to the distant town of Kamiah in the Clearwater Valley and the far horizon beyond, toward the Coeur d'Alene and Mica Peak country and the rolling prairies near Spokane. In a cottonwood grove by a small creek below our house, a large hawk has taken to perching on a dead branch just below the top of one of the largest trees. Sometimes he spreads his wings, drops off his perch, gains momentum, and then sails high into the sky, circling north, becoming only a faint spot on the distant horizon, until disappearing from sight. In my imagination, I see him soaring in effortless flight over Uncle Pete's cabin, the creek where I used to fish for speckled trout, and the faint and distant memories of my childhood past.

June 1, 2001
Wayne C. MacGregor, Jr.

RECOMMENDED READING

Altobella, Brian. *Into the Shadows Furious: The Brutal Battle for New Georgia*. Novato, CA: Presidio Press, 2000.

Appleman, Roy E. [et al.]. *Okinawa, the Last Battle: United States Army in World War II*. Washington, DC: Center of Military History, 1948.

_____. *The XXIV Corps in the Conquest of Okinawa*. Washington DC: Historical Division, War Department Special Staff, 1946.

_____. *Lewis and Clark: Historic Places Associated with Their Transcontinental Exploration (1804–06)*. Washington, DC: U.S. Department of the Interior, 1975.

Astor, Gerald. *Operation Iceberg: The Invasion and Conquest of Okinawa in Word War II*. New York: D.I. Fine, 1995.

Bahrenburg, Bruce. *The Pacific: Then and Now*. New York: Putnam, 1971.

Baldwin, Hanson W. *Battles Lost and Won: Great Campaigns of World War II*. New York: Harper and Row, 1966.

Belote, James and William. *Typhoon of Steel: The Battle for Okinawa*. New York: Harper and Row, 1970.

Berry, Henry. *Semper Fi, Mac: Living Memories of the U.S. Marines in World War II*. New York: Arbor House, 1982.

Costello, John. *The Pacific War*. New York: Atlantic Communications, 1991.

Dunnigan, James F., and Albert A. Nofi. *The Pacific War Encyclopedia*. New York: Checkmark, 1998.

Feifer, George. *Tennozan: The Battle of Okinawa and the Atomic Bomb*. New York: Ticknor and Fields, 1992.

Foster, Simon. *Okinawa 1945: Final Assault on the Empire*. London: Arms and Armour, 1994.

Fussell, Paul. *Doing Battle: The Making of a Skeptic*. Boston: Little, Brown, 1996. [Based in Europe, but an outstanding example of World War II literature.]

Gailey, Harry A. *The War in the Pacific: From Pearl Harbor to Tokyo Bay*. Novato, CA: Presidio Press, 1995.

Gow, Ian. *Okinawa, 1945: Gateway to Japan*. New York: Doubleday, 1985.

Greening, C. Ross. *Not as Briefed: From the Doolittle Raid to a German Stalag*. Pullman: Washington State University Press, 2001.

Hallas, James H. *Killing Ground on Okinawa*. Westport, CT: Praeger, 1996.

Harries, Meirion and Susie. *Soldiers of the Sun: The Rise and Fall of the Imperial Japanese Army*. New York: Random House, 1991.

Herndon, Booton. *The Unlikeliest Hero: The Story of Pfc. Desmond T. Doss, Conscientious Objector Who Won His Nation's Highest Honor*. Omaha: Pacific Press, 1967.

Hynes, Samuel. *Flights of Passage: Reflections of a World War II Aviator*. Annapolis: Naval Institute Press, 1988.

Keegan, John, ed. *Atlas of the Second World War*. London: HarperCollins, 1989 [reprint edition 1997].

Leach, Paul R. *Narrative of the Operations of the 77th Division on Okinawa*, 3 Vols. Washington DC: Historical Division, War Department Special Staff, 1946.

Leckie, Robert. *Okinawa: The Last Battle of World War II*. New York: Viking, 1995.

Linderman, Gerald F. *The World within War: America's Combat Experience in World War II*. New York: Free Press, 1997.

Manchester, William. *American Caesar: Douglas MacArthur, 1880–1964*. Boston: Little, Brown, 1978.

————. *Goodbye, Darkness: A Memoir of the Pacific War*. Boston: Little, Brown, 1980.

Mulligan, William. *Neuropsychiatry in World War II, Vol. 2, Overseas Theatres*. Washington DC: Office of the Surgeon General, 1973.

Murray, Williamson, and Allan R. Millett. *A War to Be Won: Fighting the Second World War, 1937–1945*. Cambridge, MA: Harvard University Press, 2000.

Nalty, Bernard C. *War in the Pacific: Pearl Harbor to Tokyo Bay*. Norman: University of Oklahoma Press, 1999.

Official Narrative of the Operations of the 77th Division on Okinawa. National Archives and Records Division, RG:319, Stack 270/19/8/5, Box 337.

Ours to Hold It High: The History of the 77th Infantry Division in World War II. Washington, DC: Infantry Journal Press, 1946.

Skates, John Ray. *The Invasion of Japan: Alternative to the Bomb*. Columbia: University of South Carolina Press, 1994.

Sledge, E.B. *With the Old Breed, at Peleliu and Okinawa*. Novato, CA: Presidio Press, 1981.

Spector, Ronald H. *Eagle against the Sun: The American War with Japan*. New York: Free Press, 1985.

Toland, John. *The Rising Sun: The Decline and Fall of the Japanese Empire, 1936–1945*. New York: Random House, 1970.

Van der Vat, Dan. *The Pacific Campaign: World War II, the U.S.-Japanese Naval War, 1941–1945*. New York: Touchstone, 1991.

Wodnik, Bob, *Captured Honor: POW Survival in the Philippines and Japan*. Pullman: Washington State University Press, 2003.

Yahara, Hiromichi. *The Battle for Okinawa*. New York: John Wiley and Sons, 1995.

Index